MW00827246

Israel's Feasts
and their
Fullness

by
Batya Ruth Wootten
Foreword by Angus Wootten

To Leah

from Bob + Amber

*I cast of
trumpets*

Israel's Feasts Fullness
by Batya Ruth Wootten

© 2002, Batya Ruth Wootten, Saint Cloud, FL.

Edited by Michele Libin

Cover by Crystal Lenhart, Sheridan, Wyoming

All rights are reserved under International and Pan-American Copyright Conventions. To use or reproduce any part of this book, electronically or otherwise, written permission must first be secured from the publisher. Brief quotations with credits may be used in critical reviews or articles.

Published and Distributed by:
Key of David Publishing, PO Box 700217, St Cloud, FL 34770
http://www.mim.net/keyofdavid

Printed in the United States of America.
All quotations used by permission.

Unless otherwise noted, Scripture quotations are from the *New American Standard Bible* (NASB), © 1995, The Lockman Foundation, published by Holman Bible Publishers, Nashville; and the *New New American Standard Bible*, Quick Verse for Windows, © 1992-1999, Craig Rairdon and Parsons Technology.
Verses marked KJV are from the *King James Version* Bible.
Verses marked NRSV are from *The New Revised Standard Version With Apocrypha*, © 1998 by Electronic Edition STEP Files, Parsons Technology, Inc. Cedar Rapids, Iowa.
Verses marked NIV are from the *New International Version*, © 1995 by The International Bible Society, published by Zondervan Publishing House, Grand Rapids.
Verses marked TAB are from *The Amplified Bible*, © 1994 by the Zondervan Publishing House, Grand Rapids.
Verses marked TNKH are from the *Tanakh, A New Translation of The Holy Scriptures*, © 1995 by The Jewish Publication Society. New York.
Verses from *26 Translations of the Holy Bible*, © 1985 by the Zondervan Corporation, Mathis Publishers, Atlanta, are marked according to the particular translation.

Note:
To emphasize some Scriptures, italics or an alternate word choice has been used, especially for the names of the Father and Son. Also, with all verses, except the Amplified Bible (TAB), brackets [] indicate text added by the author.

ISBN 1-886987-02-5

I
will gather
those who grieve
about the appointed feasts,
They came from you, O Zion;
The reproach of exile
is a burden on them
(Zephaniah 3:18).

Dedication

To all the children of Israel.

May we learn to celebrate our Heavenly Father's
feasts in a way that brings glory to Him
and to His Son, Messiah Yeshua.
May we learn to honor His feasts in a way that
brings unity and joy to the whole house of Israel.

Acknowledgments

There are many who are to be thanked for
helping in various ways with this book.
Friend and Messianic Israel Alliance Administrator,
Mark Huey, strongly encouraged me to collect my
writings about the feasts and to put them into book form.
Fellow editor, Michele Libin, diligently labored over every
word, ever cutting, changing, correcting, and clarifying
the text. We worked hard, laughed much, and together
grew in grace. It has been a blessing to have worked
with someone like her. If my writing is now easier
to read, give thanks to Michele, even as I do.
Once more, I am beholden to friend and talented artist,
Crystal Lenhart, who has again produced a wonderful
cover that greatly enhances the printed pages inside.
Thanks to those not mentioned here, and to friends:
Rabbi Mordechai Silver, John McKee, Toby Janicki,
Scott Diffenderfer, Lenny and Varda Harris,
and my daughter-in-law, Rene´e Wootten.
Each one proofed the text and offered helpful suggestions.
In addition, I want to again thank my husband, Angus,
for always encouraging me in my call to declare the truth
about the restoration of both the houses of Israel.

May each of you be blessed for the kindness you have
shown me. May He who sees the things that are done
in secret openly reward you for your goodness.

In Messiah Yeshua,
Batya

Contents

Part Four — The Fall Feasts: Yom Teruah, Yom Kippurim, Tabernacles

The Father's Feasts
(Leviticus Twenty-three)

The LORD, YHVH,[a] the Creator of the Universe, the Holy One of Israel, spoke to Moses, saying,

"Speak to the sons of Israel and say to them, 'YHVH's appointed times which you shall proclaim as holy convocations—My appointed times are these:

'For six days work may be done, but on the seventh day there is a sabbath of complete rest, a holy convocation. You shall not do any work; it is a sabbath to YHVH in all your dwellings.

'These are the appointed times of YHVH, holy convocations which you shall proclaim at the times appointed for them.

'In the first month, on the fourteenth day of the month at twilight is YHVH's Passover.

'Then on the fifteenth day of the same month there is the Feast of Unleavened Bread to YHVH; for seven days you shall eat unleavened bread. On the first day you shall have a holy convocation; you shall not do any laborious work. But for seven days you shall present an offering by fire to YHVH. On the seventh day is a holy convocation; you shall not do any laborious work.'"

Then YHVH spoke to Moses, saying, "Speak to the sons of Israel and say to them, 'When you enter the land which I am going

---

a YHVH: We use these four letters to indicate the Name of the one true God, which is often mistranslated "The Lord." This may be due to the Jewish tradition of not wanting to pronounce His Name, and Christianity simply followed suit. The Father's Name is comprised of four Hebrew letters, יהוה, yod, hey, vav, hey, and there are various opinions as to how it is to be pronounced: Yahweh, Yahveh, Yahvah, Yehovah, etc. Some believe this Divine Name is made up of four vowels, and pronounce it, Ih-Ah-Oo-Ah. We use the four English letters that best duplicate the sound of the four Hebrew letters as pronounced in modern Hebrew (YHVH), and let the reader determine if, and how, to pronounce it.

to give to you and reap its harvest, then you shall bring in the sheaf of the first fruits of your harvest to the priest. He shall wave the sheaf before YHVH for you to be accepted; on the day after the sabbath the priest shall wave it. Now on the day when you wave the sheaf, you shall offer a male lamb one year old without defect for a burnt offering to YHVH. Its grain offering shall then be two-tenths of an ephah of fine flour mixed with oil, an offering by fire to YHVH for a soothing aroma, with its drink offering, a fourth of a hin of wine. Until this same day, until you have brought in the offering of your God, you shall eat neither bread nor roasted grain nor new growth. It is to be a perpetual statute throughout your generations in all your dwelling places.

'You shall also count for yourselves from the day after the sabbath, from the day when you brought in the sheaf of the wave offering; there shall be seven complete sabbaths. You shall count fifty days to the day after the seventh sabbath; then you shall present a new grain offering to YHVH. You shall bring in from your dwelling places two loaves of bread for a wave offering, made of two-tenths of an ephah; they shall be of a fine flour, baked with leaven as first fruits to YHVH. Along with the bread you shall present seven one year old male lambs without defect, and a bull of the herd and two rams; they are to be a burnt offering to YHVH, with their grain offering and their drink offerings, an offering by fire of a soothing aroma to YHVH. You shall also offer one male goat for a sin offering and two male lambs one year old for a sacrifice of peace offerings. The priest shall then wave them with the bread of the first fruits for a wave offering with two lambs before YHVH; they are to be holy to YHVH for the priest. On this same day you shall make a proclamation as well; you are to have a holy convocation. You shall do no laborious work. It is to be a perpetual statute in all your dwelling places throughout your generations. When you reap the harvest of your land, moreover, you shall not reap to the very corners of your field nor gather the gleaning of your harvest; you are to leave them for the needy and the alien. I am YHVH your God.'"

Again YHVH spoke to Moses, saying, "Speak to the sons of Israel, saying, 'In the seventh month on the first of the month you shall have a rest, a reminder by blowing of trumpets, a holy convocation. 'You shall not do any laborious work, but you shall present an offering by fire to YHVH.'"

YHVH spoke to Moses, saying, "On exactly the tenth day of this seventh month is the day of atonement; it shall be a holy convocation for you, and you shall humble your souls and present an offering by fire to YHVH. You shall not do any work on this same day, for it is a day of atonement, to make atonement on your behalf before YHVH your God. If there is any person who will not humble himself on this same day, he shall be cut off from his people. As for any person who does any work on this same day, that person I will destroy from among his people. You shall do no work at all. It is to be a perpetual statute throughout your generations in all your dwelling places. It is to be a sabbath of complete rest to you, and you shall humble your souls; on the ninth of the month at evening, from evening until evening you shall keep your sabbath."

Again YHVH spoke to Moses, saying,"Speak to the sons of Israel, saying, 'On the fifteenth of this seventh month is the Feast of Booths for seven days to YHVH. On the first day is a holy convocation; you shall do no laborious work of any kind. For seven days you shall present an offering by fire to YHVH. On the eighth day you shall have a holy convocation and present an offering by fire to YHVH; it is an assembly. You shall do no laborious work.

'These are the appointed times of YHVH which you shall proclaim as holy convocations, to present offerings by fire to YHVH—burnt offerings and grain offerings, sacrifices and drink offerings, each day's matter on its own day—besides those of the sabbaths of YHVH, and besides your gifts and besides all your votive and freewill offerings, which you give to YHVH.

'On exactly the fifteenth day of the seventh month, when you have gathered in the crops of the land, you shall celebrate the feast of YHVH for seven days, with a rest on the first day and a rest on the eighth day. Now on the first day you shall take for yourselves the foliage of beautiful trees, palm branches and boughs of leafy trees and willows of the brook, and you shall rejoice before YHVH your God for seven days. You shall thus celebrate it as a feast to YHVH for seven days in the year. It shall be a perpetual statute throughout your generations; you shall celebrate it in the seventh month. You shall live in booths for seven days; all the native-born in Israel shall live in booths, so that your generations may know that I had the sons of Israel live in booths when I brought them out from the land of Egypt. I am YHVH your God.'"

So Moses declared to the sons of Israel the appointed times of YHVH (Leviticus 23).

Foreword

It is time for a paradigm shift. It is time for us to take a fresh look at an ancient topic. It is time for us to look at the feasts of Israel in a new light. Some topics are so important that, as our understanding of Scripture grows, they must be reexamined. Today the God of Israel is opening the eyes of His people to truths that were previously hidden from partially blinded eyes.

This is not just another book about the feasts. This is a liberating book that shows a better way. It is a book that is filled with effervescent new wine. However, as Messiah Yeshua said,"New wine must be put into fresh wineskins" (Luke 5:38).

The prophet Daniel was told to, "Go your way, Daniel, for these words are concealed and sealed up until the end time," when godly understanding will be increased (Daniel 12:9-10). That time is now. The truths of the Father are being revealed in a new way. He is especially revealing the truth about the feasts of Israel and how they fit into His plan for the restoration of His Kingdom to both the houses of Israel—Judah and Ephraim.

Over thirty years ago the God of Israel called me and my wife, Batya, into the ministry that is now called Messianic Israel. He entrusted us with an understanding of how He is restoring the two houses of Israel, and called us to write and teach about how His plan is to be accomplished. We do not claim to know all the answers, but after three decades of study and ministry, we believe we are able to provide clarity in the midst of muddied waters and murky doctrines concerning the people of Israel and the feasts of Israel.

Much has been written about these feasts. Some of it is very good, and Batya has referenced much of it in order to draw upon the knowledge and understanding of others. However, a great deal of what has been written about the feasts is mired in ancient tradition. The meaning the Father intended for these feasts has been lost as people throughout the ages have developed a reverence for the traditions of men above the truths of God.

Batya has been researching the feasts and writing articles about them for many years, but recently she was asked to compile her work and dig more deeply into the truths that have been hidden until these "times of the end."

She writes about these feasts because many people in these latter days are hungry to understand their Hebraic roots and the meaning of the feasts. They ask many questions. What does the Father intend? What do the Scriptures really say? What is simply Jewish tradition and what is appropriate for Believers in Messiah Yeshua?

We know we must celebrate because our Messiah celebrated. And we *want* to celebrate, because the God of Israel commanded us to do so. But how? And when? And where? A dozen questions surface.

At last there is a book that clearly answers with solid scriptural authority. This is a book that is, in essence, the "new wine."

Ezekiel spoke of a day when reunited Israel would have one King over them—the Kings of Kings; they would keep His commandments; and they would forever live on the land that the Father gave to their forefathers (Ezekiel 37:15-28).

As the people of Israel, do we have a part in bringing about the day of which Ezekiel speaks? What can we do to help bring it about?

Both Moses and Ezekiel gave excellent answers to these questions. Moses tells us, "YHVH has today declared you to be His people, a treasured possession, as He promised you, and that you should keep all His commandments" (Deuteronomy 26:18). And Ezekiel defines the people who will dwell with the God of Israel as those who "will walk in My ordinances and keep My statutes and observe them" (Ezekiel 37:24).

The feasts of Israel are key ordinances and statutes that God expects His people to observe. But, again, how do we observe them?

The New Covenant is not silent on the subject of the feasts of Israel. The Gospel accounts of Yeshua's ministry revolve around the feasts. The very core of the gospel deals with the first three of the seven feasts: Passover, Unleavened Bread, and First Fruits. On the fourth feast, Shavuot, or Pentecost, the Holy Spirit, or Ruach HaKodesh, was poured out on His people, empowering them to carry forth the gospel. The Fall feasts of Yom Teruah, Yom Kippur (HaKippurim), and Tabernacles, while celebrated by Yeshua, were not as prominent in the Gospel accounts because their fulfillment was yet future.

Israel's Feasts and their Fullness sheds much needed light into an area where there has been a great deal of darkness. This, Batya's latest book, will do as her past books have done—change lives. Reading it will change your life.

Her past books have primarily dealt with the identity of Israel. In these books she has encouraged Believers to see themselves as full citizens of the commonwealth of Israel, and that awareness has changed their lives. As you read this new book, be prepared for more changes, because it guides those who have shed the partial hardening and blindness of Romans 11 into a further understanding of their identity and call.

Many Believers are like Apollos, who was mighty in the Scriptures, fervent, and instructed in the way of the Lord, yet in need of a teacher to tell him the rest of the story. There are countless Believers today who feel led to celebrate the feasts of Israel, yet have only been taught how the Church and rabbinical Judaism have celebrated the feasts. They are in need of a Spirit-led teacher to show them the rest of the way.

Just as Apollos needed a Priscilla and an Aquila to take him aside and explain "the way of God more accurately" (Acts 18:24-26), so Believers today need a modern-day Priscilla to explain how the Father would have us understand His feasts more accurately. This modern-day teacher is my wife, Batya. Her teachings and writings are clear and concise. She is a diligent student and a meticulous researcher. Her explanations will give you an understanding of the feasts of Israel that will entertain you as well as set your feet on solid scriptural ground. Get ready for a book that will change your life and deepen your walk with the Holy One of Israel.

We are instructed to ask for the ancient paths of our forefathers, and when we find them, we are to walk in them. Many of us are now hearing the Father call out to us, "Return, O virgin Israel" (Jeremiah 6:16; 31:20-21).

This book will set your feet on a new, yet ancient path. It a glorious path of celebration that leads to Zion.

Shalom in our generation,

Angus Wootten
Director
Messianic Israel Alliance
Saint Cloud, Florida
June 2002

Introduction

A s Believers [b] in the Messiah of Israel, how do we honor Messiah Yeshua (Jesus),[c] and at the same time celebrate the feasts of the Holy One of Israel? Do we simply follow present Jewish traditions, many of which have been developed over the years, or is there something more we need to understand?

To answer these questions we will first address *why* we have the desire to celebrate. Once we understand *why* so many non-Jewish Believers now feel sovereignly called to honor these ancient feasts, our answer will help us reexamine *how* we celebrate. This answer will encourage us, help us understand why we feel as we do, and add a rewarding sense of purpose to our celebrations.

We will especially look at the role of the non-Jew in honoring Israel's feasts, and hope to encourage them to arise and take their part in the Divine plan.

---

b We use *Believer* to describe those purchased by Messiah Yeshua's blood, rather than *Christian,* because the latter title is often misused (Mat 7:23; 1 Cor 6:20; 1 Pet 1:17-19).

c *Yeshua* (ישוע) is the Messiah's given Hebrew name, it means "Salvation" (Mat 1:21). When transliterated into Greek, due to linguistic differences, *Yeshua* became *Iesous* (Ιησους). In Old English, "Iesous" was then rendered "Iesus" (pronounced *Yesus*), and was spelled with a beginning letter "J," which at the time had a "Y" sound. Later the "J" came to have a harder sound, and it came to be pronounced as "Jesus." Since this name is the result of linguistic differences, we prefer to use the Messiah's given Hebrew/Aramaic Name, Yeshua (See "*Is the Name 'Jesus' Pagan?*" by John K. McKee, *Messianic Israel Herald,* Volume 2, Issue 2).

To identify these celebrants, we ask, "*Who are these?*" Could they actually be "of Israel"? Is that why they feel a deep yearning to commemorate her feasts?

As to the probable identity of these non-Jews, our assumption is that the majority (though not necessarily all) are sons of Jacob and are indeed Israelites. Countless Scriptures that validate this truth have been meticulously enumerated in our previous book, *Who Is Israel?* This solution-driven book is causing a worldwide reexamination of the way Believers define "Israel." It clearly shows that the Father is still dealing with "both the houses of Israel" (Isaiah 8:14). We invite you to read this book for a deeper understanding of Israel's divided house—Israel (or Ephraim) and Judah. The book addresses the separate dispersions of the two houses of Israel, and outlines their present call to become a fully reunited house, or "one stick in the Father's hand" (Ezekiel 37:15-28). Additionally, we offer a summary book called *Ephraim and Judah: Israel Revealed*, which provides a concise overview of these teachings.

In our search for the truth about Israel's feasts, we do not propose that Jews become exactly like westernized Christians, or that Christians become exactly like "Rabbinic" Jews. We hope to help raise up a restored Israel that will have some characteristics of both houses, but will walk away from all false religious beliefs and practices and become the nation the Father ordained from the beginning.

The ancient feasts of Israel regularly bring us back to the Almighty. They remind us of His awesome plan for our lives and of His plan for a restored Kingdom of Israel. They also encourage us to rehearse that plan.

The principal gift found in the feasts is that they give us a sweet taste of the Almighty and provide us with times to gather together with His people. He gives us these special seasons so we can come together and learn to fulfill the two great commandments: To love Him with all our hearts, with all our souls, and with all our strength; and to love one another.

However, when it comes to the traditions of the feasts, we must realize that while tradition can be the glue that holds families together, it can also be the glue that keeps people stuck. Therefore, the primary focus of our study will not be on *how* to celebrate the traditions, but on the wondrous answer to *why* we celebrate.

With this book we hope to do what Priscilla and Aquila did, which is to suggest a "more excellent way" (Acts 18:26). It is written to explain more accurately the purposes of our Father's feasts and to suggest ways in which we might help fulfill them in these end times.

It is not our intent to simply create another feast book, for there are countless resource books currently available on this subject. However, most of these books teach about the traditional observances of the feasts, and we will address the feasts from a different perspective.

Our goal is to help you enter into a more deeply passionate and personally rich path of celebration.

We are addressing those who are crying out in their inner being for a more intimate understanding of the Father's present purposes in the earth. We do not want to provide mere knowledge that only leads to further questioning, but instead to present an understanding that touches the profound yearnings of your heart—the part of you that cries out to the God of Israel and begs Him to show you more of Himself.

On a personal basis, my prayer is that this book will help you know how very much the Father loves *you*. I pray that these words will help you catch a vision and know that you are personally part of the Father's end-time plan for His chosen people. It is my hope that as you understand about Ephraim and Judah, you will be inspired and filled to overflowing with new hope as you learn anew how to celebrate some very old feasts.

This book is not about the traditions of man, but about the purposes of Israel's God. What we want to present is not about the outward manifestations of celebration, but about deeper spiritual attributes—the very call of God on our lives.

The words on these pages speak of a deep yearning for both the houses of Israel, Judah and Ephraim, Jewish and non-Jewish Believers alike, to enter into more intimate, profound, and meaningful celebrations with the Holy One of Israel. This book is about a desire for Judah and Ephraim to come together and enter into the true spirit of the feasts. It is a prayer in print.

May we together, Judah and Ephraim, learn to celebrate our Father's feasts in all their fullness.
Amen. So be it.

Batya Ruth Wootten
Saint Cloud, FL
November 2001

Part One

Who Is Celebrating
and Why

Holy Rehearsals

We are presently seeing a phenomenon in the earth. Non-Jewish Believers in Israel's Messiah are beginning to celebrate the feasts of Israel in unprecedented numbers. There is a true move among the people to return to their Hebraic roots.

Many are discovering that each of these ordained feasts were meant to be a holy assembly, a holy *miqra*/מקרא, or *rehearsal* (Exodus 12:16). The Father calls them *rehearsals*, because in commemorating them we *rehearse*, or *depict*, our entire walk with Him. When we celebrate them, we "re-hear" valuable lessons that help us get our personal lives in order.

These feasts are divided into three primary categories that outline the Father's plan of redemption for His people. They portray a broad three-phase plan for our lives: Passover/*Pesach* (personal redemption); Pentecost/*Shavuot* (in filling of the Spirit), and *Tabernacles/Sukkot* (restoration of the kingdom of Israel).

The feasts are times of remembrance of physical events that typify spiritual events. They have to do with *physical* harvests and offerings that portray *spiritual* harvests and offerings. These important times of convocation detail the Father's past redemption and continued provision for His people. They foretold Messiah's first appearance, and they foretell His Second Coming. They forecast His sacrifice on our behalf, and they foretell the full redemption of His people. The feasts were first given by the Father to a people wandering in the desert. They foretold His plan to establish them as a Kingdom, and they now foretell His plan to restore that Kingdom. The feasts speak of many events in both the natural and the spiritual realms.

Israel's seven annual feasts come in clusters. The first three are, Passover (*Pesach*), Unleavened Bread (*Matzah*), and First of First Fruits (*Bikkurim*). These times occur in the spring during an eight-day period, and they often are collectively called "Passover."

The next feast, *Shavuot*, comes by itself fifty days after the waving of First Fruits. Many know this early summer feast by its Greek name, *Pentecost*, meaning *fifty*. It is also sometimes called the Feast of Weeks (Exodus 34:22).

The long, dry summer culminates in a collection of three fall feasts: Day of Blowing (*Yom Teruah*), Day of Atonement (*Yom Kippur*), and Tabernacles (*Sukkot*). These latter feasts cover a twenty-one-day period, which are collectively referred to as the "Fall Feasts," or just "Tabernacles."

These events represent times when the God of Israel reached down from Heaven to deal with His people. Remembering them provides special times for us to gather together with family and friends, to be encouraged in our faith, and to pass on our faith. The feasts give us an excellent opportunity to convey to our children the very thing for which Abraham was honored. The Father said of Abraham, "I have chosen him, so that he may command his children and his household after him to keep the way of YHVH [1] by doing righteousness and justice" (Genesis 18:19).

---

1 YHVH: We use these four letters to indicate the Name of the one true God, which is often mistranslated "The Lord." This may be due to the Jewish tradition of not wanting to pronounce His Name, and Christianity simply followed suit. The Father's Name is comprised of four Hebrew letters, יהוה, yod, hey, vav, hey, and there are various opinions as to how it is to be pronounced: Yahweh, Yahveh, (continued...)

When we honor the feasts, our quiet actions speak loudly to family and friends about our faith. They depict our obedience to the Father, and they portray the truth that He blesses and provides for us. Moreover, because our children tend to imitate what they see more than what they hear, it is good for them to see us rejoicing in these seasons of joy.

Feast Proclamations

Leviticus Twenty-three describes these feasts, which are called *mo'edim* (מועדים), or *appointed times*,[2] The Holy One said to Moses, "Speak to the sons of Israel, and say to them, 'These are the appointed times of YHVH, holy convocations which you shall proclaim at the times appointed for them'" (Leviticus 23:4).

At these set apart times we are to proclaim the truths of the feasts. We are to preach and teach about their meaning as they occur. We teach about them because these are more than just times of festivities, they are times of holy convocation, set apart for us to remember that which the Holy One has done for His people, and to meditate on that which He will yet do for us.

The Father has made special appointments to meet with us during these times. He even promises to protect that which we leave behind so that we can meet with Him:

"I will drive out nations before you and enlarge your borders, and no man shall covet your land when you go up three times a year to appear before YHVH your God" (Exodus 34:24).

---

1 (...continued)
Yahvah, Yehovah, etc. Some believe this Divine Name is made up of four vowels, and pronounce it, Ih-Ah-Oo-Ah. We use the four English letters that best duplicate the sound of the four Hebrew letters as pronounced in modern Hebrew (YHVH), and let the reader determine if, and how, to pronounce it.

2 *Strong's* word # H4150, from *Strong's Hebrew and Greek Dictionaries Electronic Edition STEP Files* © 1998, Parsons Technology, Inc., Cedar Rapids (hereafter *Strong's*); also from Brown-Driver-Briggs' Hebrew Definitions Electronic Edition STEP Files, © 1999, Findex.com, Inc. (hereafter: *BDB*).

Because the feasts of Israel represent important spiritual truths, many people are becoming excited about celebrating them and about returning to the Hebraic roots of their faith.

The question is, in celebrating the feasts today, how do we relate what has been done in the past to what is to be done in the future? How do we commemorate feasts that are both historic and prophetic? We especially ask, how do we lift up and honor Messiah Yeshua in these feasts?

Legalism

Some have errantly become "legalistic" about keeping the feasts. We define "legalism" as the belief that adherence to the Law, or *Torah*,[3] is a requirement for obtaining and maintaining one's justification before God.

However, salvation is never earned—it is a gift of grace received by faith in the person and work of Yeshua the Messiah.

"Legalist" is a term frequently used to describe one who attempts to keep the letter of the Law without regard for the spirit of the instructions.

We see the futility of being legalistic regarding our observance when we review the commands about *how* the feasts are to be celebrated (Leviticus 23:14,21,31,41). The feasts absolutely cannot be kept *exactly* as outlined in Torah. Specific sacrifices were required at these feasts: they were to be offered only in the Temple in Jerusalem, and only by Levitical priests (Exodus 29:9; Numbers 18:23; Deuteronomy 12:17; 16:5). Because the Father gave us precise instructions on how to observe them, and because it is impossible to exactly follow these instructions, we cannot possibly keep them as instructed.

If we ask *why* we cannot precisely follow the instructions and *who* is responsible for our not being able to follow them, we begin to see the solution to our dilemma.

---

3 The Five Books of Moses: Genesis to Deuteronomy.

The Almighty Himself allowed the Temple, once located in Jerusalem, to be destroyed by the Romans in A.D. 70 (Jeremiah 26:18; Micah 3:12; Luke 19:44). He also permitted the genealogical records housed there to be destroyed, and He scattered the Levitical priests to the winds, even though they were the only ones who could legally offer the sacrifices that He prescribed.

Our Father in Heaven knows the requirements of the feasts and that the Temple where they were to be held has been destroyed. Since He told us to fulfill those commands, He must be sending us a message.

What is the message in this apparent contradiction? What point is the Father trying to convey to His people? Does it have to do with the non-Jews who are now being drawn to the feasts? Does it have to do with the attitudes behind our celebrations?

A Liberating Truth

We cannot legally keep the feasts and the Father knows this. So let us not be legalistic about our observances. Let us instead be liberated by the fact that, since we cannot do them exactly as they were once done, or as prescribed, then we cannot really "*keep*" them. We can only have a desire in our hearts to *honor* the feasts, and we can do what we can do (Deuteronomy 27:26; Galatians 3:10; James 2:10).

We must not be legalistic about our celebrations, nor focus on the jot and tittle of *how* we celebrate. Our primary aim must be to honor the feasts as best we can, and to do the things that we can do at this time. We must also do what we do with a clean heart, for only then will He use us to teach transgressors His ways (Psalm 51:10-14).

Let us remember what He once asked of some who had wrong motives concerning their sacrifices:

"*What are your multiplied sacrifices to Me?...I have had enough of burnt offerings...I take no pleasure in the blood of bulls, lambs or goats. When you come to appear before Me, who requires of you this trampling of My courts? Bring*

*your worthless offerings no longer, incense is an abomin-
ation to me. New moon and sabbath, the calling of assemblies—I cannot endure iniquity and the solemn assembly.
I hate your new moon festivals and your appointed feasts,
they have become a burden to Me; I am weary of bearing
them. So when you spread out your hands in prayer, I will
hide My eyes from you; yes, even though you multiply
prayers, I will not listen....Wash yourselves, make yourselves clean; remove the evil of your deeds from My sight.
Cease to do evil, learn to do good; seek justice, reprove the
ruthless, defend the orphan, plead for the widow. 'Come
now, and let us reason together,' says YHVH, Though your
sins are as scarlet, they will be as white as snow; though
they are red like crimson, they will be like wool. If you
consent and obey, you will eat the best of the land... Truly,
the mouth of YHVH has spoken" (Isaiah 1:11-20).*

A People of Solution

If we are legalistic about how we celebrate these holy
convocations, or if we are haughty with those who do not yet
see the truth as we do, or if our hearts are not clean before
the Father, then we are only following the errant footsteps
of those who have gone before us.

We do not want to add to the problem. We instead want
to be part of the solution. And that makes us a people in
need of answers...

Where Do We Go For Answers?

Where do we look for answers to our questions about the feasts? Do we look to the leaders of the traditional Church?

Probably not. Most Church[4] leaders know little about the feasts of Israel. Historically, the Church has often fought bitterly, even violently, against anyone honoring what they mistakenly call "the *Jewish* feasts." Even today many in the Church persecute those who wish to honor them.

Considering the Church's lack of knowledge, should we instead look to Jewish sources for guidance? Should we celebrate the feasts based solely on Jewish traditions?

---

4 "Church," like "Israel," is a multi-faceted name/title, and one must know what an author means with its use. For there is a "church system" that will persecute true Believers (Rev 3:16; 2 Tim 3:1-12; Matt 5:20), and there is a true *church*, an eternal *ekklesia*—which includes all who truly seek to follow the God of Israel (Acts 7:38; 2 Thes 1:1; 2:13). There is also a "Synagogue of Satan" that opposes Messiah (John 8:44; 10:33; Rev 2:9; 3:9). In this book, the word "church" is sometimes used to include those who, in this life, "*claim*" to belong to "the church." This same standard of including those who, in the end, the Father Himself may not include, also is applied in references to "Jews/Judaism." We trust that in the end the Holy One Himself will decide who among both peoples is acceptable (Mat 7:23). However, since the word "church" is often misunderstood, we will prefer the Greek *ekklesia* (*Strong's* # G1577) when referring to the *called out ones*.

Judah has given honor to the feasts for centuries and has many insights regarding them. However, Judah, as a body, does not see the all-important truth that Yeshua is Israel's Messiah. If we look solely to the people of Judah (Judaism) for instructions on how to commemorate Israel's feasts, we will miss seeing "the Light of the world" (John 8:12), Yeshua, being lifted up and celebrated.

Before looking to either Christianity or Judaism (including Messianic Judaism) to show us how to honor Israel's feasts, we must realize that both have erred in their understanding of the feasts. But more about this later...

Were the Feasts Abolished?

Another erroneous belief that is sometimes raised when Believers seek to celebrate Israel's feasts is the claim that they have been "fulfilled," and thus need not be observed.

Is this true?

Yes and no. Yes, in that Messiah Yeshua is our sacrificial lamb, and we therefore have no need of another sacrifice (1 Corinthians 5:7; Hebrews 9:26-28; 10:1-26). Yeshua has filled all the *sacrificial laws* to their fullness.[5]

But no, Israel's feasts were not abolished, because they foreshadow her Messiah (Colossians 2:17; Hebrews 10:1). He is the very substance to which they point. While such yearly sacrifices could never make men perfect (as can His shed Blood), we nevertheless cannot separate these shadows from their substance, for they would then *cease to be shadows.*

The shadows of the feasts graphically portray our redemption, and they should be attached to Yeshua's Body. Furthermore, both Zechariah and Zephaniah, and many of Israel's prophets, foretold the restoration of the feasts in the eternal Kingdom.

---

5 Yeshua said, "Do not think that I came to abolish the Law or the Prophets; I did not come to abolish, but to fulfill" (Mat 5:17). *Fulfill: Strong's Concordance #* G 4137. *pleroo,* from G4134; to make replete, level up, furnish, imbue, diffuse, influence), satisfy, execute (an office), finish (a period or task), verify, complete, fill (up), fulfil, make full, fully preach, perfect, supply. Messiah Yeshua interpreted, or walked out the Father's law (see Mat 3:15; Heb 9:23-10:10).

The Holy Miqra

We are called to be a royal priesthood (1 Peter 2:9). Like the High Priest who bore the stones of all the tribes on his breast, we too must seek the restoration of all of Israel's twelve tribes. In our service to the Most High, each of His divinely appointed feasts should be to us as *a holy assembly*, a holy *miqra*/מקרא (Exodus 12:16). They should be special times when we rehearse all that the Holy One has done for us, days set apart for us to reflect on what He yet promises to do for us.

Nonetheless, we must agree that the feasts have already been objectively "fulfilled" (or will be fulfilled) in Yeshua. Similarly, Christmas has also been "*fulfilled.*" The promised Son has been given (Isaiah 9:6). Yet people continue to celebrate Christmas.[6]

The same is true of the Fourth of July. Americans celebrate its *fulfillment*. In fact, you cannot remember an event unless it happened in the past. Thus we do not stop celebrating because the event being commemorated has already occurred. We celebrate *because* it happened. Thus the idea that they have been "fulfilled" is not a legitimate reason to stop celebrating the feasts of Israel.

Every year the feasts continue to be subjectively fulfilled in the hearts of those being gathered. Each year something takes place within the minds and hearts of the celebrants. Many who once knew nothing about these set times are now being inexplicably drawn to them by the Spirit of YHVH.

Was this end time move foretold in Scripture?

Based on a prophecy of Zechariah, many people believe that is was. But Zechariah speaks of former *enemies* of Jerusalem, not those who honor Israel and are *drawn* to her and the feasts out of their love for them: "Then it will come about that any who are left of all the nations that went against Jerusalem will go up from year to year to worship the King, YHVH of Hosts, and to celebrate the Feast of

---

6 See chapter 33, "The Roots of Christmas."

Booths [Tabernacles]. [Whoever]...does not go up to Jerusalem to worship...there will be no rain on them....it will be the plague with which YHVH smites the nations who do not go up to celebrate the Feast of Booths....And there will no longer be a Canaanite in the house of YHVH of hosts in that day" (Zechariah 14:16-21).

The Burden of Reproach

On the other hand, Zephaniah 3:18 speaks of Believers who grieve over, or long for, Israel's feasts. In this verse, the Messiah says to the Father, "I will gather them that are far from the appointed season, who are of thee, that hast borne the burden of **reproach**" (*Soncino Books of the Bible*).[7]

The New American Standard Bible translates the verse, "I will gather those who grieve about the appointed feasts— They came from you, O Zion; The reproach of exile is a burden on them."

The Book of Lamentations confirms this idea of grieving because they are far from the feasts. It says, "The ways of Zion do mourn, because none come to the solemn feasts [mo'edim]: all her gates are desolate: her priests sigh, her virgins are afflicted, and she is in bitterness....YHVH has caused her grief because of the multitude of her transgressions; Her little ones have gone away as captives before the adversary. All her majesty has departed....Jerusalem remembers all her precious things that were from the days of old..." (Lamentations 1:4-7).

Zechariah affirms a restoration of the Feast of Booths for those who once *opposed* it. Zephaniah tells of those who feel it is a *reproach* to be far from the feasts.

The prophets clearly foretell a time when the feasts are restored to, and celebrated by, a repentant people of Israel (Ezekiel 45:17; 46:3).

---

7 *The Twelve Prophets*, London: Soncino, 1980, p 251. Some Bible translations even say the feasts themselves are a *reproach*, or burden, however, the *New Revised Standard* Bible says, "As on a day of festival. I will remove disaster from you, so that you will not bear reproach for it." It is *the shame of our past behavior*, which resulted in our *loss of the feasts*, that leads us to feel *reproach*.

Sacred Signs

The "appointed season" spoken of in the Zephaniah verse is the *mo'ed* (מוֹעֵד); meaning festival, appointed place, tent of meeting, a time, sacred season, sign or signal; by implication, an assembly convened for a definite purpose, a solemn congregation. This word is related to *ya'ad* (יָעַד), which means to fix, appoint, assign, designate assemble, cause to meet, set, be placed before, betroth.[8]

From these words we get a picture of our call as a people, which is to be a nation set apart, one that has certain appointed times, or sacred seasons, wherein we assemble together. These are times that we meet with one another and place our offerings, and even ourselves, before the One to Whom we are betrothed. These divine appointments are designed to heal and restore us. Honoring them is a sign that "marks" us. Observing them sets us apart, and shows the world that we belong solely to the Holy One of Israel.

The Key to Inspiring Celebrations: Ministering to All Twelve Tribes of Israel

If we are to cooperate with what the Father is doing in this day through our celebrations of His feasts, if we are to learn how to relate to both Christians and Jews concerning this issue, if we are to minister to people from both camps, then we must first understand *Israel.*

We can celebrate the feasts of Israel without understanding about "both the houses of Israel" and their stumblings (Isaiah 8:14; Romans 11:25). However, if we are going to celebrate Israel's feasts in their *fullness*, we must first understand the Father's heart for both Ephraim and Judah. We must realize that:

♦ Both the houses of Israel have stumbled
♦ A partial hardening happened to Judah *and* Ephraim
♦ They were hardened for a season by the Almighty

8 *Strong's* #'s H4150, and H3259.

♦ YHVH Himself divided Israel into two houses (see Isaiah 8:14; Romans 11:25; 2 Chronicles 11:4).

We must realize that, Joseph/Ephraim/Israel was destined to become a *fullness of the Gentiles*—and to be *lost* among the heathen—*until* a certain point in time (Genesis 48:19; Romans 11:25; Hosea 1-2; 8:8; Amos 9:9).

The children of Ephraim were scattered by the Father among the heathen nations because of their sin. Ephraim's punishment was that they would be "*Lo-Ami*," or "Not-A-People" (Hosea 1:9-10). One of their hallmarks would be that they would *not* honor the feasts.

However, Scripture speaks of their eventual repentance and return to the God of their forefathers.

That repentance and return is now in progress because it is time for Ephraim's punishment to come to end.[9] It also is time for the two houses of Israel to be reunited, and that reunion is a wonder to behold.

Asking for the Ancient Paths
Setting up Righteous Roadmarks

Many returning children of Ephraim and companions are now hearing the Father whisper in their ears, "Ask for the ancient paths, where the good way is, and walk in it; and you will find rest for your souls." They are hearing His command to "Set up for yourself roadmarks, place for yourself guideposts; direct your mind to the highway, the way by which you went. Return, O virgin of Israel, return to these your cities" (Ezekiel 37:16; Jeremiah 6:16; 31:20-21).

Countless non-Jews are now longing to return home. They yearn to celebrate the feasts of Israel. They want to return to their Father's house, to embrace their true identity as children of Israel, and to walk hand-in-hand with their brothers and sisters of the house of Judah.

We believe these returning ones are primarily the people

---

9 See the book, *Restoring Israel's Kingdom* by Angus Wootten, "*The End of Ephraim's Punishment*," Key of David, 2000, Saint Cloud, FL.

of returning virgin Israel. Their forefathers long ago forgot the ways of the Almighty, they stumbled down a way of paganism, they left the ancient paths to walk in errant bypaths. Now their children want to make *teshuvah*—they want to return home (Jeremiah 18:15).

These returning ones are being welcomed by some in Judah, and when the two come together in celebration, the air becomes electric, it becomes pregnant with expectation.

People today are looking for revival. But they will only find revival when Israel's divided house becomes reunited. This is a divine principle, for Messiah Yeshua said, "Any kingdom divided against itself is laid waste; and any city or house divided against itself will not stand" (Matthew 12:25; Luke 11:17).

A house divided against itself falls. To be strong, to experience revival, Israel must be reunited.

The Father wants us to have revival that is beyond anything we have thus far known. Messiah Yeshua said, "Truly, truly, I say to you, he who believes in Me, the works that I do, he will do also; and greater works than these he will do; because I go to the Father" (John 14:12).

The Father wants to do a great work through us, and He wants to use our joyous celebration of His feasts to help accomplish that work.

Father, help us find our way home. Help us to understand that many of Your children have not known their true identity, because as Israelites they were blinded for a season. Lead us, Father, as we seek to establish roadmarks of righteousness for both the houses of Israel. Empower us to set up guideposts that restore your people and bring glory to Your Name. Cause us to truly be the pure virgins spoken of by our prophets. Help us to have Holy Rehearsals that bring honor to You. Put our feet on the ancient paths that we might return to You in righteousness.

In Yeshua's Name we pray.
Amen.

Israel's Feasts and their Fullness

Who Are These?

As the returning children of Israel, as *reunited* Israel, we want to experience Israel's feasts in all their fullness. We want to honor them in a way that changes lives. Therefore, we must understand about the whole house of Israel. We must see that Jacob's twelve tribes were long ago divided into two houses; that Israel was once comprised of Northern and Southern Kingdoms, known as Israel (Ephraim) and Judah, and that the Father said of their division, "This thing is from Me" (2 Chronicles 11:4).

Israel was divided into two houses *by the Almighty*. As prophesied, both Ephraim and Judah have "stumbled" over He who would be a "Sanctuary" to them. In different ways both have stumbled over Messiah Yeshua. Those whom the Father calls His "two chosen families" have tripped over Yeshua, because both were hardened and blinded by God Himself. To date, both houses have only seen *in part* (Isaiah 8:13-14; Jeremiah 33:24; John 2:18-22; Romans 11:25-26).

The veil that once shrouded the eyes of Israel's tribes was to last "until..."

We are living in the days of that *until*. These are the days in which formerly blinded Israelites are beginning to see truths in the inspired Word of God. They are seeing things they could not see before (Ecclesiastes 3:1; Daniel 12:4).

Believers are now realizing that the punishments and promises made to Ephraim are different from those of Judah, for the two houses were each blinded in different ways. Ephraim was blinded to his own Israelite roots, yet was able to see, at least in part, the truth about the Divine Messiah, Yeshua. Judah has been able to see his Israelite roots, but could not see the Divine Messiah, who is the Redeemer of his soul.[10] Judah could not see He Who is the Living Torah.

The veil of blindness is now being lifted from Jewish eyes, and many are seeing that Yeshua is indeed the *Mashiach*, the Messiah of Israel. Ephraim was blinded as to his true identity, a punishment was meted out to him by the Almighty, and it has prevailed until recently. This punishment is explained in the book, *Restoring Israel's Kingdom*, by Angus Wootten.[11] This book details Ephraim's different punishments and their length, as well as the necessary requirements for his full restoration (Ezekiel 4:5; Leviticus 26:18,21; Hosea 1-2).

Repentant Ephraim is Instructed

We are now seeing Ephraim's children coming to repentance as they return to their Israelite roots, for the Father spoke of a day when He would say of formerly wayward Ephraim, "I have surely heard Ephraim grieving."

In that day, a repentant Ephraim responds: "Thou hast chastised me, and I was chastised, like an untrained calf; bring me back that I may be restored, for Thou art YHVH my God. 'For after I turned back, I repented; and after I was instructed [Rotherham says, "after I came to know myself"[12]], I smote on my thigh; I was ashamed, and also

---

10 Our Redeemer must be Elohim (God). See Psalm 49:10,15.

11 *Restoring Israel's Kingdom* by Angus Wootten, Saint Cloud, FL: Key of David, 200, chapter 11.

12 *The Emphasized Bible* by J. B. Rotherham, *26 Translations of the Holy Bible*, Grand Rapids: Zondervan, Mathis, 1985.

humiliated, because I bore the reproach of my youth'" (Jeremiah 31:18,19).

After this outwardly "Gentile Israel" comes to know himself, after Ephraim is instructed about his own Israelite roots, he becomes ashamed of the sins of his youth, and in repentance he turns from his pagan practices.

Once properly instructed and truly repentant, Ephraim "will be like a mighty man." Then the Father "will whistle for them, to gather them together [with Judah]" and, "Ephraim will come trembling from the west." Ephraim will return in great numbers, "Until no room can be found for them" (Zechariah 10:7,8,10; Hosea 11:10).

Many are now hearing the Father as He muses to Himself, *"Is Ephraim My dear son? Is he a delightful child? Indeed, as often as I have spoken against him, I certainly still remember him; therefore My heart yearns for him; I will surely have mercy on him"* (Jeremiah 31:20).

Who Are These?

Who are these people now traveling the road of Israelite celebrations? Are they returning Israel? If they realize their true identity as Israelites, will that realization help change their understanding of their call to celebrate the feasts?

Yes it will. Seeing the truth about their own heritage will greatly enhance their celebrations and fill them with a new and invigorating purpose. It will also help them understand why the Father put a call on their hearts to celebrate.

Who are these?

This is the question Jacob/Israel asked of Joseph when he saw Joseph's two sons, Manasseh and Ephraim. At that time, the aging patriarch asked of Joseph, "Who are these?" (Genesis 48:8).

Isaiah posed a similar question, "Who are these that fly along like clouds, like doves to their nests? (Isaiah 60:8, KJV).[13] Likewise, in the Book of Revelation, one of elders

---

13 For more about these "doves" and the call on their lives, see the book, *My*
(continued...)

asks, "Who are these, robed in white, and where have they come from?" (Revelation 7:13, NRSV).

Who are these? They are a people whom most of Jewish Israel does not readily recognize. Just as Israel's sons did not recognize Joseph as their brother, in this day there are many who do not recognize Joseph's sons as their brothers.

Long ago Isaiah asked, *"Who are these?"* Today there are a company of people who fly with the Spirit, who come in the Name of the Prince of Peace, and who are so numerous that their appearance is like that of a cloud for thickness.

These people often use the symbol of the dove, and are sometimes likened to *doves*, to *yownah*, from which comes the name, *Jonah*. Like Jonah, perhaps they did not want to come in the beginning, but ultimately the Father's wishes won their hearts.

Additionally, the word for wine, *yayin*, comes from the same root word as for doves, for this is a company of effervescent people, a people who bring joy and healing.[14] Being "robed in white" signifies their call to *purity*.[15]

Virgin Israel

These non-Jewish people feel inexplicably drawn to Israel, to things Jewish, to the Jewish people and to the Land of Israel. Can there be something more to their being drawn in this way than has yet been seen?

Jeremiah speaks of a "virgin" people, who would be dressed in *white*, and he tells them to, "Set up for yourself roadmarks, place for yourself guideposts; direct your mind to the highway, The way by which you went. Return, O virgin of Israel, return to these your cities" (Jeremiah 31:22).

Are these returning people actually physical Israelites?

---

13 (...continued)
Beloved's Israel by Gloria Cavallaro, Saint Cloud: Key of David, 2001.

14 Fly: *Strong's* # H5774; Cloud: # H5645; Doves: # H3123. Wine: # H3196.

15 "Who are these?" From a message delivered by David Pavlik, Spiritual Leader of Beit Yisrael congregations in Orlando and Wildwood, FL, also Shepherds Council Member, Messianic Israel Alliance.

Only the Almighty can say whether they are or are not, but there are some things we do know. We know these celebrants have an important call on their lives and an essential end time work to do, for they are called to be the repairers of the breach (Isaiah 58:1-14).

Foundational Truths

The two houses of Israel are presently being reunited: Ephraim is returning to his roots, Judah is seeing her Messiah, and both are learning more about Yeshua, the Living Torah.

To be prepared for the exciting days that lie just ahead, it is essential that we grasp these basic truths, for we who see these things can help effect Israel's full reunion.[16] Our celebration of Israel's feasts in all their fullness will play a powerful role in their restoration.

As we address the feasts, we assume our readers have an understanding of the probable identity of the non-Jews now being drawn to their Israelite roots. Therefore, we will not enumerate the countless Scriptures that prove their potential Israelite heritage. For a complete discussion of this topic, we invite you to read the comprehensive work, *Who Is Israel?* Or you may read the condensed review of those teachings, *Ephraim and Judah: Israel Revealed.* [17]

The Melo HaGoyim

To see what is unfolding before us concerning Israel and her feasts, it is imperative that we see the truth about "both the houses of Israel" (Isaiah 8:14). We must realize that it was ordained by the Almighty that those of Joseph/Ephraim would become a "*melo hagoyim*" (מלא הגוים). For Jacob prophesied over Joseph's son, Ephraim, "His descendants shall become a fullness of Gentiles [*melo hagoyim*]" (Genesis 48:19; Romans 11:25; Isaiah 8:14).

---

16 Ezek 37:15-28; Jer 16:11-16; 31:8-9,18-19; 33:23-26; Zech 8:3,7,13.
17 Both by Batya Wootten, Saint Cloud, FL: Key of David, 2000, 2002.

Restated, those of Jacob's grandson, Ephraim, were destined to become so numerous that they would have to inhabit lands of other nations. [18]

Just as every promise made by the Holy One to the people of Judah is "Yes and Amen," so it is for His promises to Joseph/Ephraim (Ezekiel 37:19).

Just as He made many promises to Judah, so the Father made many promises to Judah's brother, Joseph, and to Joseph's heir, Ephraim. He said the scattered people of Ephraim would one day be gathered from every nation, tribe and tongue.

The prophets Hosea and Amos even foretold that the Ephraimites would be called "*Sons of the Living God*" (Hosea 1-2; 8:8; Amos 9:9)—one of the very names we now use for the non-Jewish Believers in Yeshua.

Our Father's promises are being fulfilled in this end time. He is taking one stick for Judah and his companions, and one stick for Ephraim and his companions, and He is making the two sticks one in His hand (Ezekiel 37:15-28).

Non-Jewish Believers in Messiah, whom we will collectively call Ephraim, [19] are in many ways being made one with those of Judah. Most notably, they are coming together in celebration.

---

18   The *ArtScroll Tanach Series* (*a commentary from Talmudic, Midrashic* and *Rabbinic* sources; hereafter called *ArtScroll*) says *melo*, or *m'loh*, means a "fullness" and, "connotes abundance...meaning: His seed will become the abundance of the nations...They will have to inhabit lands of other nations" (*Genesis*, Vol. 6, NY: Mesorah, 1982-95, p 2121). *Melo* also is used in Psalm 24:1: "The earth is the Lord's, and the [*melo*] *fulness thereof*, (KJV); or "*all it contains*" (NASB). *Strong's* defines melo (# 4393) as "*fulness*," and *goy* (#1471) as "Gentile, heathen, nation, people." According to Gesenius' (Hendrickson, p 163a, word # 1471), *goyim* is "specially used of the (other) nations besides Israel."

19   To call the Believers in Messiah "Ephraim," is not to say that *every* Believer is a biological descendant of Israel. Just as those who call the Jewish people "Judah" are not necessarily saying *everyone* in "Judaism" is a biological descendant of Israel. The Jewish people have made "converts" from among the Gentiles/Nations (Exo 12:38; Est 8:17; Ezra 2:59; Acts 2:10), yet all are called "*Jews.*" Similarly, we call the non-Jewish Believers in Messiah "Ephraimites." We also note that among those whom we call "Ephraim," there may be many from the people of Judah, because the Early Church was entirely Jewish. Also, to escape from persecution over the years, many from Judah hid in the Church.

This book centers on those celebrations and particularly on the call of the celebrants. It is written with the understanding that Israel's two houses have not yet been fully reunited,[20] but that the Father is using His set-apart feast times to help reunite us.[21]

How Do We Celebrate?

Since the Temple no longer stands, the feasts cannot be kept exactly as prescribed. We cannot go up to offer sacrifices, and it is no longer necessary to do so (Hebrews 9:23-26-10:10). Our Heavenly Father is aware of this fact. He even had a hand in the destruction of the Temple where the Levitical sacrifices were to be made. Most importantly, prior to its destruction, He sent a Living Temple to the sons of Israel. Long before, Moses had instructed them that they must hearken to this coming Prophet (Deuteronomy 18:18-19; John 17:8, 20,21;12:49-50).

Our celebrations must be interpreted in light of this *Living Temple*—we must lift up and delight in Israel's *Standard*, Messiah Yeshua (Isaiah 11:10-12). Rejoicing in Him will empower us to enter into Israel's promised "fullness," which is foretold in many ways.

---

20 For proof texts that the two houses have not been reunited see Zech 8:3, 7,13; 9:13; 11:14; Jer 3:14-18; 31:18-19; 50:4-5,20; Isa 11:11-14; 1 Sam 17:45; Obad 1:18; Ezek 37:23.

21 Messiah Yeshua has imputed oneness to His Body. In Him it is presently available, but all Israel has not yet fully implemented that oneness. Both the houses of Israel have failed to walk as the completely repentant, reunited, and restored people of Ezekiel 37:15-28. Similarly, Yeshua has "sat down" on the "throne of His father David." That He already has "sat down" indicates that He now rules (Luke 1:32; Heb 1:3; 10:12; 12:2; Rev 3:21). His is a Kingdom to come (Matt 6:10; Luke 11:2; also see Isa 27:9; 55:3; 59:21; Jer 31:31-34; 32:38-40; Heb 8:8-12; 10:16). There was also a specific day when Yeshua was sacrificed as our Passover Lamb, yet He is called "the Lamb slain from the foundation of the world" (Rev 13:8, KJV; also see 1 Cor 5:7; John 1:29; 1 Pet 1:19; Mark 15:34).

Israel's Feasts and their Fullness

Fullness is Coming!

Fullness is promised to Israel in the end times, specifically to Ephraim and Judah. Completion is coming to Israel. She is destined to be filled to over-flowing.

This book is titled "Israel's Feasts and their Fullness" for this reason. Its purpose is to fill the reader, especially those of Ephraim, with hope in their promised fullness, that they might be inspired to fulfill their divine call, and thus help usher those of Judah into their promised fullness.

Paul told of a "**fullness**" of the Gentiles that is to "**come in**" (Romans 11:25). And those of Ephraim were to become a "**fullness**" of the nations (Genesis 48:19).

Some believe Paul spoke of a specific *number* of Gentiles coming to faith. That could be one meaning of the verse. However, *fullness* (*pleroma*) means repletion, completion, what fills. It comes from a word that means to finish (a period or task), to verify (a prediction).[22] Moreover, the words "*come in*" mean to *enter.*[23] Thus we believe this verse indicates that the Father has a last days job for Ephraim to do. He wants him to verify something to Judah.

The "fullness of Gentiles" that is Ephraim (whatever the number) is now being called to *enter into a new era*. It is an

---

22 *Strong's* #'s G 4138 and 4137 respectively.
23 *Strong's* # G 1525.

era of celebrating the feasts of Israel as they have never been celebrated before.

We suggest that Romans 11:25 has more to do with completion of a task rather than on a magic number of non-Jews being saved. We suggest that it has to do with the maturation of Ephraim; and that it tells of a time when he presses on beyond the "elementary" (but necessary) points of the gospel (Hebrews 6:1-3). It also has to do with the end of Ephraim's punishment. It speaks of the time when he responds to Jezreel: "The sons of Judah and the sons of Israel will be gathered together, and...**great will be the day of Jezreel**" (Hosea 1:11).

Judah's Fullness

Judah too is destined to come to fullness: "Now if their transgression is riches for the world and their failure is riches for the Gentiles, how much more will their fulfillment be! (Romans 11:12).

Micah spoke of a time when Judah will "return to the sons of Israel" (Micah 5:3), and Moses said the Father will "bring him unto his people [Israel]..." (Deuteronomy 33:7).

Judah enters into fullness when he hears the Word of Messiah Yeshua, and the divine plan is for him to hear that word through the mouth of his long-lost brother, Ephraim.

Judah also needs to be *returned* to the sons of Israel, because his branches were broken off the olive tree of Israel (Romans 11:17).

The Olive Tree in its Fullness

The first time Israel is called an "olive tree" is in Jeremiah; he said, "YHVH called your name, 'A green olive tree.'" And the prophet said he was speaking to, "The house of Israel and the house of Judah" (Jeremiah 11:10,16).

Thus we see that there are two main "branches" in this tree. The first branches to be broken off and scattered among the nations were those of Ephraim. Because of their penchant for paganism, they were scattered to Assyria and ultimately to every nation, where they continued to degenerate, like a plant when it becomes *wild.* They became *Lo-Ami,* or *Not-A-People,* and were scattered among the heathen (Jeremiah 2:18,21; Hosea 1:9; 5:3; 8:8; Amos 9:9; Romans 9:21-26). [24]

Years later, many of Judah were taken to Babylon, then some returned in the days of Nehemiah to rebuild the Temple. It was the heirs of these Jews and their companions who were in the Land during the time that Paul wrote of Israel's olive tree, and explained that "wild olive branches" were being called to provoke Judah to jealousy (Romans 11).

Israel, meaning both houses, is the olive tree. Paul wrote of the same olive tree that the Father had all but denuded when He scattered Ephraim and then Judah.[25] And Paul said that those of Judah who did *not* believe in Messiah Yeshua were broken off the tree (Romans 11:17-20). The Temple in Jerusalem was destroyed, and they were scattered among the nations.

Some of Judah, however, were sent forth by the Messiah to regather the previously scattered sheep of Israel (Matthew 15:24; John 10:16,27; Acts 1:8).

Yeshua is the Root

Yeshua is the Root, or life source, of Israel's olive tree. All must be rooted in Him, including the patriarchs (Psalms 52:8; 128:3; Revelation 22:16; Romans 3:23).

The returning Ephraimites and companions are called to provoke those of Judah to jealousy. They are to walk in a way that makes Judah want what they have (Romans 11;

---

24 The Father asks of Ephraim (who was taken captive to Assyria), "What are you doing...on the road to Assyria?" And, "I planted you a choice vine, a completely faithful seed. How then have you turned yourself before Me into the degenerate shoots of a foreign vine?" (Jeremiah 2:18,21). Thus, for all outward purposes, Ephraim became degenerate foreigners or pagan gentiles.

25 To better understand Israel's Olive Tree, see the Olive Tree graphic at the end of this chapter. Also see *Who Is Israel?* chapters 12 and 18.

Ezekiel 37:16). They are not to be arrogant toward the broken branches, but are to provoke them in a positive way, that Judah might be grafted in again (Obadiah 1:12; Joel 2:32-3:1; Luke 13:1-5; Romans 11:11,17-21).

When explaining the olive tree, Paul said he spoke of a *mystery*, of a hardening, or blindness, that had befallen Israel. That hardness was to last until a certain point in time. This means that even though Paul was explaining the mystery at that time, Israel as a nation would be unable to see or comprehend the mystery until a predetermined point in time.

That time is now!

With this understanding in place, we begin to see Israel's olive tree in its fullness. We see Israel and the glory of her collective calling.

The Fullness of the Messiah

Riches come forth when Judah returns to Israel's sheepfold. With their restoration and return to the flock comes collective fullness.

We want to enter into this fullness so that together Judah and Ephraim can bring about a victory in the Earth for *YHVH Tsavaot*, the LORD of Hosts.[26]

In this present fullness of time, all things are being summed up in the Messiah, and in us. For we are His "body, the fullness of Him who fills all in all."

We want to partake of Yeshua's fullness (Galatians 4:4; Ephesians 1:10-11,23). We want to "attain to the unity of the faith and...to the fullness of Messiah." For it is the Father's good pleasure "for all the fullness to dwell in Him." In Yeshua, "all the fullness of Deity dwells in bodily form" (Ephesians 4:13; 3:19; Colossians 1:19; 2:9).

The fullness, the completion, the perfection for which Israel longs, is only found in our Divine Messiah—in He Who is truly the Israel of God.

---

26 Like their Master, some may find "victory" in death (Rev 11:8-13).

Fullness and Our Forefathers

Many Believers today are dissatisfied because they know they are missing something essential in their celebrations.

To be truly satisfied, we need to celebrate the feasts of Israel in their fullness. To do so, we must not be intimidated by men, nor by their traditions. Instead, we must be people who desire to please our Heavenly Father, for in these last days our Father is looking to fully restore His people. To accomplish His purposes in the Earth, He is looking for those who will do as was prophesied through Isaiah: "Look to Abraham your father and to Sarah who gave birth to you in pain; when he was but one I called him, then I blessed him and multiplied him" (Isaiah 51:2).

The Father seeks a people who will do even as is written by Isaiah: "Through this Jacob's iniquity will be forgiven; this will be the full price of the pardoning of his sin: when he makes all the altar stones like pulverized chalk stones; when Asherim and incense altars will not stand" (Isaiah 27:9).

Change First Comes to Ephraim

When Judah begins to see such change in Ephraim, he will be encouraged to acknowledge him as a legitimate heir in Israel.

Now is the time for Ephraim to see the Messiah in His fullness; and to see that Yeshua is the Lion of Judah (Revelation 5:5). It is also time for Judah to be reunited with Israel and to see that the Only Begotten Son, so long proclaimed by Ephraim, is truly the King of Kings and Lord of Lords (1 Kings 11:11-12,26,31-35; 12:24; Ezekiel 37:15-28; John 4:22).

Our Teshuvah

Many returning celebrants are now hearing the call of the Father, and they now want to return to the feasts of Israel. But they do not necessarily want to "become Jewish." They just want to be who they are.

We believe these repentant ones are, at least primarily, returning virgin Israel. Their forefathers long ago forgot the ways of the Almighty. They stumbled, they left the ancient paths to walk in errant bypaths. Now their children want to make *teshuvah*. They want to *return* (Jeremiah 18:15).

The children of Judah have also tripped over the Sanctuary, they have stumbled over the stumbling Stone. Now they want to embrace Him, yet without denying that they are of Judah.

So it is that many Jewish and non-Jewish Believers are now coming together as one stick in the Father's hand (Ezekiel 37:15-28).

Father, help us to understand that just as Judah was hardened, so too was Ephraim hardened. Help us in our dealings with both of these stumbling houses. Allow us to be used by You to help restore Your divided house.

Amen.

The Two Branches in Israel's Olive Tree: Ephraim and Judah
Yeshua is the Root/Life Source

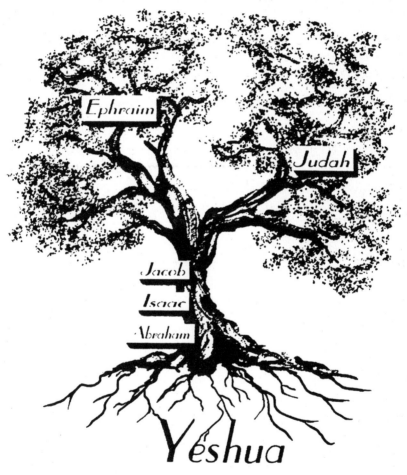

When the Father first called "Israel" an "*olive tree.*"
He specifically said He was speaking to:
"The house of Israel *and* the house of Judah" (Jeremiah 11:10).
Yeshua said, "*I am the root* and *the offspring* of David" (Revelation 22:16).

Artwork by Zion's Call Creations, Lakeland, FL

Israel's Feasts and their Fullness

The Reunion Plan
and the Prodigal

Just as shadows are attached to substance, so annual *rehearsals* of YHVH's feasts should be attached to His followers, for they remind us of our call to be His people.

As the New Covenant people of Messiah, Yeshua is now our "High Priest according to the order of Melchizedek." He has made propitiation for our sins. He is the "High Priest of our confession," and we must "hold fast" to that life-giving confession. [27]

The Blood offering provided by our High Priest differs from that of the mortal Aaronic priesthood. Those of Aaron had to repeatedly enter into the Holy of Holies once a year, but not "without taking blood offered for himself and for the sins of the people...."

But when Messiah Yeshua "appeared as a high priest ...He entered through the greater and more perfect tabernacle not made with hands." He did not have to offer Himself often, as did the priests of Aaron, who entered the holy place year by year. Yeshua "does not need daily, like

---

27 Heb 2:17; 3:1; 4:14; 5:10; 6:2; 7:26; 8:1.

those high priests, to offer up sacrifices, first for His own sins and then for the sins of the people, because this He did once for all when He offered up Himself" (Hebrews 7:27; 8:3; 9:7,11,25; Romans 6:10). Yeshua did not offer the blood of goats and calves, but through His own blood, He entered the holy place once for all, having obtained eternal redemption for all who believe in His name.[28]

We must honor our High Priest as we celebrate His feasts, for He is the One who teaches us how to celebrate. Only He can prepare our hearts and minds and enable us to come together in a spirit of love and celebration.

Jealousy Departs—Celebration Begins

Before we can fully celebrate our Father's feasts with a true spirit of love and unity, we must address the sins that hinder us: Anger, jealousy, bitterness, wrath, resentment, selfishness, and envy (Galatians 5:20-21; Ephesians 4:31-32; Colossians 3:8-10). These attitudes and behaviors inhibit our celebration and prevent our reunion.

The Father speaks of a day when "the envy and jealousy of Ephraim shall depart...and Judah shall not vex and harass Ephraim" (Isaiah 11:13, TAB).

These ancient traits characterize current Christian and Jewish relationships. Ephraim is envious, or jealous, of Judah. The Hebrew word is *kanah* (קנא), and jealous is a good translation, because both words cover a wide range of emotions. *Kanah* can be used in a favorable sense to speak of consuming zeal focused on a loved one, as in: "*Kanah* for Thy house has consumed me." It also is used to describe our Father when He says: "I, YHVH your God am a [*kanah*] jealous God" (Psalm 69:9; Exodus 20:5).

The positive, protective aspect of *kanah* is seen when Believers speak of the "unexplainable love they feel for the Jew." Even with little Biblical knowledge, some people have a desire to protect their Jewish brothers and sisters.

---

28 Heb 9:12; 10:10; John 1:12; 3:18; 10:25; 20:31; 1 John 3:23; 5:13; 1 Pet 3:18.

However, jealousy can grow into violent wrath and anger when it is distorted and left unchecked. Just as Ephraim's fierce anger once burned against Judah (2 Chronicles 25:10), such destructive anger is evident in Church history. The result of this anger is seen in the shameful anti-Semitic violence perpetrated against the Jewish people. Church history is replete with anti-Jewish actions and doctrine: The tyranny of the Crusades, the torture of the Spanish Inquisitions, the burning and pillaging of the Pogroms, plus the indescribable horror of six million Jewish lives annihilated by the Holocaust.

The record of the Church is tarnished by jealousy, marred by hatred. Her wedding gown is stained with Jewish blood. It is a stain that must be washed away—can only be washed away—with true tears of repentance.

Now is the time for Ephraim to humbly repent and seek forgiveness from his brother Judah.

A Close Relative

Judah's problem is that he "vexes" Ephraim. The word is *tsarar* (צרר), which means to cramp, afflict, besiege, bind, distress, oppress, to be an adversary, or enemy.[29] *Tsarar* speaks of restricting, tying up, or having strong emotional response to controversial decisions. This word is used in Isaiah 8:16: "*Bind* up the testimony."

"Binding" through legalism is one way that Judah vexes Ephraim.[30] Legalistic misrepresentation of Torah hinders Ephraim, because it keeps him from seeing and embracing its many truths.

In addition, Judah has also long *distressed* Ephraim by refusing to acknowledge him as an equal heir in Israel, though Judah has obviously had legitimate complaints and justifications for his actions.

The Second Book of Samuel describes an incident

---

29 Those of Judah are "*enemies* of the gospel for your sake" (Rom 11:28).

30 *Strong's* # H 6887; TWOT #1973. Restrict: see Isa 49:19; 2 Sam 20:3. Note: Hosea describes Ephraim's sin as being "bound up" (vs 13:12).

between Israel's two houses that illustrates these traits.

King David was being escorted across the Jordan, principally by the people of Judah. But they did not wait for *all* Israel to assemble and escort the king, so Ephraim became angry when he was left out of the procession.

"All the men of Israel [Ephraim] came to the king and said to the king, 'Why had our brothers the men of Judah stolen you away, and brought the king and his household and all David's men with him over the Jordan?'

"Then all the men of Judah answered the men of Israel, 'Because the king is a close relative to us. Why are you angry about this matter? Have we eaten at the king's expense, or has anything been taken for us?'

"But the men of Israel answered the men of Judah and said, 'We have ten parts in the king, therefore we also have more claim on David than you. Why then do you treat us with contempt? Was it not our advice first to bring back our king?'"

Harsh, Fierce Words

The Father's comment sums up His opinion of this matter: "Yet the words of the men of Judah were harsher than the words of the men of Israel" (2 Samuel 19:41-43).

"The king is a *close relative* to us" are *harsh*, *fierce* (KJV) words. To claim the king was "closer" to them due to biological relationship was cruel, since the Ephraimites could not change how they were born.

King David was a type of King Messiah, and a similar scenario is being played out today. For centuries, vast numbers of Ephraimite Believers have implored people everywhere to follow King Jesus (Yeshua). In this day, many Jewish Believers are claiming Messiah Yeshua is *their* close brother, and those of Ephraim are once again feeling wounded, left out, and treated with contempt.

In this state, they tend to respond with an inexcusable explosion of anger.

In opposition to the "one hope of...calling" declared in Ephesians 4:4, this type of hurtful behavior is often dismissed under the errant guise of Jewish Believers having "a different calling." But the truth is that the non-Jewish Believer may in reality be a descendant of one of Yeshua's apostles, and the supposed "Jewish" Believer could descend from one who converted to Judaism. As stated in Esther 8:17: "Many among the peoples of the land **became** Jews, for the dread of the Jews had fallen on them."

No one can prove his pedigree. A Jewish person can only *assume by faith* that he is biologically related to Yeshua. More importantly, Yeshua frowns on any who would pridefully "lord it over" another by claiming such a special relationship. He explicitly said, "Whoever does the will of My Father who is in heaven, **he is My brother...**" (Matthew 12:48-50).

Judah and the Family Album

Historically, Judah has vexed Ephraim. Jewish leaders put First Century followers of the Messiah out of the syna-gogue.[31] Judah also began reciting a curse over the Jewish Believers in their daily prayers.[32] Even today, Messiah's followers find it difficult to obtain citizenship in Israel.

In allowing this to happen, it is as though the Father gave Judah control over the "family photo album," yet Judah will not allow Ephraim's picture to be in that album.

Instruction Will Solve the Problem

These traits of jealousy and vexation must cease. We who see the truth must rise above the fray and become people of solution. We must also remember that reunion begins when Ephraim is *instructed*—which leads him to return to his own Hebraic roots, which causes his jealousy to depart, which inspires him to repent of his paganism, which allows Yeshua to heal him of his woundedness, all of which will ultimately serve to bless Judah.

---

31 John 9:22; 12:43; 16:2; Acts 26:9-11.
32 See Buksbazen quote, chapter 7, "Seventh Day or First Day." p 60-61.

When Ephraim returns to his Father's house in repentance and celebration, the stage is set for reunion with his older brother Judah. Then comes healing and restoration.

The Return of the Prodigal

In the parable of the prodigal, Yeshua tells the story of a man who had two sons, the younger of whom asked for his inheritance, then went to a distant country where he squandered it on loose living. Then came a famine, and the son had to take a job feeding swine. Hungry, he wished he could even eat of the pig's pods, but he was given nothing.

Coming to his senses, he said, "How many of my father's hired men have more than enough bread, but I am dying here with hunger!" So he determined to return to his father's house to confess his sin and renounce his disobedience. Feeling unworthy to be called his son, he would ask to become one of his father's hired men.

The son's father, having long yearned for the boy's return, saw him coming and ran to embrace and kiss him.

He said to one of his slaves, "Quickly bring out the best robe and put it on him, and put a ring on his hand and sandals on his feet; and bring the fattened calf, kill it, and let us eat and celebrate; for this son of mine was dead and has come to life again; he was lost and has been found."

The older son, who had been out in the field, upon approaching the house, heard music and dancing. After inquiring, he was told, "Your brother has come, and your father has killed the fattened calf because he has received him back safe and sound."

Unwilling to go in and join the celebration, the older brother became angry. So his father came out and began pleading with him. But he said to his father, "For many years I have been serving you and I have never neglected a command of yours; and yet you have never given me a young goat, so that I might celebrate with my friends; but when this son of yours came, who has devoured your wealth with prostitutes, you killed the fattened calf for him."

To this the father responded, "Son, you have always been with me, and all that is mine is yours. But we had to celebrate and rejoice, for this brother of yours was dead and has begun to live, and was lost and has been found" (see Luke 15:11-32).

The Prodigal Portrays Ephraim

This story can be seen as a depiction of Ephraim's return home to his Heavenly Father:

- ◆ The prodigal went to a foreign land:
- ✓ "Israel [Ephraim] will certainly go from its land into exile" (Amos 7:11).
- ◆ The prodigal lived loosely:
- ✓ Father says, "Ephraim is a trained heifer that loves to thresh, but I will come over her fair neck with a yoke; I will harness Ephraim..." (Hosea 10:11).
- ◆ The prodigal was hungry:
- ✓ "'Behold, days are coming,' declares YHVH Elohim, 'when I will send a famine on the land, not a famine for bread or a thirst for water, but rather for hearing the words of YHVH" (Amos 8:11). Today, Ephraim feels he is wasting away in gatherings that offer only the elementary milk of the Word when he needs the filling protein of meat. He craves the excitement of *doing* the Father's will (John 4:34).
- ◆ Pig's pods:
- ✓ Being close to pigs describes the younger Ephraim and not Judah. Judah does not touch pork, but Ephraim celebrates his supposed "freedom" by eating pork and Easter hams. Though he has been out wallowing in the pig's mire, Ephraim will repent and return home, and the Father will welcome him.
- ◆ The prodigal came to his senses and began to repent of his youthful sins:
- ✓ The Father says, "I have surely heard Ephraim grieving." Repentant Ephraim cries, "'Thou hast

-37-

chastised me, and I was chastised, like an untrained calf; bring me back that I may be restored, for Thou art YHVH my Elohim. For after I turned back, I repented; after I was instructed, I smote on my thigh; I was ashamed, and humiliated, because I bore the reproach of my youth" (Jeremiah 31:18-19).

♦ The father of the prodigal yearned for his son:

✓ Our Heavenly Father says, "Is Ephraim My dear son? Is he a delightful child? Indeed, as often as I have spoken against him, I certainly still remember him; therefore My heart yearns for him; I will surely have mercy on him" (Jeremiah 31:19-20).

♦ When the prodigal returned, the older son was not pleased with his reappearance. He was even angry.

✓ Like the older son, First Century Jewish leaders were not happy about the return of those once lost among the nations. They accused Paul of bringing Greeks into their Temple and defiling their holy place. Some were even angry enough to kill (Acts 21:27-31). Sadly, they walked in the same spirit as some of their fathers: "The inhabitants of Jerusalem...said [of scattered Ephraim], 'Go far from the Lord; this land has been given us as a possession'" (Ezekiel 11:15). Today, some Jewish Believers are likewise unhappy about Ephraim's reemergence; they reject the idea that the non-Jews might be equal heirs in Israel. Some want non-Jewish Believers to be in their synagogues for wrong reasons. Paul says of this type, "They make much of you, but for no good purpose; they want to exclude you, so that you may make much of them" (Galatians 4:17, NRSV). In other words, they want to appear superior, that you might look to them for acceptance.

Bringing Judah into the Party

At the time of the younger son's return, the older son was "out in the field." In the parable of the tares and the wheat, Yeshua says, "The field is the world..." (Matthew 13:38). The older son was not inside the father's house, but was "approaching" it. He was "drawing nigh" (KJV). Let all who are jealous of Judah see that it was the prodigal who was *in* the house making merry with his father. The older son was *outside*.

However, let us also be very careful to acknowledge that the father went out to meet the older son. He even pleaded with him. Such is the Father's heart toward Judah. For He has sworn and will keep His promise to *again* possess Judah:

"YHVH will possess Judah as His portion in the holy land, and will **again** choose Jerusalem" (Zechariah 2:12).

Our Father wants Judah to join the party. He would have those of Ephraim behave in a way that would make Judah want to join the celebration. Yes, that is the job long ago assigned to Ephraim: Make Judah want what you have!

To accomplish his divine assignment, Ephraim, who has so long seen himself as an orphan, must realize that he is also an heir. Only then will he no longer be jealous and be able to see Judah as a member of the family. When Ephraim ceases to feel inferior (or superior) to Judah, when Ephraim truly understands that he and Judah are brothers, then total restoration and healing will come to the whole house of Israel.

To Make Jealous—Make Merry

The secret to Israel's reunion is for Ephraim to make Judah jealous.

The older brother was provoked because he saw that his younger brother was in the house *celebrating and rejoicing,* or *making merry,* with the father.

Making merry is translated from *euphraino, euphraino* (εὐφραίνω *yoo-frah'ee-no*), meaning to be in a good frame of mind, to make glad, to be or to make merry, to rejoice.[33]

---

33 *Strong's* # G 2165.

We must realize that legalism and religion will not provoke Judah to jealousy—but celebration will.

One of the reasons so many non-Jews now feel an overwhelming urge to celebrate the feasts of Israel is because *celebration* is the key to provoking Judah to jealousy. Having others see us in a good frame of mind is the Father's plan of evangelism. When others see that knowing Yeshua makes us glad and causes us to rejoice, they will want to join in. This is the secret to our reunion.

Our assignment is simple: We must be repentant for our errant ways and rejoice in our relationship with the God of Israel. We must make merry in our Father's house. When others see true repentance and true rejoicing in us, then they will want what we have.

Father, please give us eyes to see, ears to hear, and a heart to understand. Help us to discern the problems that prevent the full restoration of Your people. Help each one of us to repent of our errant ways, then enable us by Your Spirit, by Your Ruach, to become part of the solution.

Help us now, Father, to begin a study of the days You have set apart, that You might draw us unto Yourself and into Your holy ways.

Different Dates and Directions:
The Dispersions of
Ephraim and Judah

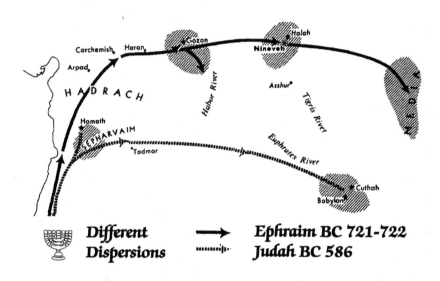

Different Dispersions	→	Ephraim BC 721-722	
	···············⫶⫶··	Judah BC 586	

To understand Israel, we must see that
Ephraim and Judah were dispersed at different times
and were sent in two different directions.
There were more than 135 years between the times of their
dispersions and up to 500 miles between the locations
to which they were dispersed.

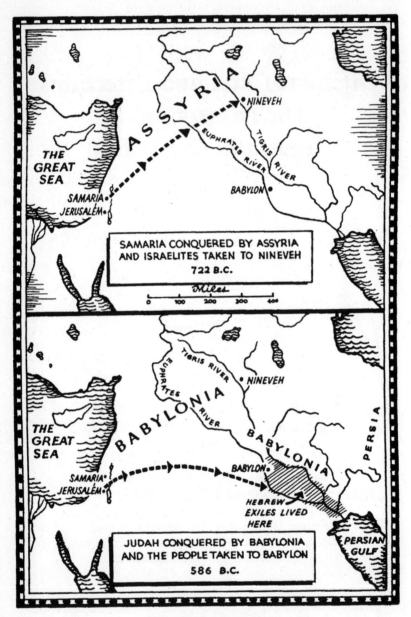

The Two Dispersions
From A Map Book For Bible Students by Frederick L. Fay,
page 18, Old Tappan, NJ: Fleming H. Revell. Used by permission.

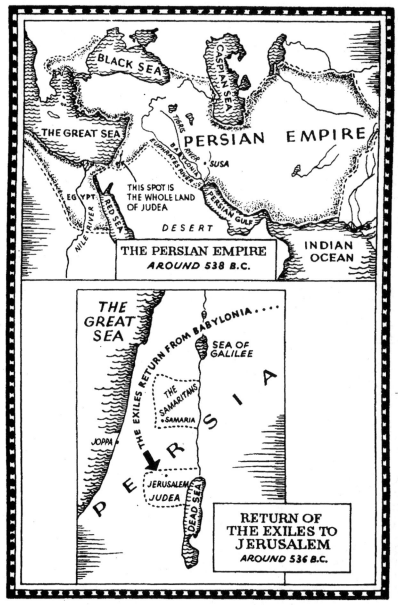

Judah's Return and Judea in the Time of Yeshua

From *A Map Book For Bible Students* by Frederick L. Fay,
page 20, Old Tappan, NJ: Fleming H. Revell. Used by permission.

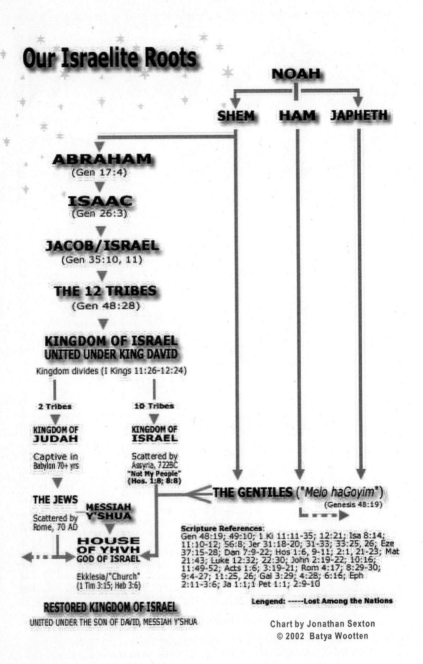

Our Israelite Roots

NOAH

SHEM   HAM   JAPHETH

ABRAHAM
(Gen 17:4)

ISAAC
(Gen 26:3)

JACOB/ISRAEL
(Gen 35:10, 11)

THE 12 TRIBES
(Gen 48:28)

KINGDOM OF ISRAEL
UNITED UNDER KING DAVID

Kingdom divides (I Kings 11:26-12:24)

2 Tribes   10 Tribes

KINGDOM OF   KINGDOM OF
JUDAH   ISRAEL

Captive in   Scattered by
Babylon 70+ yrs   Assyria, 722BC
                             "Not My People"
                             (Hos. 1:8; 8:8)

THE JEWS   THE GENTILES ("*Melo haGoyim*")
                     MESSIAH   (Genesis 48:19)
Scattered by   Y'SHUA
Rome, 70 AD

                     HOUSE   Scripture References:
                     OF YHVH   Gen 48:19; 49:10; 1 Ki 11:11-35; 12:21; Isa 8:14;
                     GOD OF ISRAEL   11:10-12; 56:8; Jer 31:18-20; 31-33; 33:25, 26; Eze
                                     37:15-28; Dan 7:9-22; Hos 1:6, 9-11; 2:1, 21-23; Mat
                     Ekklesia/"Church" 21:43; Luke 12:32; 22:30; John 2:19-22; 10:16;
                     (1 Tim 3:15; Heb 3:6) 11:49-52; Acts 1:6; 3:19-21; Rom 4:17; 8:29-30;
                                     9:4-27; 11:25, 26; Gal 3:29; 4:28; 6:16; Eph
                                     2:11-3:6; Ja 1:1;1 Pet 1:1; 2:9-10

RESTORED KINGDOM OF ISRAEL   Lengend: -----Lost Among the Nations

UNITED UNDER THE SON OF DAVID, MESSIAH Y'SHUA
                                          Chart by Jonathan Sexton
                                          © 2002 Batya Wootten

Part Two

Shabbat
Havdalah
New Moons

Shabbat: The Weekly Feast

Day of delight. A weekly rehearsal of all the goodness that we find in the Father's feasts. That is what the Shabbat should be to us.

The weekly Shabbat is the first feast listed in Scripture (Leviticus 23), because it amplifies the blessings of all the feasts. It depicts personal redemption, it is a day that is to be filled with the joy of the Holy Spirit, and it is a day that depicts the restored kingdom of Israel.

Yet many mistakenly see this day of delight as a burden to be borne rather than a blessing to be embraced.

Observing the seventh day Sabbath, or *Shabbat*, should not be regarded as a work of the Law or as a burdensome command that YHVH dealt out of our lives. It is instead the Father's gift to His people, and it is a blessed gift that most Christians have missed. But to be fair, some have missed opening this delightful gift because the package was wrapped in legalism, tied with ribbons of bondage.

The Father said to Moses, "Speak thou also unto the children of Israel, and say to them, 'Verily my Sabbaths ye shall keep: for it is a **sign** between me and you throughout your generations; that ye may know that I am YHVH that doth sanctify you'" (Exodus 31:13, KJV).

The Sabbath is the "**sign** of the Mosaic Covenant."

Can we keep perfectly this special sign?

The first commandment tells us that we are to "have no other gods" before our God, YHVH Elohim. We are to love Him with *all* our heart (Exodus 20:3; Deuteronomy 6:5). Without exception, we all fail to fulfill these basic requirements. All who think they can be saved by their works are disqualified before they ever get to the fourth commandment, "Honor the Sabbath and keep it holy." For "whoever keeps the whole law and yet stumbles in one point, he has become guilty of all" (James 2:10).

The Holy One says of mankind, "They are corrupt, and their ways are vile; there is no one who does good" (Psalm 53:1). Paul writes to the Romans, "All have sinned and fallen short of the glory of God" (vs 3:23). The Psalmist cries out, "If thou, O Yah, shouldest mark iniquities, O Adonai, who shall stand?" (vs 130:3, KJV).

While we want to strive to be obedient, we must realize that apart from the mercy and grace of God, none of us can get beyond His first commandment and have no other gods before Him. We break it continually, as we do each of His Ten Commandments. It is thus foolish for us to think we can observe the Sabbath as if by works. It is an elementary tenant of the gospel of the Kingdom that we are saved by grace and not by works (Ephesians 2:8-9; Hebrews 6:1-17).

Rising Above Legalism

To truly honor the Sabbath is to rise above man's attempts to be saved by works, or legalism. To understand the Sabbath we must see that it *predates* the Law given to Moses. It marked the end of the six days of creation. YHVH Elohim created the world in six days. "And on the seventh day God ended His work which He had made; and He rested on the seventh day from all His work which He had made. And God blessed the seventh day, and sanctified it: because in it He had rested from all his work which He created and made" (Genesis 2:2-3).

A Time of Celebration

On the Sabbath, our Creator "rested" from His work. To "rest" is to *shabbat*, meaning to desist from exertion, to cease, and to *celebrate*. He also "blessed and sanctified" this day. To *bless* is to *barach*, to praise, salute. To *sanctify* is to *kadash*, to pronounce as clean, consecrated, dedicated, hallowed. [34]

In honor of His completed work, the Sabbath was consecrated as a day of *celebration*. We are made in His image and He wants us to join Him in His celebration.

When giving His *Instructions*, or *Torah*, to Moses, the Father said to His people: "Six days you shall labor and do all your work, but the seventh day is a Sabbath to YHVH Elohim. In it you shall not do any work" (Exodus 20:9-10).

The Father set this day apart, "Because, in it He rested from all His work." For His chosen people,[35] the Sabbath is a day in which we too desist, or rest, from our works, we desist from our regular pursuits.

Restoration and Refreshment

Is this command to "shabbat" a command that leads to bondage or blessing? Is it a day to restrict or restore us?

While there are definite things that we are not to do, and things that we should do, on this day, the true answer is found in how we define *rest*.

If we tend to be legalistic in our view, to us, the Sabbath will be a command born of law, or legalism. This principle holds true whether we are *for,* or *against,* honoring this day. Both views breed talk of regulations and restrictions. Legalistic people focus on the "forbidden" things of the Sabbath, of the things you cannot do if you are going to be righteous. On the other hand, those who tend to be *anti-nomian*, or anti-law, talk about what you cannot do because you are "not free in the Spirit to do as you please."

---

34 *Strong's* #'s H7673, 1288, and 6942.
35 Deu 14:2; 1 Peter 2:9.

Riding on the High Places

Either way, we hear a "legalistic voice," and it is not the voice of the Father, nor the voice of His Son.

The Father says those who *take pleasure* in, and *honor* His Sabbath, will *delight* in Him. He says, "If because of the Sabbath, you turn your foot from doing your own pleasure on My holy day, and call the Sabbath a delight, the holy day of YHVH honorable, and shall honor it, desisting from your own ways, from seeking your own pleasure, and speaking your own word, then you will take delight in YHVH, and I will make you ride on the heights of the earth; and I will feed you with the heritage of Jacob your father, for the mouth of YHVH has spoken" (Isaiah 58:13-14).

These words were written by Isaiah long *after* the Law was given to Moses. They tell us that those who take pleasure in the Sabbath will *feast* on the inheritance of our forefather, Jacob. Isaiah tells of a *blessing* that is granted to those who honor the Sabbath, he tells of a blessed people who get to *ride on the high places.*

Restoration and refreshment are the heart and soul of the Father's Shabbat. But this day was not set aside for spiritual refreshment alone. Our Father gave us a day of rest so we can be spiritually, emotionally, and *physically* recharged. Even the ox, donkey, and stranger are included in His instructions to rest, for He prohibits "servile labor." He included servants and animals in His decree, because the Sabbath is given that all Israel, even the lowly, defenseless son of a female slave, or the foreigner who has no legal rights in the land, can still be refreshed.

The Sabbath gives us time to breathe, to slow down from the pace of earning a living, to rest, and to allow our bodies to be rejuvenated.

The Father created this day that we might be "refreshed" (Exodus 23:12). The Sabbath is especially set apart for the *Ruach*, the *Breath*, the *Spirit* of the Almighty, to breathe on us. "Refreshed" is translated from *naphash*, which means to breathe, or to be breathed upon.[36] The Sabbath is a special day wherein the *Ruach HaKodesh*, the Holy Spirit, will breathe on, and refresh, the body and spirit of those who delight in this consecrated day. As the writer of Hebrews said: "There remains a Sabbath rest for the people of God. For the one who has entered His rest has himself also rested from his works, as God did from His. Therefore let us be diligent to enter that rest..." (Hebrews 4:9-11).

We should diligently seek to live our lives in the spirit of this day. Father wants us to *live* every day of our lives in His Sabbath rest, but He also wants us to properly *honor* His consecrated seventh-day.

Desisting from Our Own Goals— Being Dedicated to the Father's Goal

We are instructed to turn our foot from doing our own "pleasure" on the Sabbath and to desist from speaking our own words (Isaiah 58:13-14). This means we are not to pursue our everyday desires, purposes, pursuits, and goals on Shabbat.[37] We are to cease pursuit and even talk of the reward of our labors under the sun (Ecclesiastes 5:18; 9:9). We are instead to especially focus on the Father's goals for our lives as outlined in His Word.

As we will later see, His plan for our salvation begins with godly families, so Shabbat is an especially good time to spend quality time with family, to focus on building up and encouraging our children in the faith.

To help us better accomplish these goals, we are instructed to have "a holy convocation" on the Shabbat. We are to gather together with those of like faith and to study, or concentrate on, our Father's Word. We are not to forsake assembling together, but are to come together that we might be stimulated, encouraged, and built up in our faith (Leviticus 23:3; Hebrews 10:23-25; Colossians 2:7).

---

36 See Exodus 23:12 and *Strong's* # H5314.
37 Pleasure: *Strong's* and *BDB* # H2656.

A Sign—to be Guarded by the Watchmen

Keeping the Sabbath is a sign to an unbelieving world that we are the people of God: "But as for you, speak to the sons of Israel, saying, 'You shall surely keep My Sabbaths; for this is a sign between Me and you throughout your generations, that you may know that I am YHVH who sanctifies you.'" By observance of this covenant sign, YHVH's people were to be known among the nations. This remains true today.

The Sabbath is a perpetual covenant: "The sons of Israel shall keep the Sabbath, to celebrate the Sabbath through-out their generations as *a perpetual covenant*. It is a *sign* between Me and the sons of Israel forever; for in six days YHVH made heaven and earth, but on the seventh day He ceased from labor, and was refreshed" (Exodus 31:13,16-17).

We are to sanctify the Father's Sabbaths and to remember that it is He Who sanctifies us. His Sabbath is a *sanctification sign* between us (Ezekiel 20:12,20).

A Sign of Belonging

A *sign* is an *oath*, a literal or figurative signal, a flag, beacon, monument, evidence, a mark, an ensign, a token.[38] To be sanctified is to be consecrated, dedicated, to be set apart.

In celebrating the Father's Sabbath, we give evidence to the world that we are consecrated to Him and that He is our source, our protection, and our provision. Honoring this day marks us as a people who belong to the God of Israel. It serves as a beacon for those drawn to His truth. But be warned: It is also evidence against those who oppose the Sabbath. This means that even if you are quiet in your observance and try not to condemn others by your actions, they will often nonetheless be convicted. But be prepared, those who are not ready for such conviction may well retaliate verbally.

---

38 *Strong's* # H226.

Despite this potential result, the Father told His people to "*keep*," to "*shamar*" His Sabbaths, meaning we are to hedge about (as with thorns), to guard, protect, attend to, take heed, mark, observe, preserve, regard, reserve, save, and to watch for His Sabbaths.[39] These words describe the duties of a watchman, and Ephraim was especially called to be a "watchman" for the whole house of Israel (Hosea 9:8).[40]

In this last day, Ephraim must learn to preserve the Father's Sabbaths in truth. He even needs to bring a fresh anointing to the Father's appointed times. Ephraim must not be anti-law, nor legalistic, in his approach. He is to simply *delight* in the Shabbat.

---

39 *Strong's* # H8104.
40 See *Who Is Israel?* chapter 21, "*Called To Be Watchmen.*"

Israel's Feasts and their Fullness

Seventh Day or First Day?

The Father hallowed the seventh day and called it His *Sabbath.* Scripture defines how a day is to be reckoned: "There was evening and there was morning, one day" (Genesis 1:5).

The Hebrew day starts at sunset; it is marked from sunset to sunset. Moreover, our Father numbered all the days in relationship to this seventh day: "And there was evening, and there was morning—the first day....the second day....the third day....the fourth day....the fifth day....the sixth day" (Genesis 1:5,8,13,19, 23,31).

Many Christians call the *first* day of the week, or Sunday, the Sabbath. But if we examine the history of this day, we find that the pagan idolaters of Rome named it "Sunday," to honor the Sun god, who was their main god. Again, Sunday is the *first* day of the week, *not* the hallowed *seventh* day Sabbath. If we look at any regular Gregorian calendar, we see that the week *begins* on Sunday.

The Christian decision to move "Sabbath" observance was largely based on the anti-Jewish sentiments of the Church, on the influence of the pagan sun worshipers that surrounded them, and on belief that the Christ was resurrected on "Easter Sunday."

The Church's emphasis on the Resurrection contributed much to their decision to commemorate Sunday rather than the Sabbath. This decision was encouraged by their understanding of Matthew 28:1: "After the Sabbath, **at dawn on the first day of the week**, Mary Magdalene and the other Mary went to look at the tomb."

Scores of books and papers have been written about the timing of the death, burial, and resurrection of our Messiah. Some say He rose on the Sabbath, others say He rose on the first day of the week, or the Day of First Fruits.

However, regardless of one's conclusion on the matter, Sunday meetings still do not meet the requirement to honor the *Sabbath*, or seventh day. The seventh day will *always* be the seventh day. Likewise, the first day of the week will *always* be the first day of the week. Sunday is simply *not* the seventh day Sabbath.

To celebrate the *concept* of the Sabbath on the first day of the week does not move the "hallowed" seventh day to Sunday. Even if you have a day of rest on the first day of the week, and even if you are worshiping Yeshua on that day, you are still not following the command to "Honor *the* Sabbath Day and keep it holy."

The Day of the Lord

Sunday is often mistakenly called "the day of the Lord." However, this term refers to a day of judgment and destruction. It is a day of wrath and burning anger; a day when Messiah Yeshua will exterminate sinners from His chosen Land.[41] For His faithful ones, "the day of the Lord" is a day of redemption and gladness, because He does away with sin in that day; it is a day wherein He is glorified (Isaiah 49:8; Ezekiel 39:13; Malachi 3:2; Luke 17:30; Ephesians 4:30). [42]

---

41 Isa 13:6,9; Lam 2:22; Eze 13:5; 30:3; Joel 1:15; 2:1,11,31; 3:14; Amos 5:18,20; Zep 1:7,8,14,18; 2:2,3; John 12:48; Acts 2:20; Obad 1:15; 1 Cor 5:5; 1 Thes 5:2; 2 Thes 2:2; 2 Pet 3:10. Also see, Isa 49:2; Rev 1:16; 2:16; 19:15,21.

42 Also see 1 Cor 1:8, 2 Cor 1:14, Phil 1:6,10, 2:16; 2 Pet 3:12.

The phrase, "the day of the Lord," is not used in Scripture to refer to the Sabbath.

When speaking of the Sabbath, this phrase is *only* used in connection with the word, *holy*, or *kadosh*, which means *sacred*.[43] For example, the Father says, "[B]ecause of the sabbath...turn your foot from doing your own pleasure on **My holy/kadosh day**, and call the sabbath a delight, **the holy day** of YHVH honorable, and honor it, desisting from your own ways..." (Isaiah 58:13).

The day the Father *hallowed*, or called *kadosh*, was the seventh day—the Sabbath day (Exodus 20:11).

Messiah Yeshua Kept The Sabbath

We also want to keep the Sabbath because Messiah Yeshua kept it. When He "came to Nazareth, where He had been brought up, **as was His custom**, He entered the synagogue **on the Sabbath**, and stood up to read" (Luke 4:16; 6:6; 13:10; Mark 1:21; 3:1-2; 6:2). However, Yeshua did not keep the Sabbath according to the customs and traditions of men. Neither did He keep it according to the precepts of some of the Pharisees. Instead, He honored the Sabbath according to the ways of YHVH Elohim.

Yeshua is "One" with the plural unity that is *Elohim*.[44] He is the Word made flesh. He was in the beginning. In and through Him all things were created—*including the Sabbath* (John 1:1-18; 10:30). Yeshua was not, is not, and cannot, ever be at odds with Elohim's Sabbath.

Messiah's Mission and The Sabbath

We see Yeshua's harmony with this set-apart day in that, at the beginning of His earthly ministry, He entered the synagogue on the Sabbath, and *"the scroll of the prophet Isaiah was handed to him. Unrolling it, He found the place where it is written: 'The Spirit of the Lord is on*

---

43 *Strong's* # H6918.

44 *Elohim.* Plural for "gods." Used especially to define the supreme God (*Strong's* # H430). See footnote #6, p 5-6.

me, because he has anointed me to preach good news to the poor. He has sent me to proclaim freedom for the prisoners and recovery of sight for the blind, to release the oppressed, to proclaim the year of the Lord's favor.' Then he rolled up the scroll, gave it back to the attendant and sat down. And, the eyes of everyone in the synagogue were fastened on him, and He began by saying to them, 'Today this scripture is fulfilled in your hearing'" (Luke 4:17-21; from Isaiah 61:1-9).

Messiah Yeshua used these verses to announce His ministry. The "acceptable year of the Lord," which He was ordained to proclaim, refers to the *sabbatical*, or Jubilee year (Luke 4:18-21). The Jubilee portrays the Sabbath, freedom, recovery, release, favor, and restoration. All who have found restoration in Messiah have at least partially experienced that Jubilee.

Yeshua did not announce His ministry in the context of fulfillment of the sabbatical Jubilee with all its liberation promises, for the purpose of *annulling* the Sabbath. No. He identified His mission with the Sabbath because it is a memorial of His redemptive actions.

Rabbinic literature links the Messiah to the Sabbath. The day is seen as a type of the world to come: The life span of the world is likened to a "cosmic week" of 6000 years, with an eschatological "seventh day Sabbath" marking the end time Messianic Age.

Most of Christianity concurs with this conclusion. They likewise associate Messiah's end of the age reign with the seventh day Sabbath. As Samuele Bacchiocchi asks in his definitive book on the subject, *From Sabbath To Sunday*: "[Since] Christ never alludes to an eventual replacement of the Sabbath, one may ask, why would Christ want to change it? What new benefit could accrue to Christians by changing the day of worship? Would such an act bespeak *stability* and *continuity* in the divine plan of salvation?"[45]

---

45 *From Sabbath To Sunday*, Samuele Bacchiocchi, Rome: The Pontifical Gregorian University Press, 1977, p 26.

The Sin of Jeroboam: Changing Feast Days

Changing the Sabbath day shows a lack of continuity, and a lack of continuity was *exactly* what the fourth century compatriots of the Roman Emperor Constantine wanted when they decided to move the Sabbath to Sunday. They wanted to put as much distance as possible between themselves and what they called the "accursed Jew." They wanted to prove that God was finished with the Jew, and that they, the Christians, had replaced them as God's chosen people.

Sadly, they were following in the footsteps of their Northern Kingdom forefather, Jeroboam, who was the first to change Israel's God-given Sabbath and feast days (1 Kings 12: 25-33; 2 Kings 17: 22,23; Jeremiah 3:21-25).

Jeroboam and His Ancient Traits

The heirs of the errant children of the Northern Kingdom often are afflicted with the same problems that plagued their parents. Their first King, Jeroboam, disdained YHVH's prescribed scriptural feasts and created his own replacement celebrations (Exodus 31:16-17; Daniel 7:25; 1 Kings 12:27-33).

Jeroboam's actions foreshadowed the grievous practices of the Christian Church, for she has also made her own proclamations, changed the Sabbath, and altered the feast days. The Church needs to repent of these sins, because Believers in Israel's Messiah are called to be a royal priesthood, one that proclaims restoration to Israel's divided kingdom.

Striking Back...

Truly, Ephraim needs to repent of this sin. He needs to repent of his errant ways.

However, in our appraisal of the actions of the Early Believers, we must remember that those who were part of the sect of Believers called "The Way," were *kicked out* of the synagogue by their Jewish brethren.[46] This action caused resentment that later turned to violence. Once the non-Jewish Believers of "The Way" outnumbered the Jewish Believers, these non-Jews struck back at the Jews. To this day they are striking back, often with hateful vengeance.

Jewish Believer Victor Buksbazen, in his book *The Feasts of Israel*, explains the situation:

"The Jewish believer in Christ was in a dilemma from the very beginning. Eventually it forced him out of the synagogue into a fellowship which was distinctly Christian, the ecclesia.

"The dilemma of the Jewish Christian was this. By the ties of blood and the affection of his heart, he felt himself to be an integral part of Israel. He differed, however, from his unbelieving brethren by his faith in the Lord, the Messiah Jesus, to whom he owed supreme allegiance. For some time after the Resurrection the Jewish believers still attended the Temple worship in Jerusalem.

"'And they, continuing daily in one accord in the temple, and breaking bread from house to house.' Acts 2:46

"Nevertheless the separation between believers and unbelievers was soon forced upon the Christians by violence and persecution. The first martyr for the faith was Stephen. Active persecution of Jewish believers, the vilification of the person of the Lord Jesus, and changes in the liturgy, which contained direct or implicit denunciation of the believers in the Messiah Jesus, drove the Jewish Christians out of the Temple and the synagogue.

"To the daily prayers of the synagogue was added the 'Birkath-Hamminim,' 'The blessing of the Sectarians,' which was in reality a malediction. This is how the strange 'blessing' was worded in the original Hebrew version: 'And for the Apostates let there be no hope, and the dominion of arrogance (probably Rome—Editor's note) may be speedily uprooted in our days. Let the Nazarenes (Jewish Christians)

---

46 See Acts 24:5,14,22; 15:5; 28:22; 9:2; 19:9,23; Jer 32:39; John 9:22; 12:42; 16:2; Isa 11:13.

and the Sectarians perish as in a moment. May they be blotted out from the Book of Life and with the Righteous ones may they not be inscribed. Blessed art thou Jehovah, who humblest the arrogant.'

"Today this prayer in a considerably changed form is used in the synagogue. But the word 'Apostates' has been changed to 'Slanderers,' and the direct reference to the Nazarenes and the Sectarians is omitted. Obviously a Jewish Christian could not stay on in the synagogue where his Lord was calumniated and he himself made the subject of malediction.

"If the Gospel was not to be confined to the narrow territorial and spiritual boundaries of Judea, the breach had to come, so that the Gospel of salvation might have free course not only among the Jews, but also among the nations.

"'As for Saul, he made havock of the church, entering into every house, and haling men and women committed them to prison.

Therefore they that were scattered abroad went everywhere preaching the word'—Acts 8:3,4.

"The final breach took place in the times of the false Messiah, Bar Kochba, who fought against the Romans and died in battle 135 A.D. The Jewish believers could not endorse his claims nor support his warfare. Believers had to leave Jerusalem and eventually Palestine. Henceforth the Church and the synagogue went separate paths, the daughter was forcibly weaned from her mother."[47]

Sabbath and Restoration

Returning to Yeshua and the Sabbath, we see that He upset *some* of the Pharisees by healing people on the Sabbath. In the Capernaum synagogue He commanded an unclean spirit to come out of a man. He healed Peter's mother-in-law. He liberated a "daughter of Abraham" from an eighteen-year-long bondage (Luke 4:16-21,31-38; 13:10-

---

[47] *The Feasts of Israel*, Victor Buksbazen, W. Collingswood, NJ: Gospel Ministry, Inc, 1976, pp 93-94.

17). On "another Sabbath...He entered the synagogue and was teaching; and there was a man there whose right hand was withered," so Yeshua healed him too (Luke 6:6-11).

Yeshua Restored the Sabbath

Yeshua healed people on the Sabbath because the day is dedicated to man's well-being. As Bacchiocchi says, Yeshua did not "intend to abrogate radically the Sabbath commandment." Rather, He "aim[ed] at restoring the institution to its original value and function." And, "This original dimension of the Sabbath as a day to honor God by sowing concern and compassion to fellow beings, had largely been forgotten in the time of Jesus. The Sabbath had become the day when correct performance of a ritual was more important than a spontaneous response to the cry of human needs." [48]

Our Messiah practiced healing and restoration on the Sabbath. He taught that acts of kindness could be done on that day.

Yeshua never spoke *against* the Biblical Sabbath, but only against the prevailing perversions of a limited number of the Pharisees that had turned Sabbath observance into bondage instead of the delight intended by the Father.

Time for the Watchmen to Watch

Israel is called to "watch" over the Father's Sabbath's. Specifically, "Ephraim was a *watchman* with my God, a prophet; yet the snare of a bird catcher is in all his ways..." (Hosea 9:8).

Ephraim's snare was that he always wanted to be like the other nations. So the Father scattered the people of Ephraim, like seed, among the nations, or Gentiles (Hosea 8:8; Amos 9:9).

There, they would remain until they had totally had

---

48 *From Sabbath To Sunday*, Samuele Bacchiocchi, Rome: The Pontifical Gregorian University Press, 1977, p 34.

their fill of being "Gentiles." There, they would languish until they wanted no more of heathen ways, and until an appointed time...

We live in that appointed time. It is a time when Ephraim is to "be instructed," that he might "repent of the [pagan] deeds of his youth" (Jeremiah 31:18-19). It is a time for them to cease all heathen practices and to again become "as mighty men" (Zechariah 10:7).

Taking The Watchman's Vow

It is also time for each Ephraimite to take the vow of a "watchman" as given in Habakkuk 2:1: "I will stand on my guard post and station myself on the rampart; and I will keep watch to see what He will speak to me, and how I may reply when I am reproved."

Ephraim, or Israel, is beginning to see how his forefathers changed the Father's feasts and Sabbath days. He is now becoming a *true watchman* of these things. He is beginning to guard against the many "Pharisaical" perversions that distort our Father's restoration truths.

Let the Ephraimite watchmen arise! Let each one ask the Father how they are to reply when He speaks to them and what they can do to help restore truth to the whole house of Israel.

Israel's Feasts and their Fullness

Celebrating Shabbat: Why and How

Why keep the Sabbath?

♦ YHVH Elohim kept it (Genesis 2:2-3).
♦ YHVH made it a commandment for His followers (Exodus 20:8-10; Deuteronomy 5:12-14).
♦ Yeshua kept the Sabbath (Mark 1:21; 3:1-2; 6:2; Luke 4:16; 13:10).
♦ The Early Believers followed the Sabbath commands even after Yeshua's death (Mark 16:1).
♦ Paul the apostle worshiped on the Sabbath (Acts 13:13-14; 17:2; 18:4).
♦ The Early Believers worshiped on the Sabbath (Acts 15:21; 16:13).
♦ YHVH pronounced a special blessing on those who keep His Sabbath (Isaiah 56:6-7).
♦ Keeping the Sabbath is a sign, a mark of belonging, between YHVH and His people (Exodus 31:13,17; Leviticus 19:3; Ezekiel 9:4; 20:12; Revelation 7:3).

May we be granted the grace to bear this glorious mark.

A Messianic Israel Shabbat Celebration

The following is a copy of a *Messianic Israel Shabbat Guide* offered by Messianic Israel Ministries. Printed and folded guides that will fit nicely in your Bibles are available at a nominal charge. Various *Celebration Guides* are offered for sale in the *Key of David Publications* section of this book. Or you may photocopy the following four Shabbat Celebration pages for your own personal use.

This Guide is a brief outline of suggestions for beginning your Sabbath celebration in your home. You may want to add your own special Sabbath touches.

We do not suggest that this is the only way Sabbath can be celebrated. The Father's instructions concerning Sabbath are minimal, and we must not add to, nor take away from, His Word. For example, many Jewish celebrations have the mother recite a prayer that includes the words, "Who commanded us to kindle the Sabbath lights," but we find no such command in Scripture.

It is important that our Sabbath celebrations be alive with new meaning and not filled with rote tradition. We must feel free to light, or not to light, Sabbath candles. We must not embrace things that are traditional yet oppose the truth of Scripture.

If concerns about "doing it right" arise, we suggest you go to the Father's Word and read every time a certain word or phrase is used: Sabbath (Sabbaths), "the Lord's Day," and so on. Once you have studied a subject in this manner, you will know what the Father says about it. Then the Holy Spirit, the *Ruach HaKodesh,* can help you remember those Words of Scripture and will use them to guide you.

We pray that this celebration Guide will help you to begin a day that is set apart solely to our Father and to His chosen way for us as a people.

May all your Sabbath celebrations be especially blessed!
Shabbat Shalom!
(Sabbath Peace!)

Erev Shabbat Celebration

The Father Begins by Reading:

"You shall remember the Sabbath day, to keep it holy...For six days you shall labor, but on the seventh day you shall cease from labor, that you...may rest and...be refreshed" (Exodus 20:8; 23:12).

"Yeshua spoke to His Disciples and said, 'Whoever continues to follow me will never walk in darkness, but will have the light which gives life.'" (John 8:12)

Seeking that "light" for "all Israel," this night we light two symbolic candlesticks: One for "the stick of Ephraim," and one for "the stick of Judah;" one to remind us to observe, the other to remember, the Sabbath day; one candle stands for Heaven and one for Earth; one for the King and one for His servants; one for the Tanach (Old Covenant), one for the Brit Chadasha (New Covenant); one for faith and one for holy deeds; one for work and one for rest.

Father, we now put aside all our cares, and turn our hearts to You, as we enter into Your Shabbat, the rest You have ordained for our good. Truly, this is the day that You have made, and we will rejoice and be glad in it.

Hadlekat Neirot (Lighting The Candles)

Mother or Daughter lights the candles and prays:
Baruch atah Adonai Eloheynu Melech ha'olam, asher natan lanu et Yeshua haMashiach, ha'or la'olam. Who tikvatanu oobeeshmo nikranu le'heyot or lagoyim. Amen.

Blessed are You, Lord our God, King of the Universe, Who has given us Yeshua our Messiah, the Light of the world. He is our hope—in Him, we are called to be a light unto the nations. Amen.

Mother's Prayer:

O God of Your people Israel, You are holy, and You have consecrated the *Shabbat*, and called the people of Israel to be Your own. You have called upon us to honor Your *Sabbath* with light, with joy, and with peace. You have given us Your Sabbath rest, as a sign that we are Your people. And so we kindle these two lights for love of Your *Shabbat*, and for love of Your people, Israel.

Almighty Father, we ask that You grant us, and all our loved ones, a chance to truly enter into Your rest on this Sabbath day. We ask that even as the candles give light to our home and family, so may Your *Ruach haKodesh* give light to our home and lives. Father, we ask that You make Your Presence known in our home, and that You bless our children with a knowledge of You. By Your grace may they always walk in the ways of Yeshua, our Living *Torah* and our Light. May You ever be their God and ours, O Lord, our Creator and Redeemer. Amen.

Family Member Reads a Scripture of Choice:

Hamotzi (Blessing of the Bread) Father Reads:

"Yeshua said, 'I am the bread that gives life, whoever comes to Me will never go hungry, and whoever puts their trust in Me will never be thirsty'" (John 6:35).

Baruch atah Adonai, Elohenu Melech ha'olam, hamotzi lechem min ha aretz, asher natan lanu lechem chaim b'Yeshua. Amen.

Blessed are You, Lord our God, King of the Universe, Who blesses us with bread, and gives us Yeshua, Who is the Bread of Life. Amen.

Kiddush (Sanctifying Prayer) Father Reads:

It was on *Hoshanah Rabbah*, the last day of *Sukkot*, that Yeshua stood and cried out, saying, "If anyone is thirsty, let him come to Me continually and drink. Whoever continues to put his trust in Me, as the *Tanach* says, 'Out of his innermost being shall continuously flow rivers of living water'" (John 7:37-38).

Baruch atah Adonai, Elohenu Melech ha'olam, boreh p'ri hagaphen. Amen.

Blessed are You, O Lord our God, King of the Universe, the Creator of the fruit of the vine.

Blessing of the Children:

Over the Son(s) the Father Prays:

Y'simchah Elohim k'Ephrayeem, v'keh M'nasheh.

May God make you a symbol of blessing as He did Ephraim and Manasseh.

Over the Daughter(s) the Father (or Mother) Prays:

Y'simech Elohim k'Sarah, Rivka, Rakhel v'Leah.

May God make you a symbol of blessing as He did Sarah, Rebekah, Rachel and Leah.

A Child Recites Ephesians 6:1-3

Eishet Chayil (Woman of Valor):

Husband Reads Proverbs 31:10-31 To His Wife.
(Or Scriptural Blessing of Choice.)

Ashrey Ha'eesh (Blessed is the Man):

Wife Reads Psalm 1 To Her Husband
(Or Scriptural Blessing of Choice.)

Israel's Feasts and their Fullness

All Sing the Sh'ma:

Sh'ma Yisrael, Adonai Elohenu, Adonai Echad. Baruch shem, k'vod malchuto, l'olam vah-ed. Amen.

Hear O Israel, the Lord our God, the Lord is One. Blessed be His Name, His Kingdom is forever, and forever more. Amen.

Father Gives Priestly Blessing:

Yevarech'cha Adonai v'yishmerecha
Yah-er Adonai panav elecha v'yechunecha
Yissah Adonai panav elechah v'yasem lechah shalom.

May the Lord bless you and keep you.
May the Lord cause His face to shine upon you and be gracious unto you.
May the Lord lift up His countenance upon you and give you peace.

Shabbat Shalom (Sabbath Peace)

© 1988-2002

Messianic Israel Ministries

PO Box 700217, Saint Cloud, FL 34770
Phone 800 829-8777   Web Site: www.mim.net
Ministering to "both the houses of Israel" (Isaiah 8:14)

Challah and Shabbat

According to Jewish tradition, challah is a specially baked braided bread that has an important role in the Sabbath celebrations. The bread is often baked at home just prior to Sabbath, and baking it can be a special event.

But before we bake challah, let us examine its history.

Our Father commanded Moses to, "Speak to the sons of Israel," and to tell them, "Present a *challah* [הלה, a cake][49] from the first of your ground meal and present it as an offering from the threshing floor. Throughout the generations to come you are to give this offering to YHVH from the first of your ground meal" (Numbers 15:20-21).

To the priests, the Father said, "Take fine flour and bake twelve *challah*, using two-tenths of an ephah for each loaf. Set them in two rows, six in each row, on the table of pure gold before YHVH. Along each row put some pure incense as a memorial portion to represent the bread and to be an offering made to YHVH. This bread is to be set out before Him regularly, Sabbath after Sabbath, on behalf of the Israelites, as an everlasting covenant for the sons of Israel" (Leviticus 24:5-8).

---

49 *Strong's* # H2471.

The people of Israel were instructed that, "on the sixth day," they were to "gather twice as much" manna, because the next day was to be a "Sabbath observance" (Exodus 16:22-29). It was to be a day of rest—for *all*. The food was to be prepared ahead of time so that even the cook would have a time of rest.

In ancient times, *challah* was typically an unleavened bread, for it is written, "You shall not offer the blood of My sacrifice with leavened bread." And, "No grain offering, which you bring to YHVH, shall be made with leaven, for you shall not offer up in smoke any leaven or any honey as an offering by fire to YHVH" (Exodus 23:18, 34:25; Leviticus 2:11).

Though the Temple was long ago destroyed, the Jewish people still uphold a tradition of offering up what has come to be known as *challah* every Friday evening (*erev Shabbat*). Typically, Sabbath candles are lit, prayers are offered, two *challot* (plural) are presented, often veiled (covered) like a bride, children and mates are blessed, and a special Sabbath meal is enjoyed.

The Blessings of Shabbat

Some people place two *challot* on the table to symbolize the double portion of manna provided each Friday while in the wilderness. God provided them with both provision and rest so the children of Israel would not have to gather food.

Sometimes the bread is sprinkled with either sesame or poppy seeds to represent the manna provided in the desert. It can be baked in special shapes, such as the menorah shape shown in the above diagram. However, the most popular form is the traditional three-strand braided challah (shown in the graphic above). [50]

---

50 Menorah Graphic: *Encyclopedia of Jewish Symbols*, Frankel and Teutsch, Northvale NJ: Jason Aronson, Inc., 1992.

To Messianic Israel, the two *challot* on the Sabbath table symbolize Israel's two houses—Judah and Ephraim.

Shabbat is meant to be a special time that can greatly strengthen the family. Since today there are so many families being torn apart, we would do well to incorporate some form of this tradition and have a family Shabbat.[51]

So use our *challah* recipe to make your Sabbath bread (or buy some at the store), then gather your family and follow the *Shabbat Celebration Guide* (or make up your own). Husbands and wives can pray for one another and then bless the children. In this way you will be blessed, because you are taking part in the restoration of all Israel—*which should begin with our families...*

Rich Symbolism

Preparing *challah* (braided Sabbath bread) for *Shabbat* can be a special experience that is rich in spiritual symbolism. The Father issued an everlasting command that bread be made and set in the Temple before Him each Sabbath: "Every sabbath day he [the priest] shall set it [the showbread] in order before YHVH continually; it is an everlasting covenant for the sons of Israel" (Leviticus 24:8).

Braided challah serves as a symbol of our call to unity. Plus it is a savory reminder that we are called to be a covenant people. Baking challah for Shabbat is an act that is steeped in ages of tradition, faithfully brought forth by our Jewish brethren.

Today, as Believers in Yeshua, challah can depict His Body, because the bread is made of diverse ingredients, each with its own distinctive taste, each one necessary to make the loaf complete. Although each ingredient is different, when they are blended together as dough they cannot be separated one from another.

Just as the oil mixed into the dough keeps it from stick-

---

51 There is a wonderful depiction of how the family can celebrate the traditional Jewish Shabbat in the classic movie, *Fiddler on the Roof,* starring Zero Mostel (available at video stores everywhere).

ing to the bowl, so the oil of the Holy Spirit keeps us from "sticking," or conforming, to this world:

"Do not be conformed to this world, but be transformed by the renewing of your mind, that you may prove what the will of God is, that which is good and acceptable and perfect" (Romans 12:2).

During the baking process, the dough is set aside and left alone to rise. This waiting process can remind us that we sometimes feel forsaken by our God as we are "set aside" to grow. Fortunately, He does not leave us for too long, though it sometimes seems like it. He is only watching and waiting for us to come to maturity.

Besides, being left alone is a necessary step if the bread is to be all that it is called to be: "For a small moment have I forsaken thee; but with great mercies will I gather thee ....with everlasting kindness will I have mercy on thee" (Isaiah 54:7,8, KJV).

Anyone who has faced seasons of loneliness understands this.

The next step in bread making is that the dough is "punched down." Have you ever felt pressed down? The Father deals with us just as does the potter; we are but "clay" being molded in His divine hand (Jeremiah 18:6).

Challah must be subjected to fire before it becomes a blessing to hungry souls. Likewise, YHVH places us in His furnace to test our hearts that we might be purified. He refines us in His "furnace of affliction." He brings us out of the iron furnace that is "Egypt," so we can become "a people for His own possession" (Proverbs 17:3; Isaiah 48:10; Deuteronomy 4:20; 1 Kings 8:51; 1 Peter 2:9).

If we walk as His blessed people are called to walk, He promises us, "Blessed shall be your basket and your kneading bowl" (Deuteronomy 28:5). So, as we knead our challah, we pray over it, that it might prove to be bread of blessing to all whom the Father calls to share at our table:

"*Baruch atah Adonai Elohenu Melech ha'olam, asher kidshanu b'mitzvotav v'tzivanu lehafrish challah.*"

"Blessed are You, O Lord our God, King of the Universe, who has sanctified us and commanded us to make challah."

Before we braid our dough, we divide it into three equal parts, which remind us of the Father, the Son and the Holy Spirit. Each part is then rolled out into three dough "ropes," which are then braided together, reminding us that, "If one can overpower him who is alone, two can resist him. But a cord of three strands is not quickly torn apart" (Ecclesiastes 4:12). Similarly, we have a three-fold foundation in our faith, as we are being built on "the foundation of the **apostles** and **prophets,** [and] **Messiah Yeshua**..." (Ephesians 2:20).

The ropes are pinched together, first on one end, then braided together, then pinched together on the other end; just as we are to be "fitly joined together" (Ephesians 2:21, KJV).

To make the loaves shine and be more beautiful, we brush them with whipped egg whites as we remember the promise: "YHVH takes pleasure in His people; He will beautify the afflicted ones with salvation" (Psalm 149:4).

When we place our bread into the oven we remember, "Beloved, think it not strange concerning the fiery trial which is to try you, as though some strange thing happened unto you." Instead, we "rejoice, in that we are partakers of Messiah's sufferings" (1 Peter 4:12-13). We remember that Isaiah told us to "Glorify YHVH in the fires, even the name of YHVH Elohim of Israel in the isles of the sea" (vs. 24:12).

Fire purifies. The fires of life forge spiritual character. And as the aroma of fresh baking bread wafts through our home, we pray that our lives will be as "a fragrant aroma, an acceptable sacrifice, well pleasing to our God" (Ephesians 5:2; Philippians 4:18).

When we examine our freshly baked bread, we remember the covenant of salt our Father made with His people: "I have given to you and your sons and your daughters...a perpetual allotment...an everlasting covenant of salt before YHVH to you and your descendants with you" (Numbers 18:19).

Today at many Shabbat tables, Jewish families dash a little salt on the challah, or on a plate in which pieces of challah are to be dipped, as a reminder of the Father's covenant with His people. We may want to continue this tradition, since Yeshua told us in Matthew 5:13, "You are the salt of the earth."

Challah. A beautiful symbol that regularly depicts blessing to the Father's chosen people.[52]

Blessed are You, O Lord our God, who brings forth bread from the earth.

---

52 Thanks to friend Carol Knox for much of this challah inspiration.

Challah Recipe (for two Challot)

4   cups all purpose flour
1 cup whole wheat flour
4 packages dry yeast (quick rising)
3 Tablespoons honey
1 tablespoon salt
1/4 cup olive oil
3 eggs
2 cups water

♦ Preheat oven to 350 degrees
♦ Dissolve yeast and honey in   cup warm (not hot) water
♦ Let stand 10 minutes, until it foams
♦ Beat 3 eggs lightly in a large bowl
♦ Add oil, salt, 2 cups water, and yeast mixture to eggs
♦ Add flour 1 cup at a time until all is added to egg mix
♦ Knead on lightly floured board for 10 minutes
♦ (or until flour is smooth and elastic)
♦ Oil large bowl
♦ Put dough in oiled bowl and turn dough over to cover with oil
♦ Cover bowl with cloth, let rise in warm place for 1 to 2 hours
♦ Punch down dough and divide into two loaves
♦ Divide each loaf into 3 long strands, or braids
♦ Braid challah (three strands per loaf: see diagram)
♦ Arrange loaves on oiled baking sheet
♦ Cover and let rise to twice original size
♦ **Egg Wash:**
♦ Beat egg yolk with 1 teaspoon water and   teaspoon oil
♦ Brush challot with egg mixture
♦ Bake challah for 45 to 50 minutes
♦ Challah is done when it sounds hollow when tapped

How To Braid Challah

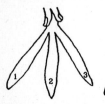   

Roll out 3 strips. Gather ends and pinch together

Fold strip #1 over strip #2

Fold strip #2 over strip #3

Braid to end, and pinch ends together

Finished
Braided
Challah

A Personal Havdalah Story

To this author, *Havdalah*, a celebration that marks the end of Shabbat, is inextricably linked to a personal experience.

It happened in Jerusalem many years ago, and it changed my life, as well as the life of my husband Angus. This is a story about Believers, a Jewish family, a Jewish tradition, and a hope.

The story began as we were on our way to Israel to finalize plans for an upcoming tour to the Land. We had been to Israel several times, taking small tour groups that joined with other larger tour groups, but now we wanted to host our own. So there we were, flying on *El Al* Airlines, going back to our "homeland."

Batya's Story

"Father, I ask that You please lead and guide us on this trip," I prayed silently. "With all my heart I want You to do a work in and through us. Though we have a lot of ideas about our tour itinerary, we have no set plan for this planning visit..."

The prayer in my heart trailed off. I felt a little anxious, a little foolish. We had no real itinerary. We were just going to Israel to work out a tour that would be "different."

I returned to my prayer, almost pleading, "Please Father, I *really* want *You* to do a work in us. I *really* want *You* to guide us..."

I had plenty of time to get lost in my quiet prayer with the Father, because Angus, who was sitting next to me, was totally engrossed in a conversation with the man seated next to him. So I continued praying and rejoicing in this opportunity to return to Israel.

After a short while, Angus introduced the man. "Sweetheart, this is Uzi Wexler," he announced, "He lives in Jerusalem."

"Hi," Uzi said warmly, "Let me be the first to officially welcome you to Jerusalem."

"Thank you," I replied. Then I commented on his gold lapel pin which had a lion poised on hind feet as if taking a stand, ready to defend. He explained that the pin was an "official logo," and that he was the Treasurer of the City of Jerusalem.

"Angus certainly has an interesting seat mate," I thought, but it was difficult for me to enter into their conversation because of the noise on the plane. As I watched the Orthodox Jewish men gather together on the east side of the plane for morning prayers, I tried to contain my excitement about approaching Israel.

Just as we were arriving at Ben Gurion Airport, Uzi invited us to join his family in a few days for their "little family Havdalah celebration." We readily accepted the invitation.

Uzi also said he wanted to help us to see a bit of Israel, so he arranged for us to join a brief tour that was being hosted by the Israeli Minister of Tourism.

The next day we joined a private group of wealthy Jewish people who were helping to fund the State of Israel. They were being given a private showing of some new excavations in Jerusalem, such as the Tower of David. They were also meeting with the current Prime Minister, Yitzhak Shamir.

"Wow! Talk about getting a Tour Guide!" I exclaimed to Angus after we left the group. "This sure is the way to see the city!"

Our brief tour had been inspiring and fun and exciting. Plus the Tourism Minister had given each of us some decorative posters as mementos.

The next day, Uzi arranged for us to meet one of the leading artists in Israel, Yossi Stern, a man who had been painting pictures in Jerusalem for more than a quarter of a century. As Yossi said, he painted portraits of the Prophets, and of "The people of the Book."

"I cannot escape a constant recognition of the great heritage of this place and our people. It cries out from every corner of this City of David and the Prophets," he said.

Yossi liked Angus, joking that he looked like one of the Prophets, or a great Angel that had come to make an announcement from on high. He jokingly nicknamed him "Gabriel."

Yossi also asked us to, "Just scribble something on a piece of paper." Then he graciously did some interesting caricatures of

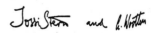

both of us, all the while explaining that he also painted, "*With* the people of Israel." Meaning, at his art shows he would ask an individual to scribble on a piece of paper, then he would amaze them as he turned their scribbling into a caricature of the individual.

This kind man also blessed us with autographed gift copies of his books of artwork, plus some black and white prints. Later that evening, one of his employees hand-delivered autographed prints of two of his pictures of Jerusalem, with a little note addressed to "Gabriel and Mrs. Gabriel."

Since we had shared briefly with him about the "two houses of Israel," and about how "Ephraim also needed to come home," Yossi encouraged us to "Come and be my neighbor and make Israel your permanent home." We were deeply touched.

Although our trip was filled with unusual experiences and wonderful encounters, probably the most moving experience was celebrating Havdalah with the Wexler family.

The Tradition of Havdalah

In Jewish tradition, both the beginning and the end of the Sabbath day is celebrated. Havdalah is an end of the Sabbath ritual. It consists of a brief ceremony in which blessings are recited over a cup of wine (to be shared), over a braided candle (to be lit), and over aromatic spices (to be passed and sniffed).

In Hebrew, *Havdalah* means division and distinction. It is used as a rite that separates the holy from the profane, marking the end of the holy Sabbath and the beginning of the commonplace work week.

During the service, some people fill the wine cup to overflowing to symbolize their hope of a coming week that is overflowing with blessings. Thus, goblets that are especially designed for Havdalah usually come with a small saucer.

The Havdalah candle is braided and has more than one wick, which corresponds to the many "lights" in the prescribed benediction. Woven in colorful strands, the most popular color combination is blue and white.

The spice box *(hadas)* used in the ceremony is usually decorated. Some are ornately crafted in silver, brass, ceramic, wood, or other materials. They frequently become family heirlooms. Whether they are brand new, or passed down from generation-to-generation, these boxes are usually filled with a mixture of cloves, nutmeg, and bay leaf.

According to the *Dictionary of the Jewish Religion*, by Isaacson and Gross, "Spices were used extensively in ancient times....It was customary to burn spices after a meal and recite a blessing before smelling them," which, they say, "Is the probable origin for sniffing spices at the Havdalah service." [53]

In *The Jewish Book of Why* by Alfred J. Kolatch, we are told, "The origin of this ceremony is attributed to the fourth and fifth century B.C.E. Men of the Great Assembly (Berachot 33a)." [54]

Many people add their own special touches to this ancient tradition. For example, some wives may utter a farewell to the Sabbath in the form of an old Yiddish hymn:
"Dear Sabbath Day doth now depart—
May the coming week be blessed
With good fortune and good deeds."

Our Story Continues...

Since our Sabbath in Jerusalem was quickly departing, Angus and I hurried to Uzi's place, which we later learned was the Wexler family compound.

Uzi's father had commanded the Israeli Army forces in Jerusalem during the War of Independence in 1948, and most of his family lived on the very hill that he had battled for and taken. Mr. Wexler and his family had built their family compound on this same hill. The elder Mr. Wexler and his wife were also present for the Havdalah celebration.

---

53 Englewood, NJ: Bantam Books, 1979, p 153.
54 NY: Jonathan David Publishers, 1981, 1995, p 178.

We discovered that he had become one of the leading publisher's of Judaica in the State of Israel.

Uzi's wife, a Supreme Court Justice for the State of Israel, was also present at the celebration, as was his sister, minus her husband, a Texas oil developer who had to be away on business. Also present was Uzi's youngest brother, who was being groomed to take over the family publishing business. Then there was Uzi's other brother, who greeted us at the door. He was one of the world's leading brain surgeons, but was also a painter who specialized in stark, telling, painful, black and white Holocaust paintings.

This week the Havdalah celebration was at Dr. Wexler's home, and it seemed that almost immediately we were in his lower level studio. There, he showed me his brutally frank Holocaust paintings.

Looking around, I could feel his anger, as well as his desire to be polite, even hospitable, to someone he thought was a "Christian."

"How would you explain the Holocaust?" he asked, after I had viewed some of his lithographs.

I could feel his inner turmoil. I also felt as though he were almost "baiting" me.

"I believe words fail when one tries to explain the Holocaust," I replied quietly.

I wanted this man to know that I did not feel I had the right to speak in this matter. I had not been there. I had not lost family members, nor did I have a favorite aunt who had been forced to be a "field whore," then later hung when drunken and pawing men grew tired of her. I did not have little cousins that had been forced to help dig mass graves, only to be shot and thrown in with hundreds of others. None of my family had been forced to wear the "yellow star" that marked millions for incarceration and death.

Dr. Wexler watched me go through the fifteen piece set of lithographs several times, each time no less shocking, or telling, than before.

"Would you like to have a set of the prints?" he asked.

It touched me that this man, who had experienced so much grief, seemed to be reaching out to me.

"I would be very honored to have them," I answered.

He put the prints in a special packet and handed them to me. "Let's go up for Havdalah," the doctor said, pointing up the steps.

I could feel his change in demeanor, and followed him up to the living room, carrying under my arm a package that spoke volumes.

In the living room, we all chatted for a while, getting acquainted. Everyone was asking us questions about our faith and our family. Since Angus and I had put our two families together years before, I told them, "We came home from our honeymoon to a house full of seven children, and then the fireworks started."

"Yes. But so far we've survived!" Angus chimed-in. Everyone laughed as we told story after story about our many children.

After a time, Uzi called the grandchildren in from their play for Havdalah. Excitedly, they all gathered around their grandfather, each one vying for a spot closer to him. Small servings of wine were poured for all, including the children. The senior Wexler lifted his glass and said the *Barucha*. After another blessing, he lit the candle; then another blessing and he passed the spices for all to smell.

I watched as this beautiful, lively family blessed the God of Israel and thanked Him for giving them the blessing that is the Sabbath. Then, at grandfather's leading, everyone lifted their glasses, drank, and then shouted, "*Shavu'a Tov!*"

"Yes," I thought, "This fine family will have a 'Good Week!'"

I was truly moved by their faith. I knew that while they did not know Messiah, they were praying to the same Father God to whom I prayed. I could feel His pleasure in the closeness of their family.

After this, In true Orthodox fashion, the men all gathered around the dining room table, while the women moved toward the living room.

As we were taking our seats, everyone was talking at once. The men were asking Angus questions and the ladies wanted to hear more about Angus' third daughter, Linda.

Taking a seat on the sofa, I began, "Linda is our miracle child." I told them how she had once had so little hope and had to face the many battles that came with her premature birth and resultant cerebral palsy—but had experienced many answers to the prayers made to the God of Israel.

One answer to prayer is that Linda had met Marsden, a big, good looking guy, who worked in the hospital where she had stayed when she had to have one of her more than twenty operations. Although the need for an another operation appeared to be a curse at the time, the Father used the opportunity for them to meet.

"Linda always had to wear leg braces and a lift on her shoe," I explained. " At their wedding, the pastor tried to get her to come in a door close to the altar. 'So she won't have very far to walk,' the pastor had said."

"But Linda was firm, 'No. All my life I've dreamed of walking down the aisle on my Father's arm,' she told the pastor. 'And nothing is going to steal that dream from me.'"

"Believe me," I told the Wexler ladies, "When Linda walked down that long aisle, holding onto her father's arm for support, there was not a dry eye in the place. They all knew her story."

I must admit that while I was very happy sharing with

the women all the wonderful things that had happened to Linda, I have never been so double-minded in my life. I wanted to both talk and listen at the same time! Because when I had started talking about Linda, at the same time I could hear Mr. Wexler saying to Angus, "Now Angus, tell us...."

Angus Tells His Story...

"Angus, tell us what the House of David is all about," was the question the patriarch of the Wexler clan asked.[55] Personally, as a retired Army Colonel, I appreciated this man very much. In the 1948 War of Independence, he had commanded the forces of Israel that had battled to keep a portion of the city of David in Jewish hands. Then, at the end of the 1967 war, he had seen the entire city once again in the hands of the descendants of David.

As I searched for an answer to give this orthodox Jew and his sons, many thoughts raced through my mind. I felt presumptuous talking to these men about restoring David's fallen tent. I was well aware of the deep divisions that exist between Christians and Jews. And here I was in the City of David, a son of Joseph, remembering that Joseph was the son who had received the birthright and the double portion, and I was talking to sons of Judah. Yet Judah was the son who had received the promise of the "scepter," and who became the progenitor of King David, from whom came Yeshua, the Messiah.

I also knew of the chasm that was created when YHVH divided Israel into the Northern and Southern Kingdoms of Israel and Judah. Almost three thousand years had passed since that fateful division. Over twenty-seven hundred years had passed since the last vestige of Israel, or the Lost Ten Tribes, as they are popularly known, had been absorbed into the Gentile nations. This was in fulfillment of the punishment about which Hosea had warned: *"You will become a people who are not a people."*

---

55 This was the name of our "Catalogue" ministry at the time.

While Israel's punishment (not knowing who they were and not understanding their roots) had been extremely effective over these long centuries, it was obviously coming to a close. We personally knew people around the world who were having the blindness removed from their eyes. They were beginning to see and understand their own heritage as part of the people of Israel. They were beginning to experience a "knowing" like the "knowing" one has of their personal relationship with the God of Israel.

And now a son of Joseph, an Ephraimite, one who knew who he was (one who also had a Jewish grandmother), had just finished celebrating the close of the Sabbath with men of Judah, men who knew very well who they were as sons of Judah. And it had all taken place in the ancient City of David!

I thought back to the time when all Israel had gathered at Hebron to turn the kingdom of Saul over to David, in fulfilment of the word of the Lord. I remembered that of the 300,000 plus men of Israel who gathered at Hebron to make David the king of all Israel, only 6,800 were from Judah. So I was confident that in the restoration of David's kingdom, and the return of His Greater Son, the tribes other than Judah would once more play a significant role. I perceived that the playing out of that role had commenced.

I knew that even though my grandmother was Jewish, because I believed in Yeshua, the Wexler's saw me as a "Christian," though not the run-of-the-mill tract distributor whose mission was to convert Jews to their particular denomination. Further, on the plane, in my conversation with Uzi, I had made it clear that we were not missionaries, at least not in the usual sense. "Our mission is not to convert Jews," I told him, "but to restore relationships between the two houses of Israel. Not by having one house convert to one of the many doctrines of the other house, but by reestablishing the fact that we are 'family.' And as a united family, it will be much easier to have a united belief in the Holy One of Israel, as He is revealed in the fullness of His Glory."

Uzi had seemed to receive what I said on the plane, but now, I wondered, "How can I convey all of my thoughts in my answer?" The elder Wexler's question, "What is the House of David all about?" hung in the air. Drawing a deep breath, and asking the Holy Spirit to speak through me, I answered:

"We believe Scripture clearly shows that there were, and still are, two houses of Israel: Ephraim and Judah. Furthermore, remnants of these two houses exist today, not only among the Jewish people, but also among those who are called Christians. Our hope is to identify that remnant, especially among Christians, and to encourage them to return to their Hebraic roots, which we believe is a prelude to the reunion of all Israel into one united house. Last, but certainly not least, we seek to encourage members of both houses to have the same personal relationship with the God of Israel that Abraham, Isaac and Jacob had."

The smiles on their faces, and comments like, "We certainly agree with that," told me the Wexler men had no problem with my answer. They were also in agreement that many from the Northern Tribes of Israel had been scattered among the nations, and in fulfillment of Scripture, would one day be regathered. They applauded the idea of modern-day Israelites having the same relationship with the God of Israel as did the Patriarchs. And they appreciated our interest and participation in the Havdalah celebration that closed out the Sabbath day.

"It seems that, rather than man-ordained feast days that once honored pagan gods, the members of the family of Israel should keep the feasts of Israel. Especially since they are the feasts given them by the God of Israel," I said.

Their response was that we had a "more challenging" job in trying to present our message to the Christian community than to the Jewish people.

After a while, Batya and I thanked the Wexler family for an enjoyable evening and began to make our way to the front door. Uzi followed us.

"Feel free to call on me if ever you need me for anything," he told us as we were leaving.

"Thanks, Uzi. Thank you very much."

"Wonderful evening," I told Batya as we made our way down the walkway.

"Wonderful people," she replied.

Our Story Ends

"I felt the Spirit of God there when we were praying," I told Angus, as we were driving back to our Jerusalem hotel.

"It was encouraging that their whole family gathered together and thanked the God of Israel for the Shabbat."

"What we experienced is so precious to me that I hardly want to talk about it. Sometimes words fall short," I said softly.

Treasured Times of Fellowship

Our visit with the Wexler family is something we still cherish—it left such a deep and lasting impression on us. We also cherish all the Havdalah celebrations that have since followed. These include times spent with just the two of us in sweet times of prayer and intercession. They also include intimate times with dear friends, plus joyous celebrations with various congregations. Most wonderful are the prophetic Havdalah celebrations we have experienced at our Messianic Israel Alliance Conferences.

The format for these wonderful celebrations is given in a later chapter.

First Century Believers and Havdalah

How did the first century Believers celebrate Havdalah?

We who desire to put an end to all our religious mistakes and to build on the ancient foundational truths of our forefathers, must go back to the beginning. We must inquire as to how the First Century Believers celebrated Havdalah.

The Meaning of "The First Day of the Week"

The Early Believers gathered together at the end of the Sabbath day. In Acts 20:7 we read, "On the first day of the week, when we were gathered together to break bread, Paul began talking to them, intending to depart the next day, and he kept on talking until midnight."

As previously noted, a scriptural day begins at evening (Genesis 1:5), so when we read that the early Believers gathered "on the first day of the week," we understand that they were actually gathering on what most Westerners call "Saturday night."

Why did they choose this time to get together?

One reason is because they were busy ministering throughout the day on the Sabbath. The Word speaks of Peter and John "going **up to the temple** at the ninth hour, the hour of prayer." An angel of the Lord told the apostles to, "Go and speak to the people **in the temple** the whole message of this Life." We also see that "Paul took men, and ...purifying himself along with them, **went into the temple**, giving notice of the completion of the days of purification, until the sacrifice was offered for each one of them" (Acts 3:1-8; 5:18-25,42; 21:26).

The apostles were in the Temple on the Sabbath praying, ministering, and being witnesses to those who had not yet heard the good news of the restoration of Israel's Kingdom. At the end of the Sabbath day, in the evening, they gathered together with other Believers on what was technically called, "the first day of the week."

Midrashing

These disciples gathered *to break bread*, which means they were sharing a meal, or were breaking bread just as Yeshua "broke bread."

Paul the apostle was talking to those gathered at one of these meetings. He continued with his speech, or *logos*, until midnight. He talked so long that a young man named Eutychus, who was possibly overcome with fumes from the many lamps burning in the room (extra lights for Havdalah?), fell out of an upper window, died from the fall, and was miraculously raised from the dead (Acts 20:8-10).

At this meeting, Paul was "talking," or *dialegomai*, which means to discuss, exhort, dispute, preach, reason with.[56] The apostle to the Nations was delivering a "*logos*," meaning he was giving a speech, preaching, teaching a doctrine, reasoning, questioning, or just plain "talking."[57]

What took place that night is what still takes place

---

56 *Strong's* # G256.
57 *Strong's* # G3056.

today when Jewish disciples gather around their rabbis. The evening describes the animated, "everyone speaks his opinion" Jewish *Yeshiva.* It describes something Judaism calls *midrashing,* which is the process of discussing various interpretations of a text.

A System that Stymies Growth

Instead of using a stimulating discussion format like this, the organized Church has chosen to use one where "one man speaks and all the others listen." This practice has frequently resulted in churches being filled with weak sheep that have never been taught how to flex their spiritual muscles.

Most congregants have never had the opportunity to question, exhort, or reason with the leadership. Most dare not question what is taught from the pulpit.

Certainly there is a place in the Body of Messiah for leaders to teach. After all, they are there to *lead.* Furthermore, disciples must "appreciate those who diligently labor among" them "and have charge over them in the Lord" and "give them instruction" (1 Thessalonians 5:12).

However, there must also be a place for *talmidim* to grow. Disciples must be allowed to fulfill their Divine command to, "Speak the truth in love," and thus, "to grow up in all aspects into Him, who is the head, even Messiah" (Ephesians 4:15). Students must have the opportunity to follow the Biblical command: "Beloved, do not believe every spirit, but **test the spirits** to see whether they are from YHVH; because many false prophets have gone out into the world" (1 John 4:1). Believers must be encouraged to "put to the test those who call themselves apostles, but are not." They must learn to discern between real and false leadership (Revelation 2:2). Such discernment is especially needed in these end times, when "false Messiahs and false prophets will arise and will show great signs and wonders, so as to mislead, if possible, even the elect" (Matthew 24:24).

We all need to have our spiritual senses sharpened.

This sharpening happens best when we exercise our spiritual muscles in the ancient pattern of Jewish Yeshiva-type discussions.

As a people, we need to build anew on ancient, God-given, original truths. If we follow in the footsteps of the apostles, the most appropriate time for us to gather is Saturday night. And the most appropriate program is the talking, debating, Yeshiva approach portrayed in Scripture.

Celebrating Havdalah

*A*gain, we ask our important question: *How do we celebrate?*

On Saturday evening, gather together with friends for a "potluck" supper and a Havdalah celebration. Begin before the end of Shabbat so you can bid it goodbye.

For your celebrations, use our Havdalah Guide (below), or use a friend's format, or a combination of both. Eventually, you may want to develop a modified version of your own. The point is to not be ritualistic about the celebration, but to have it be a time of blessed fellowship and sharing with friends.

When you gather with friends or a congregation, do not gather *because* of the Havdalah ceremony, instead, let your celebration be an outgrowth of the most important thing that is happening, which is *fellowship*. True fellowship is the ingredient that makes Havdalah, and for that matter, all "religious" celebrations, a treasure. Without true fellow-ship our gatherings can turn into little more than dead tradition. This is true whether the origins of the celebration are Christian or Jewish.

Havdalah Opportunities

For those who seek the reunion of the two houses, a Havdalah celebration can be especially meaningful for several reasons.

The timing of Havdalah meetings allows us to spend time during the Sabbath day with our family, as well as to rest physically. When we truly desist from all labor, it becomes evident that our Provider is caring for us in all things, in that we do not *have* to work. It is an amazing principle: The Father teaches us about His love and provision for us by allowing us to *rest*.

The Father defines that rest when He says through Isaiah: "If because of the Sabbath, you turn your foot from doing your own pleasure on My holy day, and call the Sabbath a delight, the holy day of YHVH honorable, and shall honor it, desisting from your own ways, from seeking your own pleasure, and speaking your own word, then you will take delight in YHVH, and I will make you ride on the heights of the earth; and I will feed you with the heritage of Jacob your father, for the mouth of YHVH has spoken" (Isaiah 58:13-14).

The Blessing of Questioning

When we gather like the Bereans of old and discuss the Word (Acts 17:10-12), many things can happen. We can exhort others, and if necessary, be exhorted. When we hear something that we believe opposes Scripture, we can question it. And whatever we say can also be questioned.

We can, and should, question each other. We need to know how to reason with one another and not be quick to discount someone because they do not believe precisely as we do on every issue. Moreover, if we force ourselves to reason with others, it will enable us to hone and sharpen the truth of what we believe. As the Scripture says: "Iron sharpens iron, so one man sharpens another" (Proverbs 27:17). Also, if a point in Scripture becomes alive to an individual, then they have an opportunity to teach or preach about it to their group. This is how the gifts of the Spirit are developed in each of us.

When we get together to pursue a *midrash*-type question and answer format, we give the Spirit the opportunity to use each of us in marvelous ways. If we will trust the *Ruach HaKodesh*, He will see that everyone uses their spiritual muscles, regardless of size. The result is spiritual growth for all!

"Speaking the truth in love, we are to grow up in all aspects into Him, who is the head, even Messiah, from whom the whole body, being fitted and held together by that which every joint supplies, according to the proper working of each individual part, causes the growth of the body for the building up of itself in love" (Ephesians 4:15-16).

Havdalah: An Ancient Tradition

To help us begin to rebuild on original truths, we point out the following about Havdalah traditions.

Havdalah means separation, or division. How appropriate that this should be a time for the Father's formerly divided and separated house to seek reunion. The tradition itself, which marks the end of the Sabbath and divides it from the rest of the week, is said to have begun several hundred years before the time of the apostles.

We read in *The Jewish Book of Why*, by Alfred J. Kolatch: "The origin of this ceremony is attributed to the fourth and fifth century B.C.E. Men of the Great Assembly (Berachot 33a)."[58]

In his excellent source book, Kolatch answers many questions about Jewish traditions, some of which we may *not* want to follow. For example, when he is asked, "Why is the *Havdala* cup of wine filled to overflowing?" Kolatch responds, "Filling the cup to overflowing is considered a good omen, an expression of hope that the week to follow

---

58 Jonathan David Publishers, NY, 1981, 1995, p 178.

will bring with it goodness in abundance. The origin of the custom is rooted in the belief, common in early societies, that the spilling of wine is a safeguard against evil spirits. These spirits, it was believed, could be bribed with a bit of wine (Eruvin 65a)."

Kolatch's answer to why women traditionally do not drink from a Havdalah glass is equally interesting: "She might grow a beard."[59]

Because the people of old did not have the same access to the Scriptures that we have today, their understanding was often darkened. Thus, superstitious beliefs were very common in early societies—both Jewish and Christian. In this day of reexamining, and sometimes incorporating traditions into our renewed celebrations, we would do well to investigate whether the tradition was begun because of superstitious beliefs. We do not want to simply trade one set of errant traditions for a different set.

Tradition and Legalism

Once, when chastening some Pharisees, Yeshua said to them, "Go and learn what this means: 'I desire mercy, *more than* sacrifice.' For I have not come to call the righteous, but sinners" (Matthew 9:11-13). (Note: the correct translation is "*more than*," not "instead of" as some may think.)

Those who concentrate on *sacrifice* tend to look to the *letter* of the Law, which kills. Those who concentrate on *mercy tend to* look to the *spirit* of the Law, which gives life (2 Corinthians 3:6; Romans 8:2).

To find the ancient paths we must be delivered from *all* religious bondage. We must also walk where no man has walked before. To return home, we must travel a road that is paved with kindness.

Mercy, and not the fine details of sacrifice, is the foundation upon which we must build. For the Father's mercies are *new* every morning (Lamentations 3:23). He is

---

59 See pp 178, 180.

always doing a *new* thing. In these latter days, if we will walk according to His ways, He will do a new thing *in and through us*. But first, a golden road of mercy must be made to run through our hearts.

While we must not *ignore*, or be oblivious to, the errors we see around us, any and all corrections must first be rooted in a heart of compassion. For it is God's "*kindness*" that leads us to repentance (Romans 2:4). He warns, "He has shown you, O man, what is good. And what does YHVH require of you? To act justly and to love mercy and to walk humbly with your Elohim" (Micah 6:8).

Making A Prophetic Havdalah Declaration

In our Havdalah celebrations we often take two lighted *Sabbath* candles, one for Ephraim and one for Judah, and have two people (to represent the two houses) use their lighted Sabbath candles to light the braided *Havdalah* candle. Let this candle prophetically typify the "one stick" of Ezekiel 37:15-28.

After lighting the Havdalah candle, and extinguishing their individual candles (symbolizing the end of their separateness), Ephraim and Judah together then lift high the one braided and brightly lit Havdalah candle and declare their unity in Messiah.

For our spice box we use two sticks of cinnamon (the two houses), twelve cloves (twelve tribes), one ball of nutmeg (one people) and two bay leaves (wings of the Holy Spirit). For good measure we throw in a little allspice.

Before passing the box we pray that our lives might be as "a fragrant aroma, an acceptable sacrifice, well pleasing to our God" (Philippians 4:18), and that He might use us in the coming week to help make the "two sticks of Israel" one in His hand.

When we finish our little celebration, we wish everyone *Shavua Tov!* Or, *"Have a good and blessed week!"*

To further your celebration, you may want to order the newest CD from our good friends, Lenny and Varda. This stirring CD is entitled, *We Proclaim!* [60]

The music of this precious Jewish couple has been bringing healing to the whole house of Israel because they especially focus on the restoration of all Israel—both houses.

On their newest CD, they have a haunting Havdalah song that will keep you singing all week long:

---

60 Available through Messianic Israel Ministries. See <www.mim.net>, or write for a free Catalogue. Contact them at: <lennyandvarda@juno.com>

Shavuah   tov   u-meh-vo-rach [61]
Shavuah   tov   u-meh-vo-rach
Shavuah   tov   u-meh-vo-rach
Shavuah   tov   u-meh-vo-rach
It's   only   six   days
Until   shabbat! [62]

Havdalah can be a very prophetic, hope-filled celebration. In our hearts we can declare to the spirit realm,
and to the world, that we believe our Father's glorious
promises that He is making us "one people," and that He
will yet return us to the mountains of Israel where we will
live an unending, *Shavu'a Tov!* We will forever have a truly
"good week"!

The following copy of our Havdalah Celebration Guide
is offered by Messianic Israel Ministries. You can order a
printed and folded 51/2" x 81/2" copy to keep in your Bible,
or you may photocopy the following four pages for your
personal use. Celebration Guides are offered for sale in the
Key of David Publications section of the book.

---

61 "Have a good and blessed week."
62 Copyright Lenny Harris, 2002, Adonai Echad Music, Cocoa, FL.

Israel's Feasts and their Fullness

Havdalah Celebration

Leader:

(With two lit Shabbat candles burning, the leader says:)

Father, you have given us the blessing of Shabbat, and You have told us to honor it and to keep it holy, to keep it set apart unto You. We thank you, Father, that we have been able to rest our bodies and to be refreshed in You on this special day. We now ask that Your Spirit continue to be upon us, as we begin another week in Your service.

Heenay El Yshuatee evtach velo efchad. Kee azee vezeemrat ya Adonai, vayehee lee leeYeshuah. Ooshavtem mayeem b'sason meemah-ahyahney ha-Yeshuah. LaAdonai haYeshuah al amchah beerchatecha selah. Adonai tzevaot eemanoo meesgav lanu Elohey Ya'akov selah.

Behold, God (is) my Salvation: I will trust (Him) and not be afraid. For the Lord is my strength (might), and my song, and He has become my salvation. With joy you shall draw water from the wells of salvation. Salvation is the Lord's. Your blessing is upon Your people. The Lord of hosts is with us, the God of Jacob is our fortress.

All Say:

Father, You are Lord of all the Universe. Happy is the man who trusts in You. You are our help, O Lord of Hosts, You answer us when we call on You.

The Cup (Leader Says):

Wine represents joy, and so now we fill our wine cup—signifying the joy that comes from celebrating the Father's Sabbaths.

All Say:

The people of Israel have been blessed with light, gladness and honor which our Father's miracle of deliverance brought to our ancestors—and which Yeshua is bringing to us. We too lift up the cup of Salvation and call on the name of our God.

Blessing of The Wine (Leader Says):

Baruch atah Adonai, Elohenu Melech ha'olam, boreh p'ri hagaphen. Amen.

Blessed are You, O Lord our God, Ruler of the Universe, the Creator of the fruit of the vine.

Blessing Over the Spices (Leader Says):

Baruch atah Adonai Eloheynu Melech ha'olam boray meenay besameem.

Blessed are You, O Lord our God, King of the Universe, Who creates diverse spices.

Pass the spices around for all to smell—as a reminder for us to live our lives as "a fragrant aroma, an acceptable sacrifice, well pleasing to our God" (Philippians 4:18).

Lighting The Havdalah Candle:

Representatives for Ephraim and Judah stand on either side of the Havdalah candle—each uses their lighted Shabbat candle to light the Havdalah candle—after they say the following blessings.

Ephraim Says:

Behold the stick of Ephraim. I desire to share with you, my brother Judah, the light of redemption and truth—through our beloved Messiah Yeshua, who is our eternal Shabbat. In His name I pray that He grant you perfect peace, health and blessing.

Judah Says:

Behold the stick of Judah. I likewise desire to share with you my brother Ephraim, the light of redemption and truth— through our beloved Messiah Yeshua. In His name I bid you peace, health and blessings. In Him, I pray that we might be empowered to walk together in all His Truth.

(Both simultaneously light the Havdalah candle, then extinguish their individual candles in the dish of wine. Together they hold up and lift high the lighted candle, and...)

Judah and Ephraim Together Say:

We cast aside our differences, and embrace one another in the true spirit of unity, that we may be one stick in the hand of our Father, the God of all Israel.

The Havdalah Blessing (Leader Says):

Baruch atah Adonai Elohenu Melech ha'olam, Hamavdeel bayn kodesh l'chol, bayn or l'choshech, Bayn Yisrael l'ameem, Bayn yom ha-shveeyee le-shayshet y'may ha-ma'aseh. Barukh atah Adonai, ha-mavdeel bayn kodesh l'chol.

Blessed are you, Lord our God, King of the Universe Who makes a division between the sacred and the secular, between light and darkness, between Israel and the other nations, between the seventh day and the six working days. Blessed are you, Lord, who makes a distinction between the secular and the sacred.

All Sing The Sh'ma:

Sh'ma Yisrael, Adonai Elohenu, Adonai Echad.
Baruch shem, k'vod malchuto, le'olam vahed. Amen

Hear O Israel, the Lord our God, the Lord is One. Blessed be His Name, whose glorious Kingdom is forever, and ever. Amen.

Israel's Feasts and their Fullness

Ephraim and Judah:

Ephraim and Judah are holding high the Havdalah candle and together...

All Proclaim in Unison:

Through the blood of Yeshua we are no longer two separate houses, we are now one stick in the Father's hand, united for His purpose—our two sticks forever burning as one flame.

Ephraim and Judah lower the candle and...

Leader Says:

Baruch atah Adonai Eloheynu Melech ha'olam, asher natan lanu et Yeshua haMashiach, ha'or la'olam.

Blessed are You, Lord our God, King of the Universe, who gives us Messiah Yeshua, the Light of the World.

All Say:

Shavua Tov! (Good Week!)
Shavua Tov! (Good Week!)

Have a good and blessed week!

© 1988-2002

Messianic Israel Ministries

Box 700217, Saint Cloud, Florida 34770
Phone 800.829.8777   Fax 407.348.3770
www.mim.net
Since 1977
Ministering to "both the houses of Israel" (Isaiah 8 14)

New Moon Celebrations

The Father says He made the moon to "mark the seasons," the *mo'edim*, the feasts (Psalm 104:19). As returning children of Israel, we see that the moon plays an important part in the feasts, and so we learn the importance of celebrating the New Moon, or *Rosh Chodesh*.

The Lunar calendar was of great importance to our forefathers because the timing of the feasts was calculated according to it. Whereas the weekly Sabbath is not affected by the moon, the rest of the feasts are. The seven month long cycle of *mo'edim* was regulated according to the appearance of the New Moon. It is a cycle that began in the month of *Abib* (Spring). The first feast, Passover, was reckoned according to the appearance of the moon, with it their calendar began, so the Israelites were very scrupulous about observing the appearance of the New Moon.

The New Moon in Scripture

On *Rosh Chodesh*, the New Moon, the children of Israel blew silver trumpets, offered sacrifices, and feasted together (Numbers 10:1-10). [63]

---

63 For more information on the silver trumpets see the Yom Teruah chapter

The Father had told them, "In the day of your gladness and in your appointed feasts, and **on the first days of your months**, you shall blow the trumpets over your burnt offerings, and over the sacrifices of your peace offerings; and they shall be as a reminder of you before your God. I am YHVH your God" (Numbers 10:10).

The Psalmist tells us to "blow the trumpet at the new moon [beginning of the months], at the full moon, on our feast day" (Psalms 81:3). Businesses closed for the occasion and kings celebrated with banquets (Amos 8:5; 1 Samuel 20:5,6,24,29). The Levites had a new moon offering and the prophets were often active (1 Chronicles 23:31; Isaiah 1:13; Haggai 1:1; Ezekiel 26:1; 29:17; 31:1; 32:1). The new moon of the seventh month was given special attention, as its siting marked the beginning of the feast of Yom Teruah (Leviticus 23:24; Numbers 29:1-6; Ezra 3:6; Nehemiah 8:2).

From this brief introduction, we see that the New Moons were important to the sons of Israel. However, although Judah has continued to sight the New (Dark) Moon, the dispersion of Ephraim among the Nations brought a cessation of the celebration to those of the former Northern Kingdom (Nehemiah 10:33; 7:73-8:2; Ezra 3:1-6; Hosea 2:11).

We encourage celebration of this special time with an informal gathering in the home and blowing of trumpets. You might want to have your friends join you for a covered dish dinner so you can share a meal and a time of worship.

You can involve the children by having them sound the trumpets or shofar when they sight the new moon. Teach them that the moon does not produce light, but rather reflects the light of the sun. So it is with the Body of Messiah: we are called to reflect His light. Celebrating the New Moon gives us opportunity to share the truth of His shining glory with others.

The Forgotten Feast

The following is an excerpt from an article written by our friends, Toby and Shannon Janicki. The article, called "Forgotten Feast," appeared in the Messianic Israel Herald Magazine.[64]

There is one feast which is often neglected, yet it is perhaps one of the most important. It is Rosh Chodesh, the Head of the Month.

History and Significance

We begin in *Bereshit* (Genesis), chapter 1, verses 14-16:

"God said, 'Let there be lights in the expanse of the sky to separate day from night; they shall serve as signs for the set times—the days and the years; and they shall serve as lights in the expanse of the sky to shine upon the earth.' And it was so. God made the two great lights, the greater light to dominate the day and the lesser light to dominate the night, and the stars."

These two great lights are the sun, *shemesh*, and the moon, *yare'ah*, respectively.

It is also important to note that the word for *set times* here is *mo'edim* (appointed times), which is the very word that YHVH chooses to use to describe His festivals.

One more passage that speaks of these two lights is found in *Tehelim* (Psalms) chapter 104, verse 19: "He made the moon to mark the seasons; the sun knows when to set."

This passage clearly sets the moon apart as the main marker of the seasons, while the sun is to mark the day. But how does the moon do this?

In *Bamidbar* (Numbers) 28:13, we read of an offering to take place on a day referred to as the New Moon. Here the Hebrew reads *ra'shei chodsheikhem* meaning, "the head of

---

64 Volume 2, Issue 1
Toby and Shannon Janicki, their son, Aharon, and their daughter, Channah, live in Loveland, Colorado, where they lead the congregation, Kehilat Y'shua Toby is a regular guest speaker at the Messianic Israel Alliance Conferences and he graciously contributed several good points to this book

the crescent/month." It is from this that we get the term *Rosh Chodesh*. Therefore, the biblical new moon marks the first day of a new month. The moon's full cycle of illumination lasts a little over 29 days. Thus we have our biblical months of either 29 or 30 days.

Calendar Problems

Looking at our own Gregorian Calendar, we see it is not based on the cycles of the moon at all. Before turning to the rabbinical calendar, we will first need to view the ancient history and practice of citing the new moon.

According to *Bamidbar* (Numbers) 10:10, the New Moon day was to be a "joyous occasion." In fact, in punishment for Israel's disobedience, YHVH threatens to take the New Moon celebration away (Hosea 2:13). In Israel, witnesses would wait and watch for the new moon, based upon when the last crescent was seen. They would then report the sighting to the Sanhedrin (council of elders) and trumpets were blown to announce to the people the beginning of the month. The people truly did not know ahead of time when the month would begin.

During the period of Syrian-Greek persecution (the time of the Maccabees and Chanukah), the celebration of the New Moon was forbidden by Syrian law along with Shabbat and circumcision. The Syrians knew that if the Hebrews did not observe and celebrate Rosh Chodesh, they would not know when the other feasts would be.

The idea of having no calendar and not knowing ahead of time when the month will begin, or on which day the festivals will be, brings to mind the words of Yeshua in Mattityahu (Matthew) 24:36:

"But when that day and hour will come, no one knows —not the angels in heaven, not the Son, only the Father."

Rabbinical Calculations

Today the rabbinical calendar is based on calculations

set up by Rabbi Hillel the Elder in the mid fourth century. Around his time, the Sanhedrin (the high court of ancient Israel) ceased to exist. Hillel felt so strongly that the New Moon could not be declared visually without a Sanhedrin to affirm its sighting that he decided that rabbinical authorities must calculate it. Unfortunately, as Astronomy has improved, the rabbis now admit that Hillel's calculations are incorrect. Sometimes his calculations are off by as much as two days, which in turn means the festivals, *mo'edim* (appointed times) are not celebrated on the correct day.

However, the rabbis refuse to change their calendar until a Sanhedrin is once again established. Nevertheless, there are groups like the Karaites, who, throughout the ages, have rejected these traditions and still site the New Moon monthly. Unfortunately they have no printed calendar.

Being Renewed

Before we conclude, let us look at an important concept that is interwoven into the celebration of Rosh Chodesh. Rabbi *Sh'aul* (Paul) wrote in his book to the Colossians 2:16-17:

"So don't let anyone pass judgment on you in connection with eating and drinking, or in regard to a Hebrew festival or Rosh-Chodesh or Shabbat. These are a shadow of things that are coming, but the body is of the Messiah."

Here Sh'aul exhorts us not to let others judge us for celebrating Rosh Chodesh. He also adds that these things are a "shadow of things that are coming." How is Rosh Chodesh a shadow of things coming?

To explain, we first need to see that, in Hebrew, "chodesh" means more than just "new." It literally means "renewed."

It is from this same root that we see a word appear in *Yirmeyahu* (Jeremiah) 31:31: "See a time is coming, declares YHVH, when I will make a **new** covenant with the House of Israel and the House of Judah."

"New" here comes from the word chodesh, so this really means that the covenant that we have through Yeshua is a B'rit Chadasha, a "Renewed Covenant."

Sun of Righteousness

Yeshua is designated as the sun in Malachi 4:2: "But for you who revere My Name a sun of righteousness shall rise to bring healing."

So, if Yeshua is represented by the sun, and the sun "renews" the moon, then the moon might be said to be a picture of us—the Believers. Just as the phases of the moon are renewed, we are constantly renewed through Yeshua and His atoning death!

A Picture of our Redemption in Messiah

Each new month, each Rosh Chodesh, presents a picture of our redemption in Messiah. Colossians 3:9-10 explains: "...you have stripped away the old self, with its way, and have put on the new self, which is continually being renewed in fuller and fuller knowledge, closer and closer to the image of its Creator." The New Moon serves to remind us of our ever-present opportunity to start over through Messiah's grace. In fact, Rabbi Samson Raphael Hirsch in his commentary on the commandments, Horeb, describes the new moon as having a "rebirth," hence the messianic concept of being "born again" (See *Yochannan* [John] 3:3).

What a beautiful concept to celebrate each month!

Celebrating Rosh Chodesh

Mark Huey is the Administrator of Messianic Israel Alliance. The following is excerpted from his article, "Rosh Chodesh," which appeared in the Messianic Israel Herald. [65]

When the Holy One created Adam, and then a people for His own possession, He instilled in them an inherent desire to praise, worship, and celebrate. This innate desire makes us want to pray, worship, praise, sing, and dance. Even the fallen angels were originally designed this way.

However, when the chief cherub, HaSatan (the Accuser), fell, he began encouraging worship-oriented man toward a type of worship that leads to debauchery and perversion.

Our Heavenly Father created us to celebrate, and in His perfect design He gave us festivals so we would have times and seasons in which to participate in these celebrations.

What do the Scriptures say about such celebrations?

"Sing aloud unto God our strength: make a joyful noise unto the God of Jacob. Take a psalm, and bring hither the timbrel, the pleasant harp with the psaltery. Blow the trumpet in the new moon, in the time appointed, on our solemn feast day. For this was a statute for Israel, and a law of the God of Jacob. This he ordained in Joseph for a testimony..." (Psalm 81:1-5).

Overlooking Benefits

We are missing out on blessings. We have been told that celebrating the feasts is no longer necessary, that the Law (Torah) has been done away with, and that we are no longer under it. The enemy of our souls has even cleverly changed the times and seasons, and God's people, due to their lack of knowledge, are missing out (Hosea 4:6; Malachi 2:7-8).

One of the days of celebration that was given to us is

---

65 Volume 1, Issue 1

Mark Huey lives in Kissimmee, Florida with his wife, Margaret, who is the Accountant for Messianic Israel Alliance The Huey's have five children You can write to him at: mark@mim net

Rosh Chodesh. What does our God say about honoring this day?

"In the day of your gladness, and in your solemn days, and in the beginnings of your months, ye shall blow with the trumpets over your burnt offerings, and over the sacrifices of your peace offerings; that they may be to you for a memorial before your God" (Numbers 10:10).

"In the beginnings of your months ye shall offer a burnt offering unto the Lord....every month throughout the months of the year" (Numbers 28:11-15).

Our ancestors had seasons where they actually honored these instructions. In the time of Saul and David, Rosh Chodesh feasts were conducted: David said to Jonathan, "Behold, tomorrow is the new moon, and I should not fail to sit with the king at meat: but let me go, that I may hide myself in the field unto the third day at even....Then Jonathan said to David, Tomorrow is the new moon: and thou shalt be missed, because thy seat will be empty" (1 Samuel 20:5,28).

David spoke of standing, "every morning to thank and praise the Lord, and likewise at even; and to offer all burnt sacrifices unto the Lord in the sabbaths, in the new moons, and on the set feasts..." (1 Chronicles 23:30-31).

Solomon also obeyed and reaped rewards: "Behold, I build a house to the name of the Lord my God, to dedicate it to him, and to burn before him...the burnt offerings morning and evening, on the sabbaths, and on the new moons..." (2 Chronicles 2:4).

In the days of Elisha there is mention of new moon recognition: "He said, Wherefore wilt thou go to him to day? it is neither new moon, nor sabbath..." (2 Kings 4:23).

Ezra said of Judah's return to the land, "They kept also ...the new moons, and all the set feasts of the Lord..." (Ezra 3:4-5; also see Nehemiah 10:33).

Hard times come when we harden our hearts to YHVH's instructions. Isaiah described our wandering ways in his first chapter, but concludes in his final chapter with the reestablishment of new moon celebrations: "And it shall come to pass, that from one new moon to another, and from one sabbath to another, shall all flesh come to worship before me, saith the Lord" (Isaiah 66:23).

During Ezekiel's day there was a perverted attempt to honor the new moons (Ezekiel 45:17; 46:1-6). But Hosea said the Lord would put a stop to them.

Hosea was a prophet to those of the Northern Kingdom of Ephraim, and he said of her, "She shall follow after her lovers, but...not overtake them; she shall seek them, but... not find them: then shall she say, I will go and return to my first husband; for then was it better with me than now. For she did not know that I gave her corn, and wine, and oil, and multiplied her silver and gold, which they prepared for Baal. Therefore will I return, and take away my corn...my wine... and will recover my wool and flax given to cover her nakedness. And...uncover her lewdness in the sight of her lovers, and none shall deliver her out of mine hand. I will also cause all her mirth to cease, her feast days, her **new moons**, her sabbaths and all her solemn feasts" (Hosea 2:7-11).

Because we perverted our ways, our Father caused our "mirth," or celebration, to cease. Thankfully we are now closer to the days forecast by Isaiah, and our Creator is allowing us to worship Him in Spirit and truth on the Holy Days—including Rosh Chodesh.

The Father's plan of the ages is unfolding in these latter days. As Israelites from both Ephraim and Judah walk together in obedience to His ways, we are beginning to break down many of the barriers that have existed between us and our Heavenly Father. This happens as we joyfully walk by faith, and through obedience to the ways of Torah, as led by the Ruach HaKodesh.

The Key to Revival

If we want revival, we must first be obedient. Therefore, at the next new moon, gather informally with family and friends and look to the sky. Once you spot the new moon, sound silver trumpets if you have them,[66] or do as Judah does and sound the shofar (ram's horn). Celebrate with thanksgiving to our Creator for His magnificent plan.

When you see the new moon, rather than just making mental ascent to the lunar cycle, give praise, worship and adoration to the One who reminds us monthly that He is the author of new life. For it is new life that is reflected in the new moon that shines upon His people Israel.

NEW MOON

FULL MOON

---

66 See chapters on Yom Teruah

Part Three

The Early Feasts:
Passover
Unleavened Bread
First Fruits
Shavuot

Seven Feasts—Nine Days

As stated in an earlier chapter, Israel's annual feasts come in three clusters: "**Three times** a year you shall celebrate a feast to Me [and]...all your males shall appear before the Lord YHVH."

These three appointed times occur in the first, third, and seventh months, and they are called the Feast of Unleavened Bread [often called Passover]; the Feast of the Harvest [also called the Feast of Weeks and *Shavuot*]; and the Feast of the Ingathering [often called Tabernacles] (Exodus 23:14-17; 34:23-24; 2 Chronicles 8:13).

When we read about these three prescribed holy convocations in Scripture, we discover that there are *seven* different feasts, and *nine* appointed days that are to be honored during these appointed times. We do not point this out to settle disputes over seven versus nine days, but to help us better understand these nine consecrated days. Prior to Yeshua's return, we will probably never settle the many arguments concerning the finer details and timing of Israel's feasts. Moreover, the thrust of this book is not intended to be about the precise timing of the feasts, but about their prophetic call to the whole house of Israel.

We recognize that there is probably no more hotly

contested subject than the timing of the death, burial, and resurrection of our Messiah. The dating of Shavuot is also passionately debated, as are the sightings of the New Moon, the different calendars, and so on.

Rather than trying to determine actual feast dates, our purpose is to enable Believers to see the feasts in a new light and to encourage them to honor these feasts.

Seven Sabbath Feasts—Nine Appointed Days

Of the nine days mentioned in descriptions of the feasts, two of them are not Sabbaths. This argument is based on defining a feast as a Sabbath,[67] and a Sabbath by the command to do no servile work: "Six days you shall labor and do all your work, but the seventh day is a sabbath of YHVH your God; in it you shall not do any work...For in six days YHVH made the heavens and the earth, the sea and all that is in them, and rested on the seventh day; therefore YHVH blessed the sabbath day and made it holy" (Exodus 20:9-11).

Two Feasts—Four Sabbaths

To help us properly define Israel's seven feasts, we note that two of them have *two* Sabbath days. These *double* feasts are Unleavened Bread and the Feast of Booths, or Tabernacles. We are commanded to do no servile work on the *first* and *last* days of *both* of these feasts.

Unleavened Bread: "On the fifteenth day...is the Feast of Unleavened Bread...for seven days you shall eat unleavened bread. On the **first day** you shall have a holy convocation; **you shall not do any laborious work**. But for seven days you shall present an offering by fire to YHVH. On the **seventh day** is a holy convocation; **you shall not do any laborious work**" (Leviticus 23:6-8; also Numbers 28:17-18,25).

Tabernacles: "On the fifteenth of this seventh month is the Feast of Booths for seven days to YHVH. On the **first day** is a holy convocation; **you shall do no laborious work** of any

---

67 The late Dr Harry Veerman of Israel, who wrote under the pen name, Phinehas Ben Zadok, stated this in a private letter to the author dated 3/1/95

kind. For seven days you shall present an offering by fire to YHVH. On the **eighth day** you shall have a holy convocation and present an offering by fire to YHVH; it is an assembly. You shall **do no laborious work**" (Leviticus 23:34-36,39).

Two "Work Days"—Passover and First Fruits

Two of the nine days to be remembered are not Sabbaths: *Passover* and *First Fruits.* These have no prohibition of work, and even call for *specific work* to be done on those days. On the day of Passover (also called the day of Preparation), fathers had to kill a lamb at twilight, mark the house by putting some of the blood on the doorposts and lintel, then roast the lamb with fire (Exodus 12:3-15). However, we are commanded in Exodus 35:3: "You shall not kindle a fire in any of your dwellings on the sabbath day."

We also see that this was a work day in that the Father said, "You shall observe this **rite**" (Exodus 12:25). In the Hebrew, *rite* is *abodah*, which speaks of work, of labor.[68]

Of the Day of First Fruits, it is said, "You shall begin to count seven weeks from the time you begin to **put the sickle to the standing grain**. Then you shall celebrate the Feast of Weeks..." (Deuteronomy 16:9-10). Putting the sickle to the grain speaks of working to harvest barley. Once harvested, the men were to *bring*, or *carry*, a sheaf of the first fruits of these harvests to the priest (Leviticus 23:10). However, Jeremiah says, "If you do not listen to Me to keep the sabbath day holy **by not carrying a load** and coming in through the gates of Jerusalem on the sabbath day, then I will kindle a fire in its gates and it will devour the palaces of Jerusalem and not be quenched" (vs 17:27).

Because these two days play important roles in the collective whole that we call the feasts of Israel, and because they are work days, what message do they convey to us?

The Work of Yeshua

The shadowy days of Passover and First Fruits foretold

---

68 *Strong's* # H5656

the death and resurrection of the Lamb of God. Passover depicted His sacrifice on our behalf, by which He took away our sins. First Fruits foretold His being the first to be raised from the dead. On these days Yeshua was working. He was canceling out the certificate of debt consisting of decrees against us. He was diligently disarming rulers and authorities and making a public display of them. Yeshua was *working*—He was beginning to bring in the sheaves that are His New Covenant people (John 1:29; Colossians 2:14-15; Psalms 126:6).

These two feasts days foretold the "work of Yeshua." For the Father said of His Firstborn, Yeshua, "My covenant shall be confirmed to him. So I will establish his **seed** forever" (Psalm 89:28-29). In fulfillment of this promise, Yeshua has myriads of children who will live eternally. They are children for whom He travailed in labor (Isaiah 53:10-11; Luke 22:44). His was a painful, hard labor that was culminated on the cross. It also was a labor of love, destined to give birth to a new creation. It was a labor so painful that He died from it. Yeshua died to give birth to the sons of righteousness.

Through faith in Yeshua we become sons of God: To "as many as received Him...He gave the right to become children of God, even to those who believe in His name" (John 1:12). When one believes in the Name of Yeshua, God's "seed abides in him...because he is born of God" (1 John 3:9). These "have been born again not of seed which is perishable but imperishable, that is, through the living and abiding word of God" (1 Peter 1:23). They are the eternal descendants promised to the Firstborn. They have His imperishable seed abiding in them and are "the Israel of God" (Galatians 6:16).

In Philippians 1:6, Paul says, "I am confident...that He who began a good work in you will perfect it until the day of Messiah Yeshua." We are a good work—a work foretold by the prophets (Acts 13:40-41). We are "created in Messiah Yeshua for good works, which God prepared beforehand so that we would walk in them" (Ephesians 2:10).

One might say that we were created through Messiah Yeshua's Passover work.

How Then Do We Count the Days?

Though it is a workday, and not a Sabbath, Passover is nonetheless an integral part of the feasts. It is a *mo'ed*, an appointed time, for it is included in a description of the feasts beginning in Exodus 34:25: "Thou shalt not offer the blood of my sacrifice with leaven; neither shall the sacrifice of the feast[69] of the passover be left until morning."

Though both Passover and Unleavened Bread are often collectively called "Passover," this verse particularly mentions the *sacrifice* of Passover and the lambs slain on that day. Unleavened Bread had no sacrifice except the lambs sacrificed on the day of Passover.[70]

Passover is included in the Leviticus 23:4-6 list of the feasts: "These are the feasts [71]of YHVH, even holy convocations, which ye shall proclaim in their seasons. In the fourteenth day of the first month at even is the Lord's **passover**. And on the fifteenth day of the same month is the feast of **unleavened bread**..."

Though it is a day of work, we must count the day of Passover in the seven feasts of Israel. The same is true of the Day of First Fruits.

As we study this important day in a later chapter, we will see that it marks a pivotal point in mankind's history. (See chart below: "Seven Feasts—Nine Days").

The Meaning of the Feasts

In describing Passover and Unleavened Bread, the Father tells us what His feasts should mean to us: "'Now

---

69   Feast: *Strong's* # H2282: *chag.* from H2287; a festival, or a victim, therefore: (solemn) feast (day), sacrifice, solemnity

70   The "sacrifice of the *feast* of the passover "could refer to the "victim," or to the lamb itself See the previous footnote

71   *Strong's* # H4150: *mo'ed.*

this day will be a **memorial** to you, and you shall **celebrate** it as a **feast** to YHVH; throughout your generations you are to celebrate it as a permanent **ordinance**" (Exodus 12:14)

The feasts are to be memorials to us. They are filled with little mementos, and so are worthy of record.[72] We are to celebrate, to *chagag* them, which is to move in a circle, march in a sacred procession, observe a festival, be giddy, celebrate, dance, reel to and fro.[73] They are to be *festive.*[74] We celebrate these *ordinances* at appointed times and with certain customs, for they are statutes of our Father that are engraved on our hearts.[75]

These fixed times are called *mo'edim*. They are sacred assemblies convened for definite purposes, and they serve as an outward sign that we belong to the Holy One of Israel.[76]

Whose Feasts Are They?

These feasts often are called "the feasts of Israel," but they are actually "The feasts of YHVH" (Leviticus 23:4; 2 Chronicles 2:4). Moreover, His feasts are also to be commemorated "forever" (Exodus 12:24). We commemorate them because they are more than just records of history, they are blueprints through which He reveals His plan of redemption for His chosen people. These collective celebrations also allow us to gather together as a family, which strengthens family ties.

The Early Feasts

We begin the cycle of the feasts with the Passover Preparation Day in the first month, on Abib fourteen, when Israel was to slay their lambs (Leviticus 23:5).

Unleavened Bread immediately follows on the fifteenth of the month, and it is observed for one week—from the

---

72 Memorial: *Strong's* # H2146 *zikrown*
73 Celebrate: *Strong's* # H2287: chagag, prim root [comp H2283, H2328]
74 Feast: *Strong's* # H2282 *chag*, from H2287
75 Ordinance: *Strong's* # H 2708 *chuqqah*, femine of H2706 from H2710
76 *Strong's* # H4150, 3259

fifteenth to the twenty-first day (Leviticus 23:6-8).

First Fruits, which speaks of the first of the barley harvest, is observed during this same week of Unleavened Bread, on the day after the weekly Sabbath (Exodus 23:19).

Next comes The Feast of Weeks. On the day of the waving of the First Fruits we begin to count fifty days, and on the fiftieth is the Feast of Weeks, or Pentecost (Leviticus 23:15-21). (Pentecost is a Greek word that means fifty.)

These first four festivals are called the Early Spring and the Late Spring feasts—Passover, Unleavened Bread, First Fruits, and the Feast of Weeks.

Some consider these four spring feasts to be a unit. To them the Feast of Weeks is a conclusion to Passover; Pesach is not complete until Shavuot is celebrated. However, the Father separated their times of celebration and both require appearances in Jerusalem. Moreover, Shavuot is fulfilled in a way that differs from Passover.

The Fall Feasts

The Fall feasts cover a twenty-one-day period, and have come to be known collectively as "Tabernacles." The first of the Fall feasts is *Yom Teruah*, the Day of Blowing, or Day of Trumpets. This feast comes on the first day of the Seventh month (sometimes called the month of Tishri). This day also is mistakenly called *Rosh Hashanah*, or *Head of the Year* (see chapter 26). *Yom Teruah* marks the beginning of Israel's call to prepare for *Yom Kippur*.

Yom Kippur, the Day of Atonement (which should be called *Yom HaKippurim*, or Day of the Coverings: plural), is the only day wherein a fast is commanded. This day is considered to be the most solemn day of the calendar year.

Five days later comes the first day of *Sukkot*, or Tabernacles, which we celebrate for seven days. Then comes the "Eighth Day," the second Sabbath associated with this feast.

With the understanding that there are nine days to be honored in Israel's seven feasts, we will now begin our study of these appointed times.

Seven Feasts —Nine Days

1	*Day of Preparation for Pesach / Passover*
2	**First Day (Sabbath) of Unleavened Bread**
3	*Day of First Fruits*
4	**Last Day (Sabbath) of Unleavened Bread**
5	Shavuot (Pentecost)
6	Yom Teruah
7	Yom Kippur (Yom HaKippurim)
8	**First Day (Sabbath) of Sukkot/Tabernacles**
9	**Eighth Day (Sabbath) of Tabernacles**

Key to Feast Table:

Working Feast Day
Feast with Two Sabbaths
Feast Day

Feast Dates

The Spring Feasts:

Pesach — Passover — Day of Preparation
Slaying of the lamb
Aviv/Nisan 14 (Corresponds to March / April)

Chag Matzah — Feast of Unleavened Bread
Week of Unleavened Bread
Aviv/Nisan 15-22 (Corresponds to March / April)

Yom HaBikkurim — Day of First Fruits
Barley Harvest
First day of the week following the Sabbath after Pesach

Shavuot — Feast of Weeks
Wheat Harvest
The Seventh First day (Sunday) after the First Fruits Waving

The Fall Feasts:

Yom Teruah — Day of Blowing
(Begins the Ten Days between Yom Teruah and Yom Kippur,
often called "The Days of Awe")
Tishri 1 (Corresponds to September / October)

Yom Kippur— Day of Atonement (Yom HaKippurim)
Tishri 10 (Corresponds to September / October)

Sukkot — The Feast of Tabernacles
The First Day: Probable birth date of Messiah Yeshua
The Eighth Day: Probable day of Yeshua's circumcision.
Tishri 15-23 (Corresponds to September / October)

"Jewish" Celebrations:

(Dates correspond to December and March)

Chanukah — The Feast of Dedication —
The Festival of Lights
Kislev 25 - Cheshvan 4   (Corresponds to December)

Purim — Lots — The Feast of Esther
Adar 14

The Farmer's Year

In Bible times, most people had some involvement with farming, every family having at least a small plot of land.

Grain
The main crops were wheat and barley. Following the autumn rains, the farmer ploughed the soil and sowed the grain by hand. If there were winter rains, he could harvest the crop in April or May.

Harvest
The farmer would cut the grain with a sickle, leaving the sheaves in the field to dry. Next, he threshed the grain on a threshing-floor, where oxen trod the grain from the husks of wheat. After this, the farmer winnowed the grain, throwing it in the air to separate the grain from the lighter chaff, which blew away. Finally, the grain was sieved and stored away in sacks or large jars.

Fruit
The Israelites grew fruit such as grapes, figs, and olives, as well as melons, dates, pomegranates, and nuts. They also often cultivated vegetables such as beans, lentils, onions, and cucumbers, and some herbs.

Animals
Sheep and goats were herded both for their meat and their milk, and for their wool and hair, which could be utilized for making garments. Farmers would often use donkeys for load-bearing and oxen for pulling ploughs.

HEAVY WINTER RAIN

SPRING RAIN

DRY SEASON STARTS

WINTER STARTS

VERY HOT

AUTUMN/EARLY RAIN

January · February · March · April · May · June · July · August · September · October · November · December

SHEBAT · ADAR · NISAN · ZIV (IYYAR) · SIVAN · TAMMUZ · AB · ELUL · ETHANIM (TISHRI) · BUL (MARCHESVAN) · KISLEV · TEBETH

12 · 1 · 2 · 3 · 4 · 5 · 6 · 7 · 8 · 9 · 10 · 11

Citrus harvest

Almond blossom

Flax harvest

Barley harvest

Almonds ripen

Vine tending

Wheat harvest

Early Figs ripen

Summer figs

Walnuts ripen

Winemaking starts

Olive harvest

Dates, pomegranates ripen

Plowing

Wheat sown

From The Kregal Pictorial Guide To The Bible by Tim Dowley, Grand Rapids: Kregal Publications, 2000.

12

-128-

The Father's Passover Plan

I say to you, I shall never again eat it until...

(Luke 22:16).

We need to fully understand the above conditional clause because final fulfillment of Passover hinges on it. Furthermore, fulfillment of this "until" will require something of us. Seeing the point behind Yeshua's stipulated clause will help us walk through a new door of end time Passover celebration and fulfillment.

Many people gain greater understanding of Yeshua's "Last Supper" (sometimes called "Communion") when they see it presented in light of a *traditional* Jewish Passover *Seder,* or a *Messianic* Jewish Seder, in which traditions are modified and/or interpreted to reflect Messiah Yeshua.[77]

However, if the Father will allow the eyes of our hearts to be enlightened (Ephesians 1:18), we will see a more excellent way that will enable us to move beyond both of these beneficial illustrations.

The traditional Jewish, and later Messianic Jewish, Passover Seders both can speak volumes to Believers in the

---

77 *Seder* means *order of service.* For more information about these traditions, see Addendum A: *Traditional and Messianic Jewish Celebrations.*

Messiah. For example, according to Jewish tradition, before the feast, the mother cleans the home of all leaven.

The night before Passover eve, or *erev Pesach*, the family has a *bedikat chametz*, a search for leaven. They search, because after cleaning the house, the mother places small pieces of leavened bread in key places, and that night the father leads the children in a candlelight search for the leftover *chametz*. When the children find this leaven, the father, feather in hand, brushes the crumbs onto a wooden spoon or paper plate—all of which (feather, container and crumbs) is wrapped up to be burned the next morning.

This family practice can teach us the basic truth that leaven represents sin, and the "temples" in which we live also need cleansing from all sin by the power of the Ruach HaKodesh (the Holy Spirit), represented by the feather.[78]

The traditional Seder includes three pieces of "striped and pierced" *matzah*, or unleavened bread. Unleavened bread is used because our ancestors did not have time to wait for the bread to rise in their sudden departure for the desert. It was called the "bread of affliction" (Deuteronomy 16:3), or *poor man's bread*, because many people believe it was all the Israelites had to eat at the time.

Messianic Judaism teaches that the three matzot speak of Father, Son, and Holy Spirit, that the unleavened bread speaks of sinlessness, and that "striped and pierced" bread depicts Yeshua, Who brought us healing by His stripes when He was wounded for our transgressions (Isaiah 53:5).

Among traditional Jews,[79] different reasons are given for having three matzah. Some teach that two loaves of bread are present on the Sabbath eve table, and a third loaf is added at Passover as a reminder of the joyous nature of this "Festival of Freedom." Some say the three matzah represent the three groups of people found in Jewish religious life: Priests, Levites, and Israelites. Others say there are three because Abraham asked Sarah to make three measures of

---

78 See Exo 12:15,19; 13:7; Luke 12:1; 13:21; 1 Cor 5:6; 1 Pet 2:5
79 We refer to Jewish people who have not accepted Yeshua as the Messiah

fine meal for their Heavenly guests (Genesis 18:6).

Though the idea of "striped and pierced" matzah is used to teach about the Messiah, the historical reason for its use has to do with artistic women and the machine age.

Initially, all matzah was handmade, and since it was rolled-out dough, it was naturally circular or oval in form. To keep the dough from rising, perforations were made in it that allowed the air to escape. Ultimately, the women who baked this bread began to make their perforations in very artistic form, drawing pictures in their bread. Since these artworks could take a long time to finish, the rabbis felt they had to step in. To insure that the matzah would not be allowed to rise, and thus not meet the "unleavened" requirement, they decreed that the entire matzah process, from kneading to baking, must be executed within eighteen minutes.

This edict put a real crimp in matzah art. And with progress being what it is, in England, in 1875, a speedy matzah baking machine was invented. So began our era of "striped and pierced" square *matzot*.[80]

Those who appreciated the art form of traditional matzah were not happy with this strange looking square, uniform, uninteresting matzah brought forth by this new-fangled machine.

Perhaps the real reason for the matzah number and form is because the Father chose that representative number and chose to have it "pierced," because He clearly wants to point us to His Son.

The Afikomen

In traditional Jewish Seders, the middle matzah is broken in half, and the second half is called the *afikomen*, which is hidden away until the end of the meal. This Greek word is said to mean, *He shall come again.* Some say it means "that which comes last," because it is like *dessert*, in

---

80 See *The Jewish Book of Why*, Alfred J Kolatch, Middle Village, NY: Jonathan David Publishers, 1981, 1995, "Matzah," p 192

that it is the last thing tasted at the Seder.

For Messianic Believers, the afikomen can typify our Messiah, Who promised us, *"I will come again"* (John 14:3).

During the traditional meal, four cups of wine are served. Messianic Judaism teaches that in the Upper Room during the Last Supper, Yeshua was following this rabbinic tradition. According to them, it was before drinking the third cup, called the Cup of Redemption, that Yeshua said, "This is the new covenant in My blood" (Luke 22:15-20).

In this manner, the entire Seder celebration overflows with spiritual significance. We will elaborate on these Seder meanings in a later chapter, "Pesach Pictures."

A Messianic Jewish Passover Haggadah

We offer an abbreviated Messianic Jewish Passover Haggadah, which means "the telling of the story" (see Addendum A). This Guide, like the others, may be purchased from Messianic Israel Ministries, or the four pages may be photocopied for personal, home, or congregational use.

The Four Types of Passover

Beyond seeing the many truths in Jewish Seders, we need to see something more. To enter into a more meaningful appreciation of Passover, we first need to see that there are *four* types of Passovers in Scripture. To put this Feast into perspective, we must realize that when YHVH promised the Israelites, "I will *pass over* you," it was not an accomplished fact, but a living promise.

He said He would stand guard over, protect, and defend His children. He would refuse the destroyer entry into their homes. He would cause the destruction to "skip," or "pass," over them. As Yeshua is One with the Father, Passover likewise depicts Yeshua's promise to safeguard those who trust in Him (John 10:30; 14:18; 17:12-26).

To see the four Passovers in Scripture is to see a picture

of the Father's plan of salvation for His children. Our appreciation of this feast is deeply enriched and enhanced as we realize we are in the middle of the Father's present-day plan. When we understand these four types in their on-going, living context, we know that we have yet to experience the most glorious Passover of all. We know that we, Messiah's New Covenant followers, have much to do with the final fulfillment of Passover.

The Family Passover

We begin our year with the season of *Passover*—just as we begin our spiritual lives with *redemption.*

Our Father said of the Hebrew month, *Abib* (which corresponds to March/April on the Gregorian calendar), "This month shall be the beginning of months for you; it is to be the first month of the year to you....for in the month of Abib you came out of Egypt."

He also said, "Observe the month of Abib and celebrate the Passover to YHVH your God, for in the month of Abib YHVH your God brought you out of Egypt by night" (Exodus 12:2; 34:18; Deuteronomy 16:1).

With this first Passover our Father commanded:

"On the tenth of this month let each one take a lamb for themselves, accord-ing to their fathers' house-holds, a lamb for each house-hold. If the household is too small for a lamb, then he and his nearest neighbor are to

Picture from the book cover, *Passover Before Messiah & After* by D & M Broadhurst Available through Messianic Israel Ministries

take one according to the number of persons in them; accord-ing to what each man should eat, you are to divide the lamb ...[and] keep it until the fourteenth day of the same month, then...kill it at twilight. Moreover, they shall take some of the blood and put it on the two doorposts and on the lintel of the houses in which they eat it. They shall eat the flesh that same night, roasted with fire, and they shall eat it with unleavened bread and bitter herbs. Do not eat any of it raw or boiled at all with water, but rather roasted with fire...You shall not leave any of it over until morning, whatever is left of it you shall burn with fire. You shall eat it in this manner: with your loins girded, your sandals on your feet and your staff in your hand; and you shall eat it in haste—it is YHVH's Passover. For I will...strike down all the firstborn in the land of Egypt....and the blood shall be a sign for you on the houses where you live; and when I see the blood I will pass over you, no plague will befall you to destroy you when I strike the land of Egypt. This day will be a memorial to you, and you shall celebrate it as a feast to YHVH throughout your generations...as a permanent ordinance"(Exodus 12:3-15).

We are to diligently teach our children about all that the Father commanded us. When they ask, *"What does this rite mean to you?"*we are to answer them with all diligence and patience; we are to be dedicated to their spiritual matur-ation (Deuteronomy 6:7; 11:19; Exodus 12:26,42; 13:8,14).

The Holy One designated the first Passover to be a time wherein:

♦ Fathers were to diligently teach their children
♦ The family was to sacrifice a lamb for their household
♦ They were to put the blood on their doorposts
♦ The families were to partake of lamb, unleavened bread, and bitter herbs in their respective homes.

The emphasis of the first Passover was on the godly *household.* The Father said it was to be eaten in a single *house* (Exodus 12:46). Thus He established what we will call the *"Family Passover."*

The Congregational Passover

Later, our Father revised His Passover instructions. He moved the location of commemoration from their homes to His Tabernacle. He moved it from *their* house to *His* house. His command to observe Passover remained intact, but He changed the requirements about *where* and *how* it was to be observed.

"Observe the month of Abib and celebrate the Passover to YHVH your God, for in the month of Abib YHVH your God brought you out of Egypt by night. You shall sacrifice the Passover to YHVH your God from the flock and the herd, in the place where YHVH chooses to establish His name....You are not allowed to sacrifice the Passover in any of your towns, but at the place where YHVH your God chooses to establish His name, you shall sacrifice the Passover in the evening at sunset, at the time that you came out of Egypt. Cook and eat it in the place which YHVH your God chooses. In the morning you are to return to your tents. On the seventh day there shall be a solemn assembly to YHVH your God; you shall do no work on it...Be careful to observe these statutes" (Deuteronomy 16:2-12).

At the Temple in Jerusalem, Israelites were to sacrifice their lambs at twilight, and then roast them. This allotted day of sacrifice was immediately followed by a seven-day period called the *Feast of Unleavened Bread:* "Seven days you shall eat unleavened bread, but on the first day you shall remove leaven from your houses; for whoever eats anything leavened from the first day until the seventh day, that person shall be cut off from Israel" (Exodus 12:15-20).

This new, congregational celebration was to take place *in the Father's house.* There, His children would partake of lamb and unleavened bread.

This yearly celebration served as a collective time of commemoration, reflection and remembrance. Thus the Father established what we will call the *"Congregational Passover."*

Choose this Day...

We now must make a choice. All would agree that the above described Congregational Passover instructions were in place when Messiah Yeshua walked the earth. So how did He celebrate Passover in the last year of His life? Did He simply partake of the Congregational Passover as prescribed in Deuteronomy? Was He following Jewish tradition, as defined by the Jewish men of His day, or did Yeshua do something new? Did He change the way in which Passover was thereafter to be commemorated?

When Yeshua offered what is often called "The Last Supper," was He eating of the Passover exactly as outlined in Scripture, or was Yeshua *Himself* the Passover Lamb that year? Did He celebrate that Passover according to the tradition of His day, or did He establish a new tradition?

He could not do both. He had to do one or the other in the year that He was sacrificed for us.

Some people say that at the time of Yeshua there were two Jewish Passover traditions that were commemorated on two consecutive nights. They claim Yeshua offered His Passover meal on the first evening, and then became the Passover lamb on the next evening. But Yeshua spoke strongly against the traditions of men. He said to those who followed *unscriptural* man made precepts, "Rightly did Isaiah prophesy of you hypocrites, as it is written: 'This people honors me with their lips, but their heart is far away from me. But in vain do they worship me, teaching as doctrines the precepts of men.' **Neglecting the commandment of God, you hold to the tradition of men**" (Mark 7:6-8).[81]

Yeshua would *not* have observed Passover according to the traditions of men. He would have honored His Father's instructions to the letter. Therefore, we must choose. Was it more important that Yeshua once more *eat* of a lamb, or to fulfill Scripture and actually *become* the prophesied Lamb?

---

81 Traditions are fine as long as they do not oppose the truth of Scripture

Paul the apostle declares, "Messiah our Passover has been sacrificed" (1 Corinthians 5:7; 1 Peter 1:19). In that fateful year Yeshua became our Passover Lamb. That year He was offered as a sacrifice at the exact time the Father commanded that the lamb of redemption was to be sacrificed. When the cup of the New Covenant was raised by Messiah Yeshua on that fateful night, *it was the first cup of a new Passover tradition.*

When we see this truth, we begin to understand that new rules were again applied to Passover: Commemoration continued, but the rules were once more changed.

The Personal Passover

Our Father first established the Family Passover and then changed it to a Congregational Passover. With Yeshua, Passover instructions were again modified. This happened when He took bread and wine into His hands and said to His apostles, "I have earnestly desired to eat this Passover with you before I suffer" (Luke 22:15).

Yeshua said He "eagerly desired" (NIV)—He "earnestly and intensely desired" (Amplified)—to eat "this" particular *Pesach* meal with His disciples.

Why was He so earnest in His desire to eat of *this* particular Passover? Certainly He had participated in many Passover celebrations. Why was *this* particular Passover so special to Him?

Because it would prove to be a "Passover" meal unlike any other. The Passover that Yeshua *"desired with desire"* (KJV) to eat would prove to be *different.*

Luke says of the occasion, "When He had taken the cup and given thanks, Yeshua said, 'Take this and share it among yourselves.' ...And when He had taken some bread and given thanks, He broke it, and gave it to them, saying, 'This is My body which is given for you; do this in remembrance of Me, this is the new covenant in My blood'" (Luke 22:15-20).

Yeshua's Passover marked the end of the Old Covenant Passovers and the beginning of His New Covenant Passovers.

While Passover itself continued as a feast, on this particular Passover, Yeshua was sacrificed "once for all," and we have no need for another (Hebrews 7:27). The central focus is no longer the blood of a substitute animal, which only "covered" sin. With Yeshua's sacrifice, the focus became the pure and undefiled Blood of the Son of God, which has the power to remit, meaning to annihilate sin.[82]

Through His death on the tree (cross), Yeshua became our Passover Lamb.

Of this Passover, Paul said: "As often as you eat this bread and drink the cup, you proclaim Yeshua's death until He comes" (1 Corinthians 11:26).

We desire to proclaim Yeshua's death, because in our proclamation we declare that we belong to New Covenant Israel and not to the world.

When we partake of Yeshua's Passover elements, we declare that *He* is our Passover; the angel of the second death will "pass over" us in the final judgement because we are sanctified by the Blood of the New Covenant Passover Lamb. Through Yeshua we have an eternal sacrifice for our sins. Thus we are called the eternal "Israel of God" (Galatians 6:16).[83]

With Yeshua's Passover there came a certain fulfillment of, and another modification in, the Passover ordinance.

In and through Him, the focus of Israel's priesthood was changed from the Aaronic order to that of Melchizedek: "When the priesthood is changed, of necessity there takes place a change of law also." The sacrifices were finished.

Yeshua is our eternal High Priest according to the order of Melchizedek (Hebrews 5:6; 7:12), and as our Eternal High Priest, He instructed us to partake of *different Passover elements.*

---

82 Acts 20:28 speaks of "the church of God which He purchased with His own blood " Therefore, it was "God['s] blood " See 1 Pet 1:19; Heb 9:14, also see the book, *Who Is Israel?* chapter 10, "The Blood, The Redeemer and Physical Israel" and the "Addendum "

83 Eph 2:13-14; Col 1:20; Luke 22:16; Rom 5:9; Eph 1:7-14; Heb 9:12,15,26; 13:11-12,20

In the past, the prescribed elements were lamb and unleavened bread, but in the New Covenant the prescribed elements are bread and wine. Why?

Unlike the old Passover sacrifices, Yeshua's sacrifice is not an annual event, as was the slaying of Passover lambs. Rather, He is our ever-present, ever-available sacrifice. Commemoration of His sacrifice includes the elements from the prescribed *daily offering:* Bread and Wine.[84]

Yeshua also moved the *emphasis* of our search for leaven. Leaven typifies sin, and all leaven was to be removed from their houses for the Feast of Unleavened Bread, which immediately followed Passover. Yeshua moved the *emphasis* of that search to the areas of our hearts. That is why Paul instructs us to "clean out the old leaven of wickedness and malice from your **hearts**" (Matthew 15:18; 1 Corinthians 5:7).

In addition to having outward symbols of our faith that can help keep us on track, Yeshua wants us to deal with our hearts. "Behold," He says, "I stand at the door [of the heart] and knock....If anyone hears My voice and opens the door, I will come in to him and will sup with him, and he with Me" (Revelation 3:20).

We will call the Passover established by Messiah Yeshua the *Personal Passover*, for only those on whose heart's door He has knocked can invite Him into their lives. Only those who have personally invited Yeshua into their lives are called to partake of His intimate Passover Supper.

If you have not yet done so, invite Yeshua into your life right now. You do not need anyone to lead you in a particular prayer. You simply need to repent of your sins and ask Yeshua to come into your heart and be Lord of your life.

The Kingdom Passover

When Yeshua initiated the New Covenant Passover, He

---

84 See Heb 7:27; 9:12; 10:10; 1 Pet 3:18; Exo 29:40-42; Num 15:1-13; 28:5-7 Though incorporated into Jewish Seders, partaking of wine at Passover was *not* commanded in Scripture

lifted high the broken bread and said to His disciples, "I shall never again eat it *until* it is fulfilled in the kingdom of God." When He had taken the cup and given thanks, He said, "Take this and share it among yourselves; for I say to you, I will not drink of the fruit of the vine from now on *until* the kingdom of God comes" (Luke 22:15-18).

In saying this, Yeshua foretold a coming, glorious, eternal Passover, one that will be celebrated in the Kingdom of God. For there is a glorious Passover that is yet to come. It will take place at the Marriage Supper of the Lamb, and blessed are those who are invited to it (Revelation 19:9). One day the trumpet will sound, and we who are invited will put on imperishable wedding garments,[85] for we have been invited to a transcendent celebration.

At that time the believing family of Israel will again be "passed over." As overcomers, the second death will not be able to harm us. In utter jubilation we will ask: "Where O death is your victory? Where O death is your sting?" (Hosea 13:14; 1 Corinthians 15:55; Revelation 21:7).

Messiah Yeshua will again take the cup into His hands as prophesied, and, perhaps in honor of the rabbinic custom of His Jewish brothers, He will call it *the fourth Passover Cup*, which is known as *the Cup of Praise*.

That would certainly be an appropriate title, for when Messiah lifts high *that* cup, Hallelujah's that will ring for an eternity will begin. Death, finally and forevermore, will be swallowed up in victory.[86]

When we celebrate *that* Passover, then we will know the full and eternal glory of the *Kingdom Passover*.

Father, by your grace and mercy may we come to know the joy of that celebration!

---

85 See 1 Cor 15:51-57; Mat 22:1-14; Hos 13:14; Rev 19:7-9, and the book, *Who Is Israel?* chapter 17, "From Orphans To Heirs "
86 Rev 2:11; 20:6,14; 21:8; Hos 13:14; 1 Cor 15:55

Celebrating Passover As Never Before!

Passover can depict many things to us. In the Family Passover we see that the Father wants to save our families, for He told us to "take enough lamb for the whole **household**." Yeshua is the "*Lamb*" [87] and we can trust that there is enough of Him for our whole family—all who have a heart for Him will be satisfied.

As Messiah Yeshua's people, we need to bring our families to the Lamb. A healthy, happy family that is obedient to the Father because of their love for Him is a powerful witness. It is a witness that will encourage others to seek to belong to the God of Israel.

The Father also wants to save us as a congregation, because there are things He can accomplish in our lives only when we are gathered in an assembly with those of like faith. We can experience congregational worship, the Body can minister to one another, and we can be built up in our faith.

Additionally, the Father wants our salvation to be very

---

87 John 1:29; Pet 1:19; Rev 5:6

personal so we will learn to hear His voice for ourselves[88] and to have the faith of our forefather Abraham. We are heirs of his promise. Our God promised to provide "Himself" as a Sacrifice and to be a personal God to Abraham's children (Galatians 2:29; Genesis 22:8; 17:7).

Finally, the Father desires to save us as a kingdom. His ultimate goal is for us to be a kingdom of priests and to bring His Kingdom of Israel here to this earth.[89]

Speaking in broad terms, let us say that for a season, YHVH put emphasis on the Family Passover to teach His people the need for godly families. Then He emphasized the Congregational Passover to establish the need for fellowship. Finally, He moved the focus to the Personal Passover so we can learn to hear His voice (John 10:27).

We are now entering into a new day. Once more the Father is moving His emphasis. The God of Israel is doing a new thing: He is making the two sticks of Ephraim and Judah one in His hand. He will soon bring forth an invincible, blameless army comprised of sons who are able to take His Land. When the two houses of Israel unite as brothers they will become a mighty army. Together they serve YHVH Tzevaot, "YHVH of Hosts, the God of the armies of Israel" (Ezekiel 37:15-28; 1 Samuel 17:45). When Ephraim and Judah are fully reunited in Yeshua, when He is reigning in the Promised Land and is the King of Kings over the whole house, then we will celebrate the Kingdom Passover.[90]

We who see this Passover plan must work toward its fulfillment. We must proclaim the full, liberating, enlightening truth about Passover. We must work to reunite the two houses of Israel, that we might celebrate the most glorious of all Passovers.

The Passover Plan: It was, it is, and it is to come. It is a precious promise that is alive with new meaning.

---

88 See Eph 4:15; Heb 6:1-3; 1 Tim. 2:5.
89 See Mat 6:10; Act 1:6; 1 Pet. 2:9; Rev 1:6; 5:10; 20:6; 21:2.
90 See Isa 11:13-14; Obad 1:18; Zech 9:13; Amos 9:10; Zeph 3:11-13.

Celebration Suggestions

To celebrate the four Passovers, gather four families, groups, or individuals and assign to each a Passover: *Family, Congregational, Personal, or Kingdom.*

Also assign to each a side of the room in which you choose to meet: north, south, east, or west. When you gather, have the youngest son present ask the famous Passover question:

"*Why is this night different from all other nights?*"

Let each family take turns portraying, explaining, acting out, preaching about, or just rejoicing over, their particular Passover expression. If you do not have enough people available to play the roles, you can make and paint cardboard cutouts of the drawings found in this chapter. The leader can take the group to each venue and then explain each particular Passover. Make your gathering as elaborate or simple as you wish.

For example, you may want to have everyone dress in costume, and at each Passover station offer the guests the prescribed offering for that particular Passover.

Put the *Family Passover* station in front of a doorway and tape paper "blood" to the posts and lintel, then have a

family offer the three prescribed elements: a small piece of roast lamb, unleavened bread, and bitter herbs. Invite them in and encourage all to eat the Passover "quickly."

For the *Congregational Passover,* have someone dress as the High Priest, make an altar and put a sacrificial lamb on it (use a stuffed toy or make one from stuffed socks). Have the changes in the scriptural command (see the Passover Guide) written out

on a scroll (a rolled up paper), and have the priest read it as though it were a declaration being made to ancient Israel.

At this station have everyone partake of the prescribed elements of roast lamb, unleavened bread, and bitter herbs.

For the *Personal Passover*, feature Messiah Yeshua and the apostles reclining at a table. Here, talk about having a clean heart, one that is ready to receive Messiah's sacrifice (Psalm 51:10; 1 Corinthians 11:27-31). Then offer the Believers the New Covenant Passover Bread and Wine: The Body and Blood of our Messiah.

At the *Kingdom Passover* station, display fruits, flowers, and food to represent the endless, bountiful table from which we will partake at the Marriage Supper of the Lamb.

Decorate the table with candlesticks, a menorah, pretty brass and glass items, and so on. Try using a mirror draped in fabric and twinkle lights as a backdrop. Use anything and everything that will make your table look lush and beautiful.

Once each Passover is explained or acted out, let everyone gather in the center of the room to gaze around and appreciate the Father's glorious plan of redemption. First, that we should be raised in godly homes by godly fathers who teach their children the way of righteousness. Second, that godly congregations declare Israel's need for a covering

for sin and aid them in finding that way to righteousness. This is the ideal way for each of us to find the way to the One who gives us the Personal Passover.

In this way our children can more readily find their way to Him, because they will have seen a pattern of righteousness in their fathers, their families, and their congregations.

Explain to everyone that when these standards of righteousness are met in the hearts of our people (Isaiah 27:9; Zephaniah 3:18), when Ephraim and Judah become one stick in the Father's hand (Ezekiel 37:15-28), then we will be ready to join Messiah for the Kingdom Passover—the one that will take place in *B'olam Haba*, the eternal Kingdom to come.

Lamb Recipe
Four Passovers Celebration Guide

On the following pages we offer an excellent roast lamb recipe, in addition to four pages taken from our *Four Passovers Celebration Guide*. Like our other Guides, this too is offered for sale by Messianic Israel Ministries. You can order a printed and folded 5 1/2 x 8 1/2 copy to keep in your Bible, or you may photocopy the four copyrighted pages for use in home or congregational celebrations.

Celebration Guides are offered for sale in the Key of David Publications section of the book.

Roast Lamb Shank
With Herbs

Combine: Half ( ) teaspoon each:
powdered ginger, thyme, sage, marjoram.
One (1) teaspoon each: salt, pepper.
One (1) tablespoon each: soy sauce, olive oil.
One each: clove of crushed garlic, bay leaf.
Make slits in lamb, rub marinade into and on meat.
Marinate for at least one hour or overnight.
Place lamb in uncovered roasting pan, roast at 300º F.
(18 minutes per pound for well done, 12 for rare.)
Recipe may be doubled for stronger flavor.

Come . . .
Let Us Rehearse
The Four Passovers

*"And on the first day you shall have a holy assembly—
a miqra kodesh—a holy rehearsal" (Exodus 12:16).
We assemble because we love the Holy One of Israel—
and His Son, our Redeemer, Yeshua, Messiah of Israel.
We have a miqra because we love our Jewish brothers.
We rehearse because we long for the restoration of
the <u>whole</u> house of Israel . . .*

© 1989-2002

Angus and Batya Wootten
Messianic Israel Ministries
PO Box 700217, Saint Cloud, FL 34770

Phone 800 829-8777   Web Site: www.mim.net

The Family Passover

Before the first Passover, the Holy One declared: "On the tenth of this month let each one take a lamb for themselves, according to their fathers' households, a lamb for each household. you shall keep it until the fourteenth day of the same month, then kill it at twilight Moreover, they shall take some of the blood and put it on the two doorposts and on the lintel of the **houses** in which they eat it They shall eat the flesh that same night, roasted with fire, and with unleavened bread and bitter herbs Do not eat any of it raw or boiled with water, but roasted with fire You shall eat it in haste—it is the YHVH's Passover For I will . strike down all the firstborn in the land of Egypt and the blood shall be a sign for you on the houses where you live; and when I see the blood I will pass over you, and no plague will befall you to destroy you when I strike the land of Egypt Now this day will be a memorial to you, and you shall celebrate it as a feast to YHVH; throughout your generations you are to celebrate it as a permanent ordinance" (Exodus 12:3-15)

As priests of their homes, our forefathers were to teach their children about YHVH's deliverance of His people when their sons asked the question, "What does this rite mean to you?" YHVH designated Passover as a time for *fathers* to diligently teach their children It also marked a time to sacrifice a lamb for the household, to put the blood on their doorposts, and to have their families partake of lamb, unleavened bread, and bitter herbs in their homes

The emphasis of this Passover is on the godly "household." For He commanded that it "be eaten in a single house" (Deut 6:7; 11:19; Exodus 12:26,42,46; 13:8,14). Thus He established the "*Family Passover.*"

The Congregational Passover

Later, the Father changed the Passover instructions He moved the rite from their homes to the Tabernacle—from *their* house to *His* house: "Observe the month of Abib and celebrate the Passover to YHVH your God, for in the month of Abib YHVH your God brought you out of Egypt by night You shall sacrifice the Passover to YHVH your God from the flock and the herd, in the place where YHVH chooses to establish His name."

For seven days our forefathers ate unleavened bread and remembered the Exodus Leaven was not to be seen in all their territories "You are not allowed," commanded YHVH, "to sacrifice the Passover in any of your towns, but at the place where YHVH your God chooses to establish His name, you shall sacrifice the Passover in the evening at sunset, at the time that you came out of Egypt Cook and eat it in the place which YHVH your God chooses Be careful to observe these statutes" (Deut 16:2-12; Exodus 12:2).

This "congregational" celebration took place in YHVH's house. There, as the priests led them in a collective time of remembrance, they partook of lamb, bitter herbs, and unleavened bread Thus did YHVH establish the "*Congregational Passover.*"

©BRW

The Personal Passover

Passover instructions were again changed when Messiah Yeshua took the bread and wine into His hands He said to His apostles, "I have earnestly desired to eat *this* Passover with you before I suffer." And, "having taken bread and given thanks, He broke it, and gave it to them, saying, 'This is My body which is given for you; do this in remembrance of Me.' And in the same way He took the cup after they had eaten, saying, 'This cup which is poured out for you is the new covenant in My blood'" (Luke 22:15-20; Matt 26:26-29)

Yeshua's Passover marked the last of the Old Covenant Passovers and the first New Covenant Passover No longer would the central focus be the blood of a substitute animal, which only "covered" sin Rather, the focus became that of the pure, undefiled Blood of the Son of God that remits, even annihilates sin

Through His death on the tree, Yeshua became our Passover Lamb For "Messiah, our Passover, has been sacrificed" (1 Cor 5:7). Of this Passover, Paul explained: "As often as you eat this bread and drink the cup, you proclaim Yeshua's death until He comes."

We proclaim Yeshua's death, because in doing so we declare that we belong to New Covenant Israel and not to the world We proclaim that He is *our* New covenant Passover Lamb so the angel of the second death will *pass over* us in the final judgement. Because we are sanctified and covered with the Blood of Yeshua, we have an eternal sacrifice for our sins In Him, we are the eternal Israel of God (1 Cor 11:26; Eph 1:7-14; 2:13-14; Col 1:20; Luke 22:16; Rom 5:9; Heb 9:12,15,26; 13:11-12,20; Gal 6:16)

With Yeshua's Passover came a change in the Passover law For "when the priesthood is changed, of necessity there is a change of law also" (Heb 5:6; 7:12) Israel's priesthood was changed from the Aaronic order to that of the High Priest, according to the order of Melchizedek—to Yeshua's priesthood. Through Messiah, Israel's Passover law was changed to observance of the New Covenant Passover.

As our High Priest, Yeshua instructed us to partake of His "bread and wine." His is not an annual occurrence like the old sacrifice, but is an ever-present, ever-available sacrifice, and so includes elements from the daily offering: Bread and Wine (Heb 7:27; 9:12; 10:10; 1 Pet 3:18; Exodus 29:40-42; Num 15:1-13; 28:6).

Yeshua "knocks at the door of our heart" because He moved the emphasis of our Passover search for leaven: We are to "clean out the old leaven of wickedness and malice from our hearts" (Rev 3:20; 1 Cor 5:7) He wants us to experience more than mere outward symbols of our faith: He wants us to deal with our hearts, that we might live righteous lives To help us accomplish this otherwise impossible task, He became our personal Passover Lamb

Thus did our Messiah establish the "*Personal Passover.*" ©BRW

The Kingdom Passover

When Yeshua initiated the New Covenant Passover, He said He "desired with desire" to partake of "this Passover," for it was to be a Passover unlike any other...

Yeshua also said: "I shall never again eat it until it is fulfilled in the kingdom of God " And when He had taken the cup and given thanks, He said, "Take this and share it among yourselves; for I say to you, I will not drink of the fruit of the vine from now on until the kingdom of God comes" (Luke 22:15-18)

In saying this, Messiah was foretelling a coming, glorious, eternal Passover, one that will be celebrated in "the kingdom of God " There is a Passover yet to come. This celebration is called "the Marriage Supper of the Lamb," and "blessed are those who are invited to it " One day the trumpet will sound and Believers will put on our imperishable wedding garments, for we are invited to a transcendent celebration (1 Cor 15:51-57; Mat 22:1-14; Hos 13:14; Rev 19:7-9)

At that celebration, the believing family of Israel will again be "*passed over.*" The second death will not be able to harm us because we are *overcomers.* Then we will ask: "Where O death is your victory? Where O death is your sting?" As promised, Messiah will *again* take the cup into His hands—the Passover Cup of Praise Then Hallelujah's that will ring for an eternity will begin, for death will be forever swallowed up in victory! (Rev 2:11; 20:6,14; 21:8; Hos 13:14; 1 Cor 15:55).

We who are overcomers must help establish this Kingdom Passover!

We who long to celebrate Passover must have an ever-present desire for this Kingdom Passover in *our* hearts For we will not, we cannot, celebrate it until the house of Israel is fully reunited. To celebrate *this* Passover, Israel's Kingdom must be restored. And the Father's prescribed plan for the restoration of *all* Israel is to have those of the "wild" side of the family of Israel provoke those of Judah to want what they have

To bring about this reunion, the other house of Israel, those of Ephraim, those destined to become a "*melo hagoyim,*" or "the fullness of Gentiles"—their jealousy of Judah must depart This will happen when they see the truth of their *own* Israelite roots It will happen when they begin to walk as one who is neither superior, nor inferior, to Judah, but as one who sees Judah as an Israelite brother This is YHVH's plan of salvation for *all* Israel (Gen 48:19; 2 Sam 19:43; 1 Kings 11:31; 2 Chr 11:4; Isa 8:14; 11:13; Jer 31:18-19; Hos 1-2; Amos 9:9-11; Matt 12:25; Acts 15:16-17; Rom 8:15-17,23; 9:4; 11; Gal 4:5; Eph 1:5).

When Ephraim sees the truth about all Israel, about his own Israelite roots, and about his call to *rehearse*, then the reunion will begin

"Let us therefore celebrate the feast " (1 Cor 5:7).

©BRW

Dedicating Your Home

Passover is an excellent time to dedicate our homes to the God of Israel. Just as our forefathers painted the blood of the lamb on the doorposts of their homes, we need to envision our entire home being covered by the Blood of Yeshua—the Blood that protects from all evil.

Yeshua is the Door

Yeshua asks us to open the door of our hearts to Him. When we do, He in turn opens a door: It is a door of salvation, one that leads to Heaven's Gate, and to protection from the second death. It is the door of Passover. Beyond this Passover Door lies the Beautiful Land—a land of peace and harmony—the Land of the Israel of God.

Let us respond to Yeshua's call to come and dine at the Father's Table. Come. Gather your family, friends, and loved ones. Come and celebrate the Feast of Passover.

Marking Earthly Doors

You can begin your home dedication by affixing a *mezuzzah* to your doorpost (see instructions below). Then you can have a celebration by offering a meal of roast lamb, unleavened bread, and bitter herbs. With family gathered around, let everyone take time to remember how the Father has personally delivered them from the "bondages of Egypt." Let them rejoice over that deliverance. Finally, after everyone has examined their hearts, let all partake of the Body and Blood of the Lamb.

Remind everyone that Abib, the Passover month, marks the head of the year (Exodus 12:2), so now is the time to make "New Years Resolutions." Now is the time to dedicate ourselves to righteous acts, for they will be our only garments at the coming wedding feast of the Lamb (Matthew 22:11; Revelation 19:8-9).

You Shall Write Them On Your Doorposts... The Mezuzzah

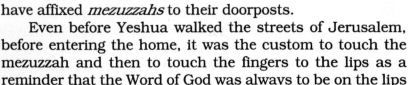

Our Father instructed the sons of Israel to write His commandments on their doorposts and gates.

Mezuzzah Scroll: Front and Back

From ancient times our Jewish brothers have followed this custom and have affixed *mezuzzahs* to their doorposts.

Even before Yeshua walked the streets of Jerusalem, before entering the home, it was the custom to touch the mezuzzah and then to touch the fingers to the lips as a reminder that the Word of God was always to be on the lips of His people.

A mezuzzah can serve to identify the homes of God's chosen people just as the blood on the doorposts served to identify them when the angel of death passed over their homes in Egypt.

The Hebrew word *mezuzzah* means *doorpost*. Traditionally, a parchment scroll with Scripture verses written in Hebrew is rolled up and placed in the mezuzzah cover (see above pictures). *Kosher* mezuzzah scrolls are hand written in Hebrew by a Scribe. Compared to the relatively inexpensive, mass-produced parchments used by most, the hand-written scrolls are very expensive.[91]

The traditional mezuzzah cover contains a scroll with Deuteronomy 6:9 and 11:13-21 Scriptures printed on it:

"Hear O Israel! YHVH is our God, YHVH is one! And you shall love YHVH your God with all your heart and with all your soul and with all your might. And these words, which I am commanding you today, shall be on your heart, and you shall teach them repetitively to your children. You must talk about them, when you are sitting at home, when you are on the road, when you are busy, and when you are at rest. And you shall bind them as a sign upon your hand, and let them serve as a symbol on your forehead. And you shall write them on the doorposts of your houses, and on your gates...And it shall come about, if you listen obediently to My commandments which I am commanding you today, to love YHVH your GOD and to serve Him with all your soul, I will give your land rain in season, autumn rain and spring, that you may gather in your grain and your new wine and your oil. And I will give grass in your fields for your cattle, and you shall eat and be satisfied. Beware, lest your hearts be deceived and you turn away and serve other gods and worship them. For YHVH's anger will flare up against you, and He will shut up the Heavens so that there will be no rain and the ground will not yield its fruit; and you will perish quickly from the good land which YHVH is giving you. You shall therefore impress these words of mine on your heart and on your soul; and you shall bind them as a sign on your hand, and they shall be as a symbol on your forehead. And you shall teach them to your children, speaking of them at home and abroad, when you lie down and when you rise up. And you shall post them on the doorposts of your house and on your gates. So that your days and the days of your children may be multiplied in the land which YHVH swore to your fathers to give them, as long as the Heavens remain above the earth."

---

91 Mezuzzot are available at <www mim net> and on the Internet

Hebrew letters
sheen, dalet,
yod spell
Shaddai
(read from
right to left)

El Shaddai

Mezuzzot (plural) covers come in many different styles and finishes. Most have the name *Shaddai*, or the initial letter for *Shaddai*, the Hebrew letter, *sheen*, written on the front. The name, *El Shaddai*, is one of the names of the God of Israel. It means "The Power," or "The God that cannot be obstructed." Thus the common translation, the *Almighty*.

In Hebrew, *Shaddai* is written with the letters, *sheen, dalet, yod.* Tradition;y, these letters also serve as an acronym for "*Shomer D'latot Yisrael*," meaning *Protector of the doors of Yisrael.*

Mezuzzah scrolls have the Name *Shaddai* printed on the back (shown above) and are rolled up with Scripture verses inside, then placed inside the cover. In this way, the *Shaddai* is visible on the rolled scroll.

Traditionally, the mezuzzah is affixed to the upper third right hand portion of the doorpost, with the mezuzzah cover and the top of the Shaddai (name or initial) pointing inside the home at a slight angle of 30 degrees.[92] (See picture.)

The Mezuzzah and our Confession

Our Father instructed us to post His commandments on our doorposts as a witness to the world of our love for Him. Yeshua, said, "Everyone therefore who shall confess Me before men, I will also confess him before My Father who is in Heaven" (Matthew 10:32). And, "I and the Father are One" (John 10:30).

---

92 The *Jewish Book of Why*, by Alfred J Kolatch, Middle Village, NY: Jonathan David, 1981, 1995, pp 113-16, 151

We who love the Son also love the Father, and out of love for Him we heed the instructions to post the Law on our doorposts.

We do this because we are blessed when we confess our God before the world. Further, this is the method the Father said we should use to declare to the world that our homes belong to Him.

So delight in, celebrate, enjoy this ancient custom that has so long been upheld by our Jewish brothers.

A Home Dedication Celebration

Have a Home Dedication Celebration and personalize it to fit your family.

For example, you may want to gather with your family to pray and then make a declaration like the Israelites made to Joshua, and which Joshua made to Israel.

The Israelites said to Joshua, "We will serve YHVH our God and listen to His voice."

Joshua responded, "Choose for yourselves today whom you will serve: the gods which your fathers served which were beyond the River, or the gods of the Amorites in whose land you are living. But, as for me and my house, we will serve YHVH" (Joshua 24:15,24).

You can actually write the verses from Deuteronomy on a "scroll" yourself and have your children participate. Simply write them on a single piece of paper, then keep reducing the paper on a copy machine until it is at a workable size.

Mezuzzah covers can be ordered from Messianic Israel Ministries, or you may find them for sale at your local Jewish or Christian bookstore, or on the Internet. A wide variety of styles is available.

To make your home dedication even more special, create your own mezuzzah cover. If your doorway is covered from the elements, the rolled up soft bark of a tree will work well, or you can design one out of clay or tin. Use your imagination.

You may want to anoint (the word actually means to *dedicate*) your home with oil for service, just as Moses anointed the Tabernacle (Leviticus 8:10). Anoint your doorpost with oil and pray the previously suggested prayers that your home might be covered in the Blood of Yeshua.

Another suggested prayer of dedication is:

"Father, may our home be a meeting place for the *wise*" (see Daniel 12:3,9).[93]

Dedicate your home and ask the Father to make it a haven from the wrong influences of the world. Then declare that your home will be a place wherein the song of YHVH is always found. Wonderful music by Lenny and Varda about the restoration of the two houses of Israel is available from Messianic Israel Ministries.

The constant sound of praise music in your home is a sure invitation to the Father's heavenly hosts. So dedicate (or rededicate) your home to the Father.

May He bless your home with His Glorious Presence.

The Mezuzzah

A mezuzzah attached the doorpost of your home can serve as a personal confession that:

- ♦ You love YHVH with all your heart (Deuteronomy 6:5).
- ♦ His Living Word/Torah (Yeshua) lives in your heart (Deuteronomy 6:6).
- ♦ You are teaching His Word to your children (Deuteronomy 6:7).
- ♦ You look to the Holy One of Israel for all your needs (Deuteronomy 11:14-15).

---

93 The Angel told Daniel that his word was "sealed" until the end time; and that in the end time, "Those who have *insight* will shine brightly like the brightness of the expanse of heaven" (Daniel 12:3,9) This insight speaks of circumspect intelligence, or watchful, detailed, discerning understanding (see *wise,* Strong's word # H7919) In this end time era, let us ask our Father to "unseal" this type of "insight" for us, to bless our homes, and to use them for the gathering of such insightful people

Pesach Pictures

The Father's feasts are so replete with pictures that instruct us, no one individual can explain them all. For example, instructions for commemorating the Passover were given in Exodus (vss. 12:1-27), and in these verses we see that the month of Passover is to be the beginning of months for us. Similarly, receiving Yeshua into our lives marks the beginning of our new life in Him.

Guidelines for Interpreting Scripture Types

To establish a principle for interpreting Scripture types and shadows we quote from *The Feasts of the Lord*, by Robert Thompson, who provides some excellent guidelines.

"Let us mention two rules for interpreting Bible symbols, or types, as they are called. Types, such as the Levitical convocations, help us to understand the Lord Jesus and His plan of salvation.

"The first rule of interpretation is this: study the symbol, and then ask the Holy Spirit to cause the main truth to rise to the surface. Do not focus too long on the details of the symbol and attempt to force the interpretation. You will get sidetracked. We see Bible truth through a glass darkly, as

Paul says in 1 Corinthians 13, and the Holy Spirit must be the One to throw light on the subject. Usually a type presents one main truth, or line of truth, and the Spirit will give us the understanding.

*"For example, Christ is the **Lamb** of God. The truth which rises to the surface is that Christ was led away as an offering for our sins, and that we eat His body and drink His precious blood as our Passover. But we can't pursue the symbol further and claim that Christ today is led around helplessly and is a prey for every wolf who appears on the scene. Again, in one setting leaven is a type of sin; in another setting leaven is a type of the kingdom of heaven.*

"Still another example is this: the Christian church is referred to as the bride of the Lamb. This symbol of marriage indicates to us that we enter into spiritual union with Christ, and are made one with Him. But we can't go on from this and state that Christians are feminine because they are called the 'bride,' and that the bride is a different group from the sons of God who are male because they are 'sons.'"[94]

Three Stages of Progression

The feasts equate symbolically with the layout of the Temple, which had an Outer Court, an Inner Court, and a Holy Place.

The feasts are also divided into three segments: Early Spring, Late Spring, and Fall. These depict the Father's three phase plan of redemption for His people:

Passover (personal redemption), Shavuot/Pentecost (in filling of the Spirit), and Tabernacles (full restoration of Israel's Kingdom).

In these two types, we see divisions of three, as well as three stages of progression. We also know that John the apostle spoke of *children, young men,* and *fathers.* He told the children that their sins were forgiven, he said the young

---

94   *The Feasts of the Lord,* Robert Thompson, Medford, OR: Omega Publications, 1975, pp 11-12

men who had overcome the wicked one were strong and that the word of God abides in them. Twice in these same verses, John addresses the fathers and says they *know* the Father (1 John 2:12-14).

Forgiveness of sin corresponds to Passover. It can be likened to the first step one takes in their relationship with the Messiah—just as the Outer Court is the first section to be entered when one walked into Israel's ancient Temple.

Being made strong, or filled with power, corresponds to the power poured out on us in our personal Pentecost experience (Acts 1:8). This feast experience is like entering into the Inner Court of the Temple.

These two feasts speak of what Yeshua accomplished during His sojourn on earth, and they depict our early experiences as Believers.

The Fall feasts, which once foretold that Yeshua would come to tabernacle with His people, now foretell His return to forever dwell with us. These latter feasts also reveal that prior to His return, a work needs to be done by the mature *fathers* in Israel (1 Corinthians 4:15). These Fall feasts foretell the Father's plan to restore all Israel. It is a plan that is precious to His heart. It is plan that is revealed in the Holy Place.

Imagine yourself as a little child who runs into the Holy place and climbs into your Father's lap. You lay your head on His chest and quietly listen to the beat of His heart. This heartbeat is like that of the father of the prodigal, who longed for the return of his lost son and for the reunion of his whole house—both his sons. This is the desire of our Heavenly Father.

The Fall feasts of Israel foretell this reunion. It is a reunion that will be effected by the mature.

May we be granted the grace to be part of that restoration.

The Three Stages of Progression		
Outer Court	Inner Court	Holy Place
Passover	Pentecost	Tabernacles
Children	Young Men	Fathers

Covered With The Blood

The Hebrew word *Pesach* is taken from a word that means to pass, or hover over.[95] This word teaches us that when we are covered by the Blood of Messiah Yeshua, the angel of the second death will "pass over" us (Revelation 2:11; 20:6,14; 218). It tells us that the Holy One will hover, and protect us from evil; He will even cause it to skip over our blood-covered houses (Deuteronomy 32:11; Ezekiel 10:19; 11:22).

Passover teaches us that there is no atonement for sin apart from the shedding of blood (Hebrews 9:22). For this reason our Father told us to put the blood of the lamb on the doorposts of our houses, and then to go in and partake of the lamb. This symbolizes protection; it reveals that even in difficult times there will be houses in which the Father will provide for us.

"None of you shall go outside the door of his house until morning." This verse reveals that no matter how dark the night, there will be a "morning," and "joy" will come with it. Though it was dark in Egypt, there was light in Goshen where His people lived (Exodus 8:22; 10:23). Similarly, we have a "lamp that shines in a dark place." That lamp is Yeshua, the "Morning star." And He will not allow the destroyer to enter into our homes.[96] We can put His Blood on our doorposts, then go in and shut the door behind us, knowing that all will be well and that we only have to celebrate our Passover and wait until morning.

---

95 *Strong's* # H6453. peh'-sakh; from H6452, *paw-sakh'*; meaning to hop, skip over (or spare), to hesitate; dance, leap, or pass over.
96 Exo 12:7,22-23; Psa 30:5; 1 Pet. 1:19.

The head of each household had to slay a lamb and sprinkle its blood on the door's lintel and two side posts. Then the lamb was to be roasted with fire and eaten with bitter herbs and unleavened bread. The Israelites were to eat in haste and be dressed and ready to leave Egypt. Their exodus from slavery would begin that night. The angel of death would pass through Egypt and judge every house that did not have the required blood covering.

The lambs that were selected had to be without blemish, and Yeshua, the Lamb of God (John 1:29), was without spot or blemish (1 Peter 1:19). The blood of the lamb was to be applied to the doorposts, and we who believe in the Messiah are of the house of God (Ephesians 2:19; 1 Timothy 3:15; Hebrews 3:6; 1 Peter 2:5). We enter this spiritual house through He Who says, "I say to you, I am the door of the sheep....if anyone enters through Me, he will be saved, and will go in and out and find pasture" (John 10:7-9). We enter through the shed blood of Yeshua .[97]

Partaking of The Lamb

The lamb was to be eaten with unleavened bread, and we are to live unleavened lives in Messiah Yeshua (1 Corinthians 5:6-8; Leviticus 11:44; 19:2; 1 Peter 1:15-16).

The lamb was to be roasted with fire and eaten with bitter herbs. Fire depicts purification, and once we come to know the Lamb, we are tested by fire. We are purified (Zechariah 13:9; James 1:12; 1 Peter 1:7; Revelation 3:18).

Bitter herbs represent the bondage of this world, which is a type of Egypt. Bondage, burdens, and bitterness come when we yield to wickedness. This is true whether the works are those of Satan or of our own doing.[98]

Israel was told, "Now you shall eat it in this manner: with your loins girded, your sandals on your feet, and your staff in your hand; and you shall eat it in haste—it is the

---

97 *The Seven Festivals of the Messiah* by Eddie Chumney, www.geocities. com/Heartland/2175/chap3.

98 *Ibid.*

Lord's Passover" (Exodus 12:11).

The lamb was to be eaten in haste; we must not harden our hearts nor delay when we hear about the Lamb, Yeshua. When He says to us, "Take, eat; this is My body," when we hear Him calling us to drink of the cup of His New Covenant Passover, we must be quick to respond. We must be hasty to leave behind the things of this world and to follow Him alone (1 Samuel 6:6; Psalms 95:8; Hebrews 3:8,5; 4:7; Matthew 4:19; 26:26-28).

Our forefathers had to be girded and shod. Similarly, our loins must be girded with a spirit of servanthood and our feet shod with the gospel of the restored Kingdom (Matthew 24:14; Luke 12:37; 16:16; Romans 10:15; Ephesians 6:14-15).

Taking Up the Staff of Reunion

In addition to being girded and shod, our forefathers were to have a *staff* in their hand. A staff, or *maqqel*, aids us in our walk.[99] Messiah Yeshua sends us the Comforter, the Holy Spirit, the Ruach HaKodesh, to aid and empower us in our walk (John 14:16-26; 15:26; Luke 24:49). Yeshua sent this Helper because the first steps of Passover lead to Unleavened Bread, which is a call to walk in blamelessness, and we cannot walk in that absolute purity unless we are Divinely empowered.

Zechariah spoke of two staffs, when, after Judah's return from Babylon (around 520 B.C.), he said, "I pastured the flock doomed to slaughter....and I took for myself two staffs: the one I called Favor and the other I called Union; so I pastured the flock....[and] I took my staff Favor and cut it in pieces, to break my covenant which I had made with all the peoples ....Then I cut in pieces my second staff Union, to break the brotherhood between Judah and Israel" (Zechariah 11:7-14)

Though the shepherd David once prayed for the Father's

---

99 *Strong's* word # H4731. mak-kale'; to germinate; a shoot, stick (with leaves, or for walking, striking, guiding, divining); rod, staff.

favor to be on all Israel, her errant sons turned the beauty of being favored into false pride. So YHVH gave them into the hands of foreigners, that they might be profaned.[100]

Of Zechariah's staff called Union, the *New International Version Study Bible* says his action is "signifying the dissolution of...the unity between the south and the north."[101] *The Twelve Prophets* calls the staff "Binders" and says, "The ...staff Binders, is now shattered, denoting the dissolution of all unity and harmony between Israel and Judah." [102]

Unity and harmony were taken from Israel and Judah. The staff that bound them together was broken, so each was free to walk in their own way. Because their house is now divided, they cannot stand. They can only stumble along in their limited and separate walks (Luke 11:17; Isaiah 8:14; Romans 11:25).

This same word for staff is used in Jeremiah 1:11-12. There, the Father asked, "What do you see, Jeremiah?" The prophet answered, "I see a rod of an almond tree." To this, the Father replied, "You have seen well, for I am watching over My word to perform it."

An almond branch is known for its ability to *quickly* blossom forth, and Yeshua is about to do a *quick* work in the earth (Revelation 22:7). We who see the truth about the reunion of the two sticks of Ephraim and Judah (as foretold by Ezekiel) must take up this end time Passover staff. We must show forth the staff of good shepherds who truly feed the flock of scattered Israel (Ezekiel 34).

Then we will truly be empowered in our walk, just as the Father promised through Zechariah: *"I will strengthen the house of Judah, and I will save the house of Joseph, and I will bring them back, because I have had compassion on them; and they will be as though I had not rejected them,*

---

100 Psa 90:17; Eze 7:20-22; 24:21; Dan 9:26; Luke 21:5-6.

101 520 B.C.: *New International Version Study Bible, Introduction,* Grand Rapids: Zondervan, 1995, Zechariah, p 1405; NIV quote (same Bible), Zechariah 11:14 footnote, p 1412. Also see "Binders," *The Twelve Prophets,* London: Soncino, 1980, p 267.

102 *The Twelve Prophets,* London: Soncino, 1980, pp 316-317.

For I am YHVH their God and I will answer them. Ephraim will be like a mighty man, and their heart will be glad as if from wine; indeed, their children will see it and be glad, their heart will rejoice in YHVH. I will whistle for them to gather them together, for I have redeemed them; and they will be as numerous as they were before. When I scatter them among the peoples, they will remember Me in far countries, and they with their children will live and come back. I will bring them back from the land of Egypt and gather them from Assyria; and I will bring them into the land of Gilead and Lebanon, until no room can be found for them....And I will strengthen them in YHVH, and in His name they will walk,' declares YHVH" (Zechariah 10:6-12).

When the two houses of Israel both humble themselves and begin to seek true reunion, then the fires of revival will spread quickly throughout the world.

We who understand these things must take this end time Passover staff of Favor and Union into our hands.

Chag HaMatzah
The Feast of Unleavened Bread

Our Father instructed Israel to sacrifice their Passover lambs on Abib/Nisan 14.[103] They were to do this at twilight, which begins at the ninth hour of the day, at 3:00 p.m. This was the exact hour when Yeshua was sacrificed for us (Mark 15:33-37).

At that time they could begin roasting their lambs, which would take several hours.

To understand Passover, we must remember that in Hebraic thought the day begins in the evening, at sunset (Genesis 1:5)—which usually happens around 6pm. We must also remember that this Passover day of sacrifice was immediately followed by a seven day period called the Feast of Unleavened Bread, or *Chag HaMatzah,* which begins on Abib 15. In other words, the first actual "day" of Unleavened Bread started before the Israelites could finish roasting their lambs, so the lamb was eaten with unleavened bread.

Of this week long feast, the Father said, "Seven days

---

103 The month of Abib became known as Nisan after the Jews returned from their Babylonian captivity.

you shall eat unleavened bread, but on the first day you shall remove leaven from your houses; for whoever eats anything leavened from the first day until the seventh day, that person shall be cut off from Israel" (Exodus 12:15-20).

For seven days leaven was not allowed in Israel's houses or territories. *Leaven* speaks of sin, and *seven* speaks of the Creation, of rest, spirituality, and perfection.[104] In this feast we see our call to walk in purity. It is a call, as Paul the apostle said, to "Celebrate the feast, not with old leaven, nor with the leaven of malice and wickedness, but with the unleavened bread of sincerity and truth" (1 Corinthians 5:8).

The Feast of Unleavened Bread reminds us of the swift departure our forefathers made from Egypt. They had to leave so quickly they did not have time to put leaven into their bread and wait for it to rise.

When bread rises, it "puffs up," and when we are puffed up with pride or self-focus, our desires are not upright. Too much focus on head knowledge can make people proud, puffed up, arrogant, and unspiritual (Habakkuk 2:4, 1 Corinthians 8:1; Colossians 2:18, NIV).

Unleavened bread depicts our Messiah. Unleavened by life, He was the perfect sacrifice for our sins. Moreover, His body was in the grave during the first days of this feast. He lay there, like a Seed divinely planted, waiting to burst forth as the eternal bread of life.

Yeshua says of Himself, "I am the bread of life; he who comes to Me will not hunger." Yeshua comes to feed hungry souls with the Bread of Life: "This is the bread which comes down out of heaven, so that one may eat of it and not die" (John 6:35,50).

Yeshua was even born in the "house of bread." The Hebrew name of His birth place, *Bethlehem*, is derived from *beit* and *lechem*. *Beit* means *house*, and *lechem* means *bread*.[105]

---

104   *The Wisdom In The Hebrew Alphabet*, Scherman and Zlotowitz, Brooklyn: *ArtScroll Mesorah Series*, 1983, pp 207-210.
105   *Strong's* words # H1035, 1004, 3899.

The Pattern Fulfilled

The Passover lamb was slain on the fourteenth of Abib, and the next day, on the feast of Unleavened Bread, our forefathers left Egypt. Fifty days after the Day of First Fruits, on the Feast of Weeks (Shavuot), the Father gave them the Ten Commandments.

Similarly, Messiah Yeshua was crucified on the fourteenth of Abib (Passover), was in the tomb on the fifteenth (Unleavened Bread), and after three days was resurrected in fulfillment of First Fruits. Fifty days later, the Ruach HaKodesh, He Who fills us with the Living Torah, was poured out on the Believers gathered in Jerusalem for Pentecost (Shavuot).

Chag HaMatzah in Scripture

The Feast of Unleavened Bread, or *Chag HaMatzah*, which is a Sabbath, is explained in Exodus and Leviticus:

"Moreover, they shall take some of the blood and put it on the two doorposts and on the lintel of the houses in which they eat it. They shall eat the flesh that same night, roasted with fire, and they shall eat it with unleavened bread and bitter herbs....Now this day will be a memorial to you, and you shall celebrate it as a feast to YHVH; throughout your generations you are to celebrate it as a permanent ordinance. 'Seven days you shall eat unleavened bread, but on the first day you shall remove leaven from your houses; for whoever eats anything leavened from the first day until the seventh day, that person shall be cut off from Israel. On the first day you shall have a holy assembly, and another holy assembly on the seventh day; no work at all shall be done on them, except what must be eaten by every person, that alone may be prepared by you (Exodus 12:7-8,14-17).

"You shall also observe the feast of unleavened bread, for on this very day I brought your hosts out of the land of Egypt; therefore you shall observe this day throughout your

generations as a permanent ordinance. On the fifteenth day of the same month there is the feast of unleavened bread to YHVH; for seven days you shall eat unleavened bread. On the first day you shall have a holy convocation; you shall not do any laborious work" (Leviticus 23:6-7).

Unleavened from Sabbath to Sabbath

The Feast of Unleavened Bread has two Sabbaths in it. We are to have a holy assembly on the first and the seventh day. During the week we are to consume no leaven. This command depicts our call to be pure from Sabbath to Sabbath. We are not to put on a spiritual face for our assemblies, then have a different face for friends and families. Peter the apostle , in quoting the Torah, said, "Be ye holy, for I am holy" (1 Peter 1:16, KJV). Week to week, day in and day out, we are called to be unleavened.

Messiah suffered for us and was an example for us. "He committed no sin, nor was any deceit found in his mouth. When being reviled, He did not revile in return; while suffering, He uttered no threats, but kept entrusting Himself to Him who judges righteously." This Sinless One bore our sins in His body on the tree, or cross, so that we might die to sin and live to righteousness. By His wounds we are healed (Isaiah 53:5 1 Peter 2:21-24;).

We are called to follow in Yeshua's righteous footsteps.

Lots of Leaven...

There are many types of leaven in Scripture, all of which can affect Believers. There is the leaven of the Pharisees and the Sadducees, which often depicts hypocrisy, dead ritualism, disbelief, and humanism. There is the leaven of worldliness and sensuality that was displayed in the Corinthians, and the leaven of legalism and pride so prevalent among the Galatians.[106]

---

106 See Mat 2:7-12; 16:5-12; 23:1-3;27-28; Mark 6:14-18; 8:14-15; Luke 11:37-44; 12:1; 1 Cor 4:17-21; 5:1-13; 6:1,9-18; 8:1; 13:4; 2 Cor 12:20-21; Gal
(continued...)

We must not be like these examples, but must keep the feasts in sincerity and truth. To do so, we must be dedicated to our Father and to His purposes in the earth. As Joshua first said, and as Paul the apostle later confirmed, We must "fear [revere] YHVH and serve Him in sincerity and truth" (Joshua 24:14; 1 Corinthians 5:7-8).

Bedikat Chametz

In a previous chapter we explained the Jewish tradition of cleaning the house of leaven, or *Bedikat Chametz* (see *The Father's Passover Plan*). In this tradition, the wife thoroughly cleans the house and removes all leaven, but she deliberately leaves behind some leaven, such as bread crumbs, for the children to find. The father then leads them in a candlelight search for leaven using a feather to brush the leaven onto a wooden spoon, then dropping it into a paper bag. The paper bag filled with the leaven is then discarded or burned.

Because we are of the house of God,[107] our house is to be cleansed of all sin: "Do you not know that you are a temple of God and that the Spirit of God dwells in you?" (1 Corinthians 3:16-19). Also, the Father's Word is a lamp: "Thy word is a lamp unto my feet, and a light unto my path" (Psalm 119:105). In this search for leaven, the candle can be said to represent the Word, and the feather represents the Holy Spirit. We must ask the *Ruach*, the Word of Truth, to reveal our sins and to cleanse our hearts and lives (Ephesians 5:26).

Though traditional Judaism would not agree with the idea, the wooden spoon can be said to represent the tree on which Yeshua was crucified (Deuteronomy 21:22-23). In the ceremony, the leaven was swept onto the spoon, and our

---

106 (...continued)
5:9; 1 John 2:16. Adapted from *The Passover Feast*, Ruth Spector Lascelle, Van Nuys, CA: 1975, p 7; *Pesach and Hag HaMatzah*, Barney Kasdan www.imja.com /maoz; and *The Seven Festivals of the Messiah*, Eddie Chumney, www.geocities. com/Heartland/2175/chap3.
107 Eph 2:19; 1 Tim 3:15; Heb 3:6; 1 Peter 2:5.

sins were put on Yeshua when He died for us on the tree (Isaiah 53; Romans 5:8; 2 Corinthians 5:21; 1 Thessalonians 5:9-10).

The leaven is burned, which depicts the price to be paid for sin (Ephesians 4:8-10; Luke 16:19-24).

This hide and seek type search is one that Believers in Messiah can use to teach their children the good news of the gospel, as well as the fundamentals of Israel's feasts.

Yom HaBikkurim
The Day of First Fruits

We need to remember a most important "Festival of Joy."

When Believers begin to discover the errors found in Church theology concerning Easter, very often they turn to Judaism. They turn away from anything that has to do with Easter and replace it with a celebration of some form of the Jewish Passover tradition.[108]

However, these worthy Jewish traditions are based on commemoration of our Passover deliverance from Egypt, and on the slaying of a lamb, but we who follow Messiah have something *more* to celebrate. He fulfills this feast, and as our "Passover Lamb," He *arose* from the grave. He came forth as a type of "First of First Fruits," and thus He is "the beginning, the firstborn from the dead" (Colossians 1:18).

If we look through the lens of mercy, we will see that the Christian celebration of the Resurrection, *apart from its errant traditions*, is a type of "First Fruits" celebration.

We do not say this to encourage anything that has to do

---

108 See footnote #3, page 5.

with the ancient pagan cult of "Ishtar," from which the word "Easter" is derived,[109] nor do we want to encourage a parade of bunnies with baskets of colored eggs. Rabbits and eggs are fertility symbols, and Ishtar was the ancient Assyrian/Babylonian goddess of love, fertility, and war.[110]

We say this because Messiah's Resurrection is an event that is *worthy of celebration*. His resurrection from the dead marks a pivotal point in history.

Yeshua is the substance of the day of the sheaf. He is the essence of the first of the first fruits offering that followed Passover. In His resurrection, He was the first of the first fruits of resurrection. He "has been raised from the dead the first fruits of those who are asleep" (1 Corinthians 15:20,23).

As our High Priest, He was presented before the Father: "He entered through the greater and more perfect tabernacle, not made with hands, that is to say, not of this creation; for Messiah did not enter a holy place made with hands, a mere copy of the true one, but into heaven itself, to appear in the presence of God for us" (Hebrews 9:11,24).

Yeshua's resurrection is a type of harvest. It marked the beginning of our Father's harvest season. Yeshua is "the firstborn among many brethren," and we, His brethren, "also have the first fruits of the Spirit." For this reason we "groan within ourselves"—because we are "waiting eagerly for our adoption as sons, [which is] the redemption of our body." Messiah Yeshua "brought us forth...that we would be a kind of first fruits among His creatures" (Romans 8:29,23; James 1:18).

As we return to our roots, we would do well to remember this special day that speaks of mankind's greatest hope. However, we must learn to celebrate it based on its shadow beginning, as described in Torah (Leviticus 23:10-15; Colossians 2:17; Hebrews 10:1).

---

109 The *American Heritage Electronic Dictionary*, Houghton Mifflin, 1994, says the third meaning of Easter is "from Old English *ēastre*, Easter, from Germanic *austrō*-, a dawn-goddess whose holiday was celebrated at the vernal equinox."

110 *Ibid*, "Ishtar."

A "Forgotten" Feast

On the Day of First Fruits, in ancient Israel, the priest waved a sheaf of the first fruits of the barley harvest before the Almighty. Today this feast is largely ignored by most of traditional Judaism. Judah does not celebrate this feast, but Ephraim does, though in an errant way.

Barley Sheaf Offering

Called *Yom HaBikkurim*, or *Day of the First Fruits*, we have much to learn about this most important day.

The word *bikkurim* is plural for *bikkur*, and speaks of the first ripe fruits of the crop. It especially refers to the first products of grain (bread) and fruits.[111]

Israel could not keep this feast until they entered into the Promised Land. They did not keep it in the wilderness where they ate only the manna from heaven. They ceased to eat manna after they had their first Passover, then they ate of the produce of the Land (Joshua 5:10-12).

Yom HaBikkurim is outlined in Leviticus 23:10-15:

"Speak to the sons of Israel and say to them, 'When you enter the land which I am going to give to you and reap its harvest, then you shall bring in the sheaf of the first fruits of your harvest to the priest. 'He shall wave the sheaf before YHVH for you to be accepted; on the day after the sabbath the priest shall wave it. Now on the day when you wave the sheaf, you shall offer a male lamb one year old without defect for a burnt offering to YHVH. Its grain offering shall then be two-tenths of an ephah of fine flour mixed with oil, an offering by fire to YHVH for a soothing aroma, with its drink offering, a fourth of a hin of wine. Until this same day, until you have brought in the offering of your God, you shall eat neither bread nor roasted grain nor new growth.

---

111 *Strong's* H1061, from 1069. bakar; to burst the womb, i.e. (caus.) bear or make early fruit (of woman or tree).; also to give the birthright:--make firstborn, be firstling, bring forth first child (new fruit). Bikkurim: See ; Exo 23:16; 2:1; Lev 2:14; 23:17; Num 13:20; 18:12,13; 2 Ki 4:42; Nah 3:12.

It is to be a perpetual statute throughout your generations in all your dwelling places. You shall also count for yourselves from the day after the sabbath, from the day when you brought in the sheaf of the wave offering; there shall be seven complete sabbaths."

Fulfilled by a Single Priest...

The picture painted by this feast is that of a priest standing alone and waving a sheaf before the Lord. It is a picture of our Messiah, Who is a priest according to the order of Melchizedek" (Hebrews 7:17).

This single priest, who alone made the proper offering, portrays Yeshua, just as does the single sheaf being waved, for Yeshua is "Messiah the First Fruits" (1 Corinthians 15:23).

This first fruit offering was to be waved "on the day after the Sabbath," meaning on the first day of the week, which corresponds to Sunday. This lone priest, who presented an offering to the Father on this day, depicts Yeshua, Who rose from the dead on the first day of the week (Luke 24:1).

Sheaves in Scripture

The first time we read of a *sheaf* in Scripture is in Joseph's dream. In this dream he saw eleven sheaves bow down before his sheaf.[112] The sheaves represented his brothers, who would ultimately bow before him (Genesis 37:5-11; 43:28).

In Scripture, sheaves (plural) can represent a person or persons. A literal sheaf speaks of a pile tied together.

The sheaf that was to be presented on Yom HaBikkurim was called an *omer*. This word comes from *amar*, which is defined as to chastise, as if piling blows, to gather grain and bind sheaves together.[113] An *omer* is a unit of dry measure equal to a tenth of an ephah (Exodus 16:36), which equals about 3.5 liters, or 3.7 quarts.

---

112 *Strong's* #'s H485 and 481, 'alummah, something bound; a sheaf. H481: 'alam, to tie fast; hence, to be tongue-tied: bind, be dumb, put to silence.
113 Omer: *Strong's* #'s H 6016, 6014.

Once more we see a shadow of our High Priest, Yeshua, in that "the chastening for our well-being fell upon Him" (Isaiah 53:5).

We also see a spirit of giving, for Israel was commanded to leave the occasional forgotten sheaf and the gleanings of the harvest in the corners of their fields so they could be used to feed the stranger, the fatherless, the widow and the poor. To do anything less would stop the flow of blessing from YHVH's hand. This principle taught the children of Israel that the joy of harvest should be expressed in charity to others (Leviticus 19:9,22; Deuteronomy 24:19-22; Ruth 2:7,15, 2:15; Job 24:10).

The Barley Sheaf

The sheaf waved on First Fruits was a barley sheaf. On the first day of the week following the regular Sabbath during Unleavened Bread, the harvest of this cereal grain began.

Sown in the winter, barley was the first grain to ripen in the spring. Because of its deep roots, it has a tremendous ability to absorb nutrients from the soil, so it gives a healthy boost to those who eat it.[114]

Similarly, we who have received Messiah Yeshua as Lord are to be firmly rooted in Him, that we might be built up, healthy, established in our faith (Colossians 2:67).[115]

We Are a First Fruits Company

"But now Messiah has been raised from the dead, the first fruits of those who are asleep" (1 Corinthians 15:20). "And not only this, but also we ourselves, having the first

---

114 Barley is said to contain all the vitamins, minerals, and proteins necessary for the human diet, and it is thought to give instant access to vital nutrients. See <http://www.aimforenergy.com/barleygreen/bgrass.htm> and <http://www.aim4betterhealthnaturally.com/morabbar.html>

115 *Strong's* # H485: 'alummah, al-oom-maw'; or (masc.) 'alum, aw-loom'.

fruits of the Spirit, even we ourselves groan within ourselves, waiting eagerly for our adoption as sons, the redemption of our body" (Romans 8:23).[116] "But each in his own order: Messiah the first fruits, after that those who are Messiah's at His coming" (1 Corinthians 15:23). For, "In the exercise of His will He brought us forth by the word of truth, so that we would be a kind of first fruits among His creatures" (James 1:18).

Messiah Yeshua is the first of a first fruit company. "He is also head of the body, the ekklesia/congregation; and He is the beginning, the firstborn from the dead, so that He Himself will come to have first place in everything" (Colossians 1:18). By reason of His resurrection from the dead, He was the first to proclaim light, to light the way (Acts 26:23). When we are illumined by His Spirit, we are called "to the general assembly and *ekklesia*/congregation of the firstborn who are enrolled in heaven, and to God, the Judge of all, and to the spirits of the righteous made perfect" (Hebrews 12:23).

Our Messiah is "The first and the last," He died (meaning His earthly flesh ceased to be inhabited by His Spirit), and He "has come to life" (Revelation 2:8). He is our resurrection hope. It is a glorious hope that must not be forgotten, for we who belong to Him will forever live in His presence. So let us rejoice in our First Fruits Priest Who made eternal life possible for us.

The Most Choice

The first fruits were considered the choicest of all. They were consecrated, or holy unto YHVH. The firstborn of man and beast belonged to Him, as did the first fruits of the earth (Exodus 13:2; 11-13, 22:29). However, some of the first fruits were presented to the priests and Levites (Leviticus 19:23-25; Nehemiah 10:34-39). All first fruits were to be offered with thanksgiving and praise.

---

116 The Spirit of adoption is mentioned only five times in Scripture. All must receive it to become sons of God, and it belongs to "the sons of Israel" (Rom 8:15, 23; 9:4; Gal 4:5; Eph 1:5); *Who Is Israel?* chapter 14, "*More Tattered Theories.*"

A List of Firsts

Yeshua fulfills the shadow of First Fruits. He is first in every way. He is given first place in everything, because all things are being summed up in Him. He is all, and can be found in all (Ephesians 1:10-11,23).

Messiah Yeshua is—
♦ The firstborn of the Father (Hebrews 1:6).[117]
♦ The firstborn of every creature (Colossians 1:15).
♦ The firstborn of Mary/Miryam (Matthew 1:23-25).
♦ The firstborn from the dead (Revelation 1:5).
♦ The firstborn of many brethren (Romans 8:29).

Yeshua is the First (*Aleph*) and the Last (*Tav*), the *Alpha* and the *Omega*, the *Beginning* and the *End* (Revelation 1:8,17; 21:6; 22:13; Isaiah 41:4; 44:6; 48:12). "He is also head of the body, the *ekklesia/congregation*, and He is the beginning, the firstborn from the dead, so that He Himself will come to have *first place in everything*. For it was the Father's good pleasure for all the fullness to dwell in Him, and through Him to reconcile all things to Himself, having made peace through the blood of His cross; through Him, I say, whether things on earth or things in heaven" (Colossians 1:18-20).

The Ceremony

To fulfill the First Fruits obligation in ancient Israel, the celebrant would take the first sheaf from his barley harvest to the priest, who would then wave the sheaf before YHVH in the Temple. As it is written, "'He shall wave the sheaf before YHVH for you to be accepted; on the day after the sabbath the priest shall wave it" (Leviticus 23:11).

In the heavens, on the day this feast saw its fulfillment, Yeshua waved a wave sheaf in our behalf. When He offered that holy sheaf, all were accepted—all who *were* His, all who

---

117 Israel is the Father's firstborn, and His "Servant," Who is Yeshua, also is named "Israel" (Exo 4:22; Isa 49:3; Hos 11:1: Mat 2:15,18).

are His, and all who *ever will be* His. "For Messiah did not enter a holy place made with hands...but into heaven itself, to appear in the presence of God for us." And He did this, "Once and for all" (Exodus 25:40; Romans 6:10; Hebrews 7:27; 9:12,24; 10:10).

Counting the Omer

On this day of waving the sheaf, Israel is to begin counting off "seven complete sabbaths." This counting process has come to be known as "counting the omer." The count begins on the Day of First Fruits, and is culminated fifty days later on Shavuot.

For this fifty day interval a special custom arose that Jewish people celebrate to this day. On each of these fifty days a "counting benediction" is recited and days are marked off on a calendar:

Blessed are You, O Lord our God, King of the Universe, Who has sanctified us the Thy commandments, and has commanded us concerning the counting of the omer.

This blessing is followed by saying:

"This is the ___ day, being ___ weeks and ___ days of the omer." [118]

The "Sabbath" Controversy
And Why it Matters

There has long been a controversy over how to interpret the command to begin the count on "the day after the Sabbath" (Leviticus 23:11). Some people think this reference to "the Sabbath" refers to the weekly Sabbath. Others think it refers to the first day of Unleavened Bread, which is a "Feast Sabbath." Since Shavuot has no assigned date beyond beginning the count on "the day after the Sabbath," we need to understand which Sabbath is meant in order to know when to celebrate Shavuot.

---

118 *The Everlasting Tradition*, Galen Peterson, Grand Rapids: Kregal Publications, 1995, pp 28-29.

Sunday to Sunday

If we say the verse speaks of the weekly Sabbath, then the waving of the First Fruits will always be on a Sunday, and Shavuot will always fall on a Sunday—exactly seven Sabbaths plus one day, or fifty days later.

Sabbath versus Shabbaton

The word "Sabbath," which is used in this verse, is the word used to speak of the *weekly* Sabbath. The word used to describe feast days of rest is "*Shabbaton.*"[119] The only exception to this rule is Yom HaKippurim, the holiest day of the year. That most holy day is called a Sabbath of complete rest, a *Shabbat Shabbaton*[120]

Restated, the weekly Sabbath can be, and is, sometimes called a *Shabbat Shabbaton* (Exodus 31:15), however, except for Yom HaKippurim. the word *Shabbat* is *not* applied to the feast days. They are days of *Shabbaton.*

Thus it would appear that "the day after the Sabbath" (Leviticus 23:11) would *not* refer to the first day of Unleavened Bread, for that is a *Shabbaton*, a *feast day.* Instead, it refers to the weekly Sabbath.

Moreover, if we were to begin the count on Unleavened Bread, then Shavuot would always fall on the sixth of Sivan (the third month), because the feast of Unleavened Bread begins on a fixed date—the fifteenth of Abib (Leviticus 23:6). Therefore, there would be no need to count the days; we would simply be instructed to observe Shavuot on the sixth of Sivan. (See charts this chapter.)

Calendar Charts

The following calendars count the omer based on the two methods previously discussed.

As you study these calendars, keep in mind that we are solely addressing the issue of the counting of the omer.

---

119 *Strong's* # H7677, from H7676; special holiday; rest, sabbath.
120 www.karaite-korner.org/light-of-israel/ pentecost_classical_proofs.shtml

The first calendar is based on the scriptural command that the count begins on the morrow after the *weekly* Sabbath, a Sunday, and it ends on a Sunday, as is required. This is the counting method that we believe is scripturally correct.

The Sabbath mentioned must be the weekly Sabbath, because there are to be "fifty" days and "seven" sabbaths in the counting: "'You shall count fifty[121] days to the day **after the seventh sabbath**; then you shall present a new grain offering" (Leviticus 23:16).

The second calendar follows the rabbinic assumption that the counting begins after the first day of Unleavened Bread—which is a *Shabbaton*, and not a regular *Sabbath* day. Our example has that day, the fifteenth of Abib, falling on a Thursday. This means their fifty day count ends on a Friday, which is *not* the day after the Sabbath, and the count must end on the day "after" the Sabbath. On that calendar, since they count the first day of Unleavened Bread as a "Sabbath," they have a total of eight Sabbaths in their count.

What First Fruits Means to Us

We celebrate this feast because, for Believers, First Fruits reminds us that our God is the source of all blessings, that we are to seek first His Kingdom, and that He is always to be our first love.[122]

This time of counting the days between the waving of the First Fruits barley sheaf and the harvesting of the wheat is a depiction of our earthly sojourn. For we are strangers and exiles in this earth. Our time here is a time of expectation, a time of knowing that the Father will provide. We know we have a coming inheritance, and we know the final "Ingathering" is coming soon (Hebrews 11:13-14; Acts 26:18; Ephesians 1:11,14,18; Colossians 1:12; 1 Peter 1:4).

Just as we are blessed when we accept Yeshua into our

---

121 *Strong's* # H2572.
122 Mat 6:33; 1 John 4:9; Rev 2:4.

hearts as the Passover Lamb, so there is something more. For Yeshua has made a way for us to enter into Eternity with the Father. We who have repented of our sins and believe in Yeshua have this hope of resurrection. We hope in the coming first fruits harvests.

Celebrating Yom HaBikkurim

One way we can celebrate this awesome day is to take individual sheaves of barley and tie them with colorful ribbons, then gather family and friends and joyously wave our individual barley sheaves before the Father. We can offer Him songs of thanksgiving and praise. Let us remember to be as priests before Him, and like Aaron, bear the burden of all the tribes on our breasts. On this day in particular, we can intercede in prayer for the whole house of Israel.

You also might want to have someone dress as a priest, and others dress as Israelites who are bringing in their sheaves. Someone can read all the appropriate verses while the people act out the feast. Give the children a calendar on which they can begin counting off the days until Shavuot. Pray! Sing! Rejoice! Give gifts! Worship and celebrate on this day that speaks of the Resurrection work of He Who is the First of First Fruits!

Scriptural Counting Method

Counting from the Morrow after the Weekly Sabbath						
Sun	Mon	Tues	Wed	Thurs	Fri	Sabbath
			Abib 14– Passover	Abib 15– 1st day of Un- leavened Bread	Abib 16	
1 Day of First Fruits	2	3	4	5	6	1st Sabbath
8	9	10	11	12	13	2nd Sabbath
15	16	17	18	19	20	3rd Sabbath
22	23	24	25	26	27	4th Sabbath
29	30	31	32	33	34	5th Sabbath
36	37	38	39	40	41	6th Sabbath
43	44	45	46	47	48	7th Sabbath
50 Shavuot= Morrow after the 7th Sabbath						

Yom HaBikkurim The Day of First Fruits

Rabbinical Counting Method

Counting from the Day of Unleavened Bread						
Sun	Mon	Tues	Wed	Thurs	Fri	Sabbath
			Abib 14–Passover	Abib 15–Day of Un-leavened Bread	Abib 16–[Day of First Fruits?]	2
3	4	5	6	7	8	1st Sabbath
10	11	12	13	14	15	2nd Sabbath
17	18	19	20	21	22	3rd Sabbath
24	25	26	27	28	29	4th Sabbath
31	32	33	34	35	36	5th Sabbath
38	39	40	41	42	43	6th Sabbath
45	46	47	48	49	50 Rabbinic Shavuot	

Israel's Feasts and their Fullness

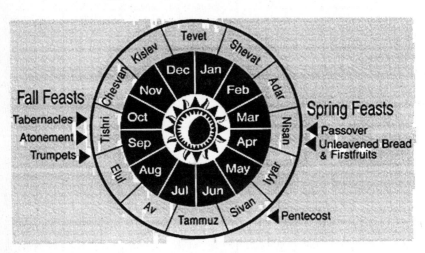

Chart from:
The Holidays of God by Kevin Williams
Martin R. De Haan II, President of RBC Ministries
http://www.gospelcom.net/rbc/ds/q0408/

The Spirit of Shavuot

Just as fulfillment of the Kingdom Passover calls for participation by Yeshua's followers in order to be fulfilled, so *Shavuot* cries for involvement by a reunited Israel that we might experience this feast in all its fullness.[123]

The word *Shavuot*, which means *Weeks*, comes from *sheva*, the Hebrew word for *seven*, the number of completion and perfection.[124]   Seven weeks after the waving of the barley First Fruits, Israel celebrated this Late Spring feast.

Shavuot is also called the "Feast of the Harvest of the First Fruits," and "the Feast of Weeks, that is, the first fruits of the **wheat** harvest" (Exodus 23:16; 34:22). In Numbers 28:26 we read, "On the day of the first fruits, when you present a new grain offering...in your **Feast of Weeks**."

In Christian circles this day is primarily known as *Pentecost* (from a Greek word meaning *fifty*) because it is celebrated seven complete weeks, or *fifty* days, after the Day of First Fruits (Leviticus 23:15-16; Deuteronomy 16:9).

---

123 This is not to imply that we can make anything happen on our own, but to say that just as the Father used Moses to deliver His people, He also continues to use *people* to accomplish His works in the earth.

124 *Strong's* # H7620.

The last of the Spring feasts, Shavuot has no specific date beyond the counting of days after the Day of First Fruits (see *"Counting The Omer"* in the First Fruits chapter).

This day of rejoicing is a High Sabbath, a *Shalosh Regalim*—one of the three required annual pilgrimages to Jerusalem (Deuteronomy 16:16; 2 Chronicles 8:13).

The Covenant of the Ten Commandments— The Spirit of Torah

Most Believers agree that the Father gave the Ten Commandments to the children of Israel on Shavuot.[125] Then, on a Shavuot day many years later, the Ruach HaKodesh was poured out on Yeshua's disciples as they were gathered together in prayer (Exodus 19:9-25; 20:1-21; Acts 2:1-4).

With this outpouring, as prophesied, that which was once written on tablets of stone by the finger of God began to be written on hearts of flesh by the Spirit of God (Jeremiah 31:31-33; Hebrews 8:8-13; 10:16-17).

When Moses was with the Lord on Mount Horeb, YHVH "wrote on the tablets the words of the covenant, the Ten Commandments." In the "midst of fire" He wrote them (Exodus 34:28; Deuteronomy 10:4). Moses said, "He declared to you His covenant which He commanded you to perform, that is, the Ten Commandments; and He wrote them on two tablets of stone" (Deuteronomy 4:13).

The Ten Commandments are YHVH's Covenant. His Covenant Tablets were carried by the Levites in what was called "the Ark of the Covenant" (Deuteronomy 31:9).[126]

---

125 Israel came to Mount Sinai on the third day of the third month, and YHVH visited the people three days later (Exodus 19:1,10-17). This is thought to have happened 50 days after they crossed the Red Sea, on the day that came to be known as the feast of Shavuot.

126 When it was placed in the Tabernacle in the Wilderness, the Ark of the Covenant contained a golden jar of manna, Aaron's rod that budded, and the tables of the covenant (Heb 9:4). However, by the time that the Ark was placed in the Temple, there was nothing in it "except the two tablets which Moses put there at Horeb, where YHVH made a covenant with the sons of Israel, when they came out of Egypt" (1 Ki 8:9; 2 Chr 5:10).

The Book Beside the Ark...

As to the *book of the Law*, the Torah, the five books written by Moses, we read that he "commanded the Levites who carried the Ark, saying, 'Take this **book of the law** and place it **beside** the ark of the covenant of YHVH your God, that it may remain there as a witness against you" (Deuteronomy 31:26-27).

The "book of the Law" was placed *beside* the Ark, but the Tablets of the Covenant were *in* it.

The Five Books Enlarge on The Spirit of Torah

When we realize that the Ten Commandments impart the *spirit* of the Father's Covenant, we more clearly see the New Covenant fulfillment of Shavuot. *The spirit of Torah was first written in flames of fire on tablets of stone by the finger of God. That Covenant was then written with tongues of fire on hearts of flesh by the Spirit of God* (Jeremiah 31:31-33; Hebrews 8:8-13; 10:16-17; Acts 2:3; Luke 24:49).

Fulfillment of Shavuot speaks of having the *spirit of the Father's Covenant* brought to life in men's hearts by His Holy Spirit. In other words, Shavuot centers around the *spirit* of His Torah.

When we do not understand the *spirit* of the Law, we tend to stumble over the minutia of the *letter* of the Law, and the letter of the law then becomes "a testimony against us."

Ten Commandments—Two Commandments

Messiah Yeshua gave a simple explanation of the Father's Covenant commands. One might even say that Yeshua consolidated the Torah and even the Ten Commandments into Two Commandments. When being tested by a certain lawyer, Yeshua was asked, "Teacher, which is the greatest commandment in the Law?"

The Messiah answered him, "You shall love the Lord your God with all your heart, and with all your soul, and with all your mind. This is the greatest and foremost commandment. The second is like it, 'You shall love your neighbor as yourself. On these two commandments depend the whole Law and the Prophets" (Matthew 22:36-40).

Torah Summed up in a Word

In saying this, Yeshua was not denying any part of Torah, but was simplifying its message, or giving an outline for the whole Torah. He was speaking of its pure *essence*, which is *love*. We must *love* YHVH with all our hearts and we must *love* our neighbor as ourselves. That is the essence of the Torah and the prophets.

One might say that the essence of the Ten Commandments was brought down to Two Commandments, and those Two Commandments have a common command, they are distilled down to one word—Love.[127]

As John the apostle says, "The one who does not love does not know God, for **God is love**" (1 John 4:8).

The Book of the Law was written by Moses to help Israel understand how to actually *walk* in that love. The *Sefer Torah*, the Book of Torah, serves a *witness* about how we are actually walking out the Father's covenant. It is a Book that testifies *against* us when we fall short of its high call, or testifies *for* us when we fulfill its commands.

The Essence of the Essence

The Ten Commandments are the *essence*, or the *spirit* of the God-inspired five books written by Moses.

Of these books of the Covenant, Moses said, *"Keep and*

---

127 The first four of the Ten Commandments were essentially summed up in Yeshua's greatest commandment, which is to love YHVH with all your heart. He then summed up the following six commandments in His second commandment, which is to love your neighbor (see Deu 6:5; 30:6; Lev 19:18).

do them, for that is your wisdom and your understanding in the sight of the peoples who will hear all these statutes and say, 'Surely this great nation is a wise and understanding people.' For what great nation is there that has a god so near to it as is YHVH our God whenever we call on Him? Or what great nation is there that has statutes and judgments as righteous as this whole law which I am setting before you today? Only give heed to yourself and keep your soul diligently, so that you do not forget the things which your eyes have seen and they do not depart from your heart all the days of your life; but make them known to your sons and your grandsons" (Deuteronomy 4:6-9).

Torah came forth from a heart filled with love. Its Holy Words might rightly be called *Loving Instructions*. They serve as defined parameters given to the children of a Father who wants to protect them, to keep them safe.

Yeshua brought out the *essence* of the *essence* of the Law. The many words of Torah can be summed up in one word. The spirit, the essence of Torah's essence, is realized in the word *love*.

If we do not have love, as Paul the apostle says, our words about Torah will only sound like a "clanging cymbal" (1 Corinthians 13:1).

The outside world will see a fulfillment of Shavuot in we who are disciples of Messiah Yeshua when they see us truly walking in love. All that we do, all that we are, all that we live and teach and preach of the Father's truths must be done from a heart of love.

Israel's Feasts and their Fullness

Shavuot
In Scripture and Tradition

*Y*ou shall celebrate the Feast of Weeks, that is, the
first fruits of the wheat harvest, and the Feast of
Ingathering at the turn of the year....You shall also count for
yourselves from the day after the sabbath, from the day
when you brought in the sheaf of the wave offering; there
shall be seven complete sabbaths. You shall count fifty
days to the day after the seventh sabbath; then you shall
present a new grain offering to YHVH. You shall bring in
from your dwelling places two loaves of bread for a wave
offering, made of two-tenths of an ephah; they shall be of a
fine flour, baked with leaven as first fruits to YHVH. Along
with the bread you shall present seven one year old male
lambs without defect, and a bull of the herd and two rams;
they are to be a burnt offering to YHVH, with their grain
offering and their drink offerings, an offering by fire of a
soothing aroma to YHVH. You shall also offer one male goat
for a sin offering and two male lambs one year old for a
sacrifice of peace offerings. The priest shall then wave them
with the bread of the first fruits for a wave offering with two

lambs before YHVH; they are to be holy to the Lord for the priest ....Also on the day of the first fruits, when you present a new grain offering to YHVH in your Feast of Weeks, you shall have a holy convocation; you shall do no laborious work....Then you shall celebrate the Feast of Weeks to YHVH your God with a tribute of a freewill offering of your hand, which you shall give just as YHVH your God blesses you.... Three times in a year all your males shall appear before YHVH your God in the place which He chooses, at the Feast of Unleavened Bread and at the Feast of Weeks and at the Feast of Booths, and they shall not appear before YHVH empty-handed" (Exodus 34:22; Numbers 28:26; Deuteronomy 16:10,16; Leviticus 23:15-20).

Shavuot and Sefirat HaOmer

As previously stated, on the Day of *First Fruits*, the Israelites brought an offering of a *barley* sheaf to the Temple. This first fruit offering was elaborately prepared and given in a very colorful ceremony to the priest for the ritual of waving. Waving the sheaf back and forth was a type of prayer before the Holy One. They were beseeching the Lord of the Harvest to protect their coming *wheat* harvest from bad weather. With this ceremony began a time of counting and anticipation of YHVH's coming provision.

This countdown from First Fruits to Shavuot is called *Sefirat HaOmer, the counting of the omer.* In Israel it is often called *Sefira* for short. *The Jewish Book of Why* says:

"The counting...connect[ed]...Passover and Shavuot... Passover marked the beginning of the grain harvest. The first crop (barley) was cut...and a small amount (an omer) was brought to the Temple as a sacrifice....For the next forty-nine days, each day was marked off (counted), and this period became known as Sefira ('the counting')....The fiftieth day was Shavuot, on which the next crop (wheat) was harvested and brought to the Temple" (pages 207-208).

Shavuot called for a holy convocation. It was to be a feast filled with joy and prayers of thanksgiving. Since

YHVH is the giver of our harvests, at this time gifts of first fruits were brought into His storehouse (Malachi 3:10).

The Israelites went to the Temple on this day and a special sacrifice was offered. The priest waved two *leavened* loaves of bread made from the finest of the newly harvested wheat flours. These were presented to the Holy One, but were not placed on the altar because YHVH had specifically declared, "No grain offering, which you bring to YHVH, shall be made with leaven, for you shall not offer up in smoke any leaven or any honey as an offering by fire to YHVH" (Leviticus 2:11).

While these two leavened loaves could be "waved" before Him, they could not be "offered up in smoke" on the altar: "As an offering of first fruits you shall bring them to YHVH, but they shall not ascend for a soothing aroma on the altar" (Leviticus 2:12).

Two lambs were also offered, and the feast was concluded with communal meals to which the poor, the stranger, and the Levites were invited. *However, bread made from the new harvest could not be eaten until after this ceremony.* This point will be important to our understanding of the fulfillment of Shavuot, which will be elaborated on it in the next chapter.

Jewish Traditions—
The Rabbis Interpret Shavuot

After the destruction of the Temple in A.D. 70, the rabbis began to associate Shavuot with the giving of the Torah. However, this was a later interpretation, and not the original meaning of it.

The Interpreter's Dictionary of the Bible explains:

"The feast, therefore, both by virtue of its relation to Passover and the entire harvest period, and as the season of the offering of first fruits, is agricultural in character. Neither the OT nor Josephus and Philo hint that it memorialized events in Israel's history. The book of

Jubilees also treats the feast as a harvest observance (22:1) but makes it a covenant-renewal ceremony for the covenant of Noah founded on this day (6:1-21). It is possible that connection with the covenant of Noah facilitated its association later with the revelation of the law on Sinai. ...the oldest reference to this is a saying in the Talmud (Pes. 68b) attributed to Rabbi El'azar ben Pedath (ca. A.D. 270): 'Pentecost is the day on which Torah was given....'

"Following the destruction of the temple, Weeks continued to be observed by its gradual transformation into a feast commemorating the gift of the law....

"But, as already noted, the association of the revelation of the law with Weeks is a later development".[128] In other words, the giving of the Book of the Law was not the original scriptural meaning of Shavuot.

In her book, *In the Jewish Tradition, A Year of Food and Festivities*, author Judith Fellner explains how the rabbis came to their interpretation.

"Once the Temple was destroyed....the idea of the omer and the counting of the days between Passover and Shavuot were in danger of being forgotten. The Rabbis, always inventive, wanted to perpetuate the ritual of the count, and recast 'the counting.' They made it part of the daily liturgy, together with a blessing....

"If Shavuot had remained a purely agricultural holiday, with no historical event attached to it—as the Exodus from Egypt is attached to Passover and the ancient Israelites wandering in the desert living in temporary dwellings is attached to Sukkot—the holiday would have surely died out.

"Recognizing this, the Rabbis wisely attached one of the greatest of all historical events to Shavuot, thereby ensuring its survival. By the third century, Shavuot became known as 'the time of the giving of the Torah' at Sinai, giving the holiday an essential spiritual component, linking it to the Exodus and Israel's journey to the promised land."

---

128 *Interpreter's Dictionary*, Abingdon, Vol. Four, "Weeks, Feast of," pp 827-828. Emphasis added.

Fellner further points out that, *"Shavuot... remains the least known and the least observed of the major Jewish festivals. Its central concept is the commemoration of revelation (God revealing Himself) at Mount Sinai and the celebration of the covenantal relationship between God and Israel, symbolized by the giving of the Torah...."*[129]
We emphasize this change in focus to convey the importance of returning to the Father's *true* meaning of Shavuot. We must remember that a "partial hardening" happened to Israel (Romans 11:25), and Jewish Israel has been unable to see the fullness of this important feast, partly because they do not recognize its fulfillment by the Ruach HaKodesh, and partly because they have not understood the importance of the *two leavened loaves.* Therefore, they have tied it almost exclusively to the giving of the Book of the Law written by Moses.

Other Jewish Traditions

Shavuot is also said to depict the marriage covenant between Israel and the Almighty. Judith Fellner writes:
"What happened at Mount Sinai was preceded by a covenantal relationship between God and Israel, a mutual commitment by the two parties pledging eternal faithfulness, much as a marriage—a popular metaphor in the Bible—in which Israel is depicted as the bride and God the bridegroom. 'And I will betroth you unto me forever' (Hos. 2:1). The marriage that took place at Mount Sinai between the children of Israel and God was sealed with the words 'we will do and we will hear.' These words committed the Israelites to an ethical and moral code that was not only binding on them, but on all future generations of Jews. Sephardic Jews have created an actual marriage document, or ketubah, for Shavuot, which specifies the obligations between Israel and God...."

---

129 *In the Jewish Tradition, A Year of Food and Festivities,* Judith Fellner, "Shavuot," Jonathan David Publishers, Middle Village, NY, 1995, pages 101-108.

Again, we recall that the Book of the Law was placed *beside* the ark of the covenant as a witness against the people, and that it was written later by Moses in the land of Moab (Deuteronomy 31:26-27; 29:1).

We also recall that the Ten Commandments represent the spirit of the Torah, and that true Torah can be reduced to one word, love. And surely love must be the essence of any true marriage contract.

In this way we can see the giving of the Covenant as being symbolic of a marriage contract, or a *ketubah*. (See graphic this chapter.)

More from Fellner:

Fellner also tells us, *"[T]he...reading designated for Shavuot...[is] the Book of Ruth. A lovely, pastoral story, the Book of Ruth describes how the young Moabite widow Ruth unconditionally embraces the faith and people of her mother- in-law, Naomi, saying, 'Do not urge me to leave you, to turn back and not follow you. For wherever you go, I will go; wherever you lodge, I will lodge; your people shall be my people and your God, my God' (Ruth 1:16). (Today, these words form part of the Jewish conversion ceremony.) The story takes place during the barley and wheat harvest season, which is another reason the Rabbis chose to read the Book of Ruth on Shavuot.....*

"The Torah reading for the first day of Shavuot is the description of the giving of the Torah on Mount Sinai, including the Ten Commandments. It is customary in many synagogues for people to stand when that portion is read, as if they were once again standing at Sinai accepting those commandments."

"According to...tradition, the period between Passover and Shavuot is a season of mourning. Marriages are not performed during this period, hair is not cut, and music is not played or heard. The reasons for this are not clear. Some suggest that a plague cost the lives of many of Rabbi Akiba's students during the Roman period and on the

thirty-third day of the omer, the plague suddenly ceased. Hence, the establishment of a special Lag Baomer (thirty-third day of the omer') celebration.

"Another tradition suggests that since this period was preparatory to receiving the Torah, these days should be set aside for reflection, study, and rededication to the principles of Jewish life and ritual. Therefore, frivolous activities were to be avoided....

"Shavuot is...known as Hag Hakatzir (Harvest Holiday). ...On Shavuot, two loaves of wheat bread from choice first wheat crops were baked and offered by priests at the Temple in Jerusalem as offerings of thanksgiving. Shavuot is...a day to commemorate the bringing of first fruits of the seven species (wheat, barley, grapes, figs, pomegranates, olives, and dates) to the Temple in Jerusalem. This vivid ceremony, described in elaborate detail in the Mishnah, marks the beginning of a new agricultural season." [130]

In Summary:

Shavuot was an agricultural feast. Its association with the giving of the Book of the Torah, which was written by Moses in Moab, was only begun by the rabbis much later, in approximately A.D. 270. The primary feature of this feast in ancient Israel was the waving of the two loaves of leavened bread.

Understanding of this offering has largely been lost, but is destined to be restored in these latter days. Fulfillment of Shavuot was *begun* with the giving of the Ten Commandments, it was further *fulfilled* with the outpouring of the Holy Spirit, and it will be greatly *enhanced* when all Israel is fully reunited.

We have yet to see a wondrous "new grain offering" being presented at Shavuot (Leviticus 23:15-16,21). When we begin to see the truth about all Israel—when we begin to properly honor both of her houses—we will fully taste of the loaves of Shavuot.

---

130 *Ibid,* pp 101-108.

The Ketubah: An Ornately Decorated Marriage Contract

Empowerment by The Spirit

The central concept of Shavuot is said to be the "revelation of God." Almost 2,000 years ago, a small group of Israelites gathered in Jerusalem on this feast day, and at that convocation the Father once again revealed Himself to His people. Just as Yeshua promised, fifty days after His First Fruits resurrection, He sent the Comforter, and His followers experienced the first *New Covenant* Shavuot—the Holy Spirit was poured out on a waiting, expectant, New Covenant people of Israel.

Today during our sojourn on earth, Yeshua gives us the opportunity to receive the *Ruach HaKodesh*, the One He promised to send, the One Who will write the eternal truths of Torah on our hearts when we ask Him (John 14:16,26; 15:26;16:7; Jeremiah 31:31-33).

With this new Shavuot outpouring of the *Ruach HaKodesh*, Yeshua began to reap a harvest and to bring forth His New Covenant *ekklesia*. As the people of this New Covenant, our generation also needs to be empowered with the Ruach HaKodesh, just as were His early disciples. There are difficult days of trial ahead, and we are in great need of the empowerment of the Spirit so we can clearly hear the Father's voice as He whispers in our ear, "This is the way, walk ye in it" (Isaiah 30:21).

Shavuot and Jubilee

In ancient Israel every fiftieth year was a year of Jubilee. Because Shavuot comes on the "fiftieth" day, it is a picture of *Jubilee*. In Hebrew, fifty represents liberty, freedom, deliverance, and jubilee.[131] In these special years of freedom and restoration, slaves were set free and debts were cancelled. Liberty was proclaimed with the sound of the Jubilee trumpets (Leviticus 25:8-17).

Today we need to hear the sound of Jubilee, for we too need to be liberated from the bonds, the chains, and the sins that hold us to our former "slavery."

From Death to Life

Passover focuses on the death of the lamb. Unleavened Bread focuses on Israel's call to sinlessness. The First Fruits barley harvest highlights Yeshua's Resurrection, and Shavuot highlights His wheat harvest of Believers.

When the Commandments of the Covenant were given to ancient Israel, they testified against the immorality of their flesh, and "about three thousand men of the people fell that day" (Exodus 32:28; 1 Corinthians 10:8).

Conversely, when the Holy Spirit was given, three thousand souls were empowered with the fullness of the Spirit and granted the gift of eternal life in the Messiah. On that New Covenant Shavuot day, a transformed and empowered apostle Peter began to preach, and "those who received his word were baptized; and that day there were added about three thousand souls" (Acts 2:41; see also Acts 1:8; 2:38; 3:12-26; 4:33).

Harvested Sheaves

The sheaves of Shavuot also foretell the coming resurrection of those who put their faith in Messiah Yeshua.[132]

---

131 *The Wisdom In The Hebrew Alphabet*, by Scherman and Zlotowitz, *ArtScroll Mesorah Series*, 1983, Mesorah Publications, Brooklyn.
132 Mat 13:39; Mark 4:26; Luke 10:2; Rev 14:14-16.

For at the end of this age of earthly sowing, "The dead in Messiah will rise first, then we who are alive and remain shall be caught up together with them in the clouds to meet the Lord in the air. And thus we shall always be with the Lord" (1 Thessalonians 4:16-17).

There are Two...

The key to the celebration of Shavuot is the waving of the two leavened loaves.

Why *two* leavened loaves? What do they represent? What is the importance of the number two?

YHVH is dealing with *two* houses of Israel. Moreover, His Word reveals that He has:

♦ Two Houses of Israel (Isaiah 8:14; Jeremiah 31:31-33; Hebrews 8:8-10)
♦ Two Nations (Ezekiel 35:10)
♦ Two Chosen Families (Jeremiah 33:24)
♦ Two Sinful Sisters (Ezekiel 23:2-4)
♦ Two Olive Branches (Zechariah 4:11-14; Jeremiah 11:10, 16-17; 2:18,21; Romans 11; Revelation 11:4)
♦ Two Sticks (Ezekiel 37:15-28)
♦ Two Witnesses (Revelation 11:3-4)
♦ Two Lampstands (Revelation 11:3-4)
♦ Two Cherubim over the Mercy Seat (Exodus 25:18-20)
♦ Two Tablets of Covenant Law (Exodus 34:29;)
♦ Two Silver Trumpets (Numbers 10:2-3)
♦ Two Leavened Loaves (Hebrews 9:28)

Quite obviously, the number two has great significance to the Father, and we must not overlook its meaning in this feast.

Making an End Time Proclamation

Concerning this feast, we are told, "On this same day you shall make a **proclamation** as well; you are to have a holy convocation. You shall do no laborious work. It is to be a perpetual statute in all your dwelling places throughout your generations" (Leviticus 23:21).

We are commanded to make a *proclamation*, a *qara*, concerning this feast. We are to proclaim, mention, publish, and preach the truth about this appointed time.[133]

But exactly what do we need to proclaim in this hour?

Twelve Unleavened Showbread Loaves
Two Leavened Shavuot Loaves

Just as the twelve *unleavened* loaves of "show bread" found in the Tabernacle represented the twelve tribes of Israel, so the two *leavened* loaves of Shavuot represent both the houses of Israel—Ephraim and Judah (Isaiah 8:14).

When designing the Tabernacle, the Father told Moses, "You shall set the bread of the Presence on the table before Me at all times." The Bread of the Presence consisted of twelve loaves of unleavened bread, which were to be renewed every sabbath day, and which served as a reminder of YHVH's everlasting covenant with the sons of Israel (Exodus 25:30; Leviticus 24:5-9).

We might say that the twelve *unleavened* loaves of the Presence spoke of the *unity* of the twelve tribes of Israel, whereas the two *leavened* loaves speak of the current *division* of the two houses of Israel.

Divided by Leaven

Of all the cereal offerings in Scripture, only the two wave loaves of Shavuot were baked with leaven.

What does this signify?

Leaven symbolizes sin, and two is the number of the

---

133 *Strong's* word # H 7121.

two houses of Israel—both of which have stumbled over the One who would be a "Sanctuary" to them. Both houses have fallen short (Isaiah 8:14; John 2:22; Romans 11:25). And they will continue to fall short so long as they are divided.

The First Piece of Dough

In Romans 11:16, we read: "If the first piece of dough is holy, the lump is also; and if the root is holy, the branches are too." With the feasts, the first piece of dough mentioned is that of Unleavened Bread. This represents our Messiah. He is "holy" dough. The second lump of dough mentioned is the two leavened loaves of Shavuot.

We are part of that latter "lump." We are made *holy* only when we abide in our holy Messiah.

Bread and the Word

Yeshua is the "Bread of life." He said of Himself, "I am the bread which came down from heaven" (John 6:48-51). Yeshua is the Living Word, the Word of Life (John 1:14; 1 John 1:1; 1 Peter 1:23). He declared, "It is written, Man shall not live on bread alone, but on every word that proceeds out of the mouth of God" (Matthew 4:4).

Our Father's Word, Genesis to Revelation, is like bread to us, and the two loaves represent the two covenant people: *Two Books of the Covenant—Two Loaves.*

The house of Judah has had charge of the Old (First) Covenant, or Torah, and they tend to eat only of that covenant loaf. The house of Ephraim, or Israel, has had charge of the New Covenant, the covenant of the heart (Jeremiah 31:31-33), and they tend to eat only of that covenant loaf.[134]

---

134 In using the words "Old and New Covenants" in this way we do not imply that the Father has "two covenant peoples," as some errantly claim. The Father promised to make a "Renewed" (New) Covenant with the houses of Israel and Judah. Both houses are being called to fully enter into that covenant, and when we do so, we will "not teach again, each man his neighbor...saying, 'Know YHVH,' for they will all know Me, from the least of them to the greatest of them,"
(continued...)

The Father has used the two houses to maintain the "loaf," or book of the Covenant, over which He has given them charge. Although the overseers of these two Covenants have made mistakes in the way they have presented His truths, nevertheless, the two leavened loaves continue to be His prescribed wave offering.

Eating of the Latter Day Bread of Shavuot

The appointed wave offering of this feast teaches us that the Father loves both the houses of Israel. They are His two chosen families (Jeremiah 33:24).

However, while fine bread of truth can be found in the teachings of both houses, both also contain leaven. We need to work to bring forth only that which is of the finest flours from our divided family. We need to leave the leaven behind.

Let us reunite! Let us eat of the latter day bread of Shavuot! As New Covenant priests of Israel, let us wave both loaves before our Father (1 Peter 2:9). Let us bring in from our dwelling places two loaves of bread for a wave offering, let them be of *very fine* flour, baked with leaven as first fruits to YHVH (Leviticus 23:17).

Only when we are fully reunited will Israel's "broken brotherhood" be restored. Only when our sin of division is ended will we be empowered to stand as an undivided house of Israel (Zechariah 11:14; Matthew 12:25; Ezekiel 37:15-28).

When we again become the reunited twelve tribes of Israel we will see the Presence of the Holy One. At that time we will be permitted to fully partake of the filling loaves of Shavuot. That holy food will propel us, it will strengthen us, it will empower us to run into the falls feasts—and into the return of our beloved Messiah.

---

134 (...continued)
declares YHVH, for I will forgive their iniquity, and their sin I will remember no more" (Jer 31:31-34).

Celebrating Shavuot

Traditionally, Shavuot marks a time of remembering, giving, and rejoicing.

Concerning giving, the Father says, "Three times in a year all your males shall appear before YHVH your God...and they shall not appear before YHVH empty-handed. Every man shall give as he is able, according to the blessing of YHVH your God which He has given you" (Deuteronomy 16:16-17).

These Holy Convocations offer a time for us to "celebrate ...with a tribute of a freewill offering of our hands." The feasts mark a time when we are to bring the whole tithe into YHVH's storehouse, that there might be meat [*physical and/or spiritual food*] in His storehouse" (Malachi 3:10).

We bring our gifts from that which we have harvested into His storehouse, and then, He "rebukes the devourer for our sake. "'Test Me now in this,' says the Lord of Hosts, 'and see if I will not open for you the windows of heaven, and pour out for you a blessing until it overflows. And, I will rebuke the devourer for you'" (Malachi 3:10-11).

Now is a good time to replace the *meat* in the storehouse. The Father has made sure that you have been spiritually fed during the past year, now it is time to give back to the storehouse, or storehouses, in which you found spiritual food (John 4:32-34).

This means that wherever you have been gleaning nourishing truth, take your gifts to that storehouse. Help replenish their supply, so that others can find like nourishment. Rejoice in giving back to the various sources from which you have harvested your spiritual food.

As a fellowship or family, pray together about the "altar" on which you lay your gifts. We must not lay our gifts on "unclean" altars. After prayer, offer a freewill offering to your storehouse of choice.

"Celebrate Shavuot to YHVH your God with a tribute of a freewill offering of your hand, which you give just as YHVH your God blesses you" (Deuteronomy 16:10).

Celebration Suggestions

The seven species: barley, dates, figs, grapes, pomegranates, olives, and wheat. From the book, *The Encyclopedia of Jewish Symbols*, by Frankel and Teutsch.

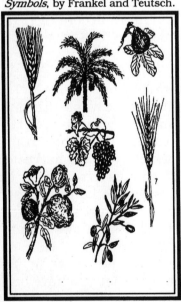

At this time our homes and places of worship and fellowship are decorated with flowers, fruit, and greenery. Among the decorations are the *Seven Species* traditionally presented before our Provider during this season (see list and graphic at left).

These Seven Species are said to symbolize the fertility of the Promised Land (Deuteronomy 8:8).

Fresh fruits and honey are the foods of choice at the celebrations.

Traditionally, the Book of Ruth is read at this time. And many Orthodox Jews stay up all night studying the Scriptures.

For New Covenant Israel, Shavuot offers a perfect time to bring our "harvest" of new Believers before the Father. It is an excellent time to present to the Body of Messiah the "new fruit," or new Believers, who have been gathered during the year. During this time, we can especially honor them in our congregations. One way to do this is to have a special "dedication ceremony" for them.

It also is a good time to renew our commitment to the Holy One, and to rejoice because we have been redeemed, and thus have been brought to this time of celebration.

Shavuot foretold the outpouring of the *Ruach HaKodesh* (Acts 2). This feast is ever foretelling that truth, because an outpouring of the Spirit continues to be available to those who partake of the Lamb (Matthew 7:9-11). Now is a good time to seek the in-filling and empowering of the *Ruach HaKodesh* (Luke 11:13).

A Wave Offering of Gratitude

Celebrate by waving two leavened loaves of bread before the Father while thanking and praising Him for the way He has used both loaves. The action is not as important as what is in the heart, so as you wave your loaves, thank Him for making His Word come alive to you and for bringing forth a harvest in your life. Although we are imperfect vessels (to whom righteousness has been imputed), if we make ourselves available, He will use us to help bring forth His reunited Kingdom. So ask Him to make His Heavenly Bread a part of your being, and to allow you to be part of the restoration of His Kingdom. As you wave your loaves, remind the Father that you long for the perfection, completion, and full reunion of both houses. Declare to Him that you long for the pure, reunited house over which Messiah reigns—the house that will never again be "plucked up" from their promised Land (Ezekiel 37:22-26).

The offerings made to our Father were to be "first fruit" offerings (Leviticus 2:12). Like the feast of the First of First Fruits (Yom HaBikkurim), offerings were first made to the

Father, then we could partake. Therefore, we want to wave the two loaves of Shavuot before Him, because it is only after they are offered to Him that we can partake of their goodness. Symbolically, it is after the offering is made that we eat of the loaves of Shavuot. Only when we rejoin the houses can we experience Pentecost, or Shavuot, in its fullness!

Tasting of the Bread of Reunion

It is just as Paul the apostle said about Judah being brought back into Israel's fold. Paul encouraged those who were formerly of the Nations (Ephesians 2:11-22) to move to "jealousy" his Jewish brothers. He explained what would happen when this is accomplished.

"If their rejection [of the gospel of the Kingdom] is [used to bring about] the reconciliation of the world, what will their acceptance be but life from the dead?" (Romans 11:13-15).

If we want revival, we must make it possible for Judah to see something glorious in those who have embraced Israel's New Covenant. We must present a way of life that will inspire him to want the same way of life.

So let us bring our gifts into the Father's storehouse and wave two loaves of bread before Him. Let us thank and praise Him for the way He has used, and will continue to use, both loaves, or both houses.

Let us thank Him for giving us the understanding and the desire to honor both the houses of Israel by waving the two loaves before Him, for only *then* will we be filled with the Spirit in a way that will enable us to move into Yom Teruah.

After this feast, and before the next feast, comes the long, hot summer, which serves as an excellent symbol of the long, hot season that exists between Messiah's two comings.

With expectant hearts we wait, knowing that our Father's unending love for us will take us beyond the Shavuot waving. One day soon His love will take us to the time when we can "Tabernacle" with Him.

Hallelujah!

Part Four

The Falls Feasts
Yom Teruah
Yom HaKippurim
Tabernacles

Yom Teruah

The sound of the Yom Teruah trumpets signaled the beginning of the Fall feasts for ancient Israel. The sound also marked the beginning of the ten days before Yom HaKippurim, the Day of the Coverings.

Yom Teruah and Yom HaKippurim together are called the "High Holy Days." These two feasts differ from the others in that they are not centered around agriculture. Rather, their focus is on preparing man to meet his Maker on the day of judgment.

These deciding days often are called the "Ten Days of Awe." Traditionally, they are times of self-examination and repentance. They mark a time when men are to make peace with their brethren—that their hearts might be prepared for Yom HaKippurim, the Day of Atonements, the day when man stands before the Almighty.

Messiah Yeshua may have made His statement about brothers who were angry with each other at this time: *"I say to you that everyone who is angry with his brother shall be guilty before the court; and whoever says to his brother, 'You good-for-nothing,' shall be guilty before the supreme court; and whoever says, 'You fool,' shall be guilty enough to go into the fiery hell. Therefore if you are presenting your offering at the altar, and there remember that your brother has something against you, leave your offering there before the altar and go; first be reconciled to your brother, and then come and present your offering. Make friends quickly with your opponent at law while you are with him on the way, so that your opponent may not hand you over to the judge, and the judge to the officer, and you be thrown into prison. Truly I say to you, you will not come out of there until you have paid up the last cent"* (Matthew 5:22-26).

In addition to the courts of this world, the court mentioned by the Messiah could refer to the court all men will one day face as they stand before the Judge of all the earth.[135] The Judge of that court has forewarned us: "If someone says, 'I love God,' and hates his brother, he is a liar; for the one who does not love his brother whom he has seen, cannot love God whom he has not seen" (1 John 4:20).

Yom Teruah especially addresses our need to make peace with our fellow man. It warns us that someday we will have to give an account of our actions.

The Fall Feasts and Completion

Yom Teruah means *Day of Blowing.* This day is also called the Feast of Trumpets, or *Zikron Teruah*, which means a *Memorial of Blowing* (Leviticus 23:24). Yom Teruah occurs in the month of Tishri, which corresponds to the Gregorian months of September and October.

The seventh day, the seventh month, and the seventh year were deemed sacred to Israel. Since Yom Teruah begins the seventh month,[136] the feasts that occur in this month are viewed as especially sacred.

Seven is related to *completion*, and we read in Philippians 1:6 that "He who began a good work in you will carry it on to completion until the day of Messiah" (NIV).

The Fall feasts tell of the completion of our walk and of the completion of the Father's work in the earth. They

---

135 Psa 67:4; 96:13; John 12:48; Heb 4:12.
136 Exo 20:8-10; Lev 25:4.

foretell Yeshua's return to earth, as well as the time when the Father will come down in the Heavenly City, the New Jerusalem.

The Feast of Trumpets symbolizes our call to warfare, to intercession, to listening for the Father's voice, to absolute obedience, and to true unity with our brethren.

Yom Teruah in Ancient Israel

We see the Feast of Trumpets being celebrated in Ezra 3:1-6. Sacrifices were offered at the blasts of the trumpets (by those of Judah who had returned to the Land after their Babylonian exile), and sweeping revival took place (Nehemiah 7:73-8:13). "Hezekiah gave the order to offer the burnt offering on the altar... the song to YHVH also began with the trumpets, accompanied by the instruments of David....While the whole assembly worshiped, the singers also sang and the trumpets sounded; all this continued until the burnt offering was finished" (2 Chronicles 29:27-28).[137]

This account depicts Yom Teruah as a time of return and revival—a time of people singing the song of YHVH.

Rosh HaShanah—The Jewish New Year

In Jewish tradition, this day is called *Rosh HaShanah*, meaning *Head of the Year*, because they say the month of *Tishri* marks the beginning of their year. But the Father said Abib was to be "the beginning of months" for Israel, as this is the month when we came out of Egypt (Exodus 12:2).

Some rabbis do acknowledge that Abib is to be the head of the year, and some claim the Tishri celebration is but a "civil" New Year. Others say Judaism celebrates on this day to commemorate the creation of the world, which they believe happened in the fall. Thus they begin their calendar in the seventh month, with Yom Teruah.

---

137 Use of the silver trumpets is further confirmed in *The Writings of Flavius Josephus*, "Antiquities of the Jews" (3:12), www.bible.crosswalk.com/History. They were to be blown by the priests over burnt and peace offerings (Num 10:10). *The song:* 2Ch 7:3 20:21 23:18 Ps 136:1 137:3,4; also see vs 89:15.

Two Scriptures are used to defend this decision: Exodus 23:16 and 34:22: "The feast of ingathering, which is in the end of the year, when thou hast gathered in thy labours out of the field." And, "You shall celebrate...the Feast of Ingathering at the turn of the year." (*Young's Literal Translation* renders it, "At the **revolution** of the year." [138])

What is meant by these verses? Did the Father change His mind about His New Year? Are these Scriptures a "slip of the tongue"? Did the Holy One forgot that He had already fixed the time for our New Year? What did He mean when He said that Tabernacles occurs at the "turn of the year"?

Could it be that the tradition is based on a misunderstanding of the meaning of the "year"?

The End of a Seven Month Long "Year"

We suggest that the year's end mentioned above refers to Israel's feast calendar, which was based on a *seven-month-long* cycle. Her feasts began with Passover and ended seven months later with Tabernacles. This agricultural year began with the spring barley harvest during the season of Passover and ended with the fall fruit harvest of Sukkot. This "calendar" was based on a *seven-month-long, lunar* cycle, which refers to the monthly rotation of the moon around the earth.

If this reasoning is accurate, then it explains why Israel's lunar-based agricultural year ended at the conclusion of Sukkot, the last feast of the agricultural year, and that the "new year" *did not begin the next day*. Instead, it began the next spring, in the month of Abib, with the barley harvest.[139]

Ancient Israel was an agriculturally-based nation, their feast celebrations involved their entire lives and they revolved around the planting seasons. Their agricultural calendar only included seven lunar-based months, which

---

138 *Young's Literal Translation*, Robert Young, *26 Translations of The Bible.*
139 *Jewish Customs And Ceremonies*, Ben M. Edidin, NY: Hebrew Publishing, 1978, pp 93,100.

began with the first harvest in the month of Abib.

However, Israel also functioned in a world that had (and still does have) a twelve-month-long calendar year related to the *solar* cycle of the *sun*, which is based on the rotation of the earth around the sun.

Israel's twelve-month-long solar calendar likewise must begin in Abib. To do less is to ignore the Father's stated calendar year, it is to ignore the decree of the One who set the sun in its place.

Babylon and the New Year

Could there be another explanation for a calendar that begins in the fall of the year?

The Jewish calendar begins with Yom Teruah, or Rosh HaShanah. Some believe that Judah renamed this feast day and changed their calendar year when they were taken captive to Babylon.

In seems that in the Babylonian calendar, this same month was known as the "Head of the Year," and Judah may have adopted that custom.

In his book, *Seasons of Our Joy*, Arthur Waskow explains how this may have happened:

"By the time the Jews had suffered the destruction of the First Temple and had wept and sung their song in Babylon, the first of Tishri [date for Yom Teruah] took on new meaning. The simple thread was woven, twirled, embroidered into a richer fabric of renewal...."

"Some scholars believe that deep in the background of this [New Year] celebration...stood a Babylonian holiday....

"[T]he successful conclusion of the Babylonian harvest was an occasion for pledging renewed obedience to the Babylonian throne....either before the Exile or during it, the Jews both borrowed and transformed this coronation—lifted it on high to assert that only God is the King, and that every year we recognize and celebrate God's power...

"Once the rabbis decided Tishri was the head of the year, they [began]...to establish the orderly procession of

time and....human community [and]....rules...for the sighti-
ng of a new moon....[and] rules of order...among all...who
must obey God's royal will toward justice. Linking these two
...the rabbis heard the call of the ram's horn, the shofar..."[140]

Did the rabbis hear the Father's call, or were they
deceived by a blast from Babylon? Did Judah fall into a
misunderstanding similar to the Christian misunderstanding of Christmas? Did Ephraim go to Rome only to learn to
errantly celebrate Christmas, and Judah to Babylon only to
learn to errantly celebrate Rosh HaShanah?

Nathan Ausubel, in his *Book of Jewish Knowledge*, says:

"Rosh Hashanah is called the Jewish New Year." [But]
"its institution showed no concern with the [Biblical]
calendar. It occurs—not as one would expect—on the first
day of the first month of the Hebrew month of Nissan
[Babylonian name for Abib]....

"Rosh Hashanah...originated in a primitive culture...in
which magic, myth, and incantation were familiar features
of religious belief...

"Since early Jewish culture was within the constellation
of...Babylonia, which dominated the... Middle East, Rosh
Hashanah followed, in its main outline, the 'Day of Judgment'
...Babylonians...considered it to be their New Year [and]...
believed that on that day there took place an awesome
convocation of all their deities in the great Temple of
Marduk, the chief god in Babylon.

"They assembled there on every New Year to 'renew' the
world and to pass judgment on human beings, and then
inscribed the fate of each individual for the ensuing year on
a 'tablet of destiny.'

"The name Rosh Hashanah was not...originally used...to
designate this day... the first mention of Rosh Hashanah is
found in the Mishnah, the code of the Oral Tradition which
was first compiled in the second century....[A.D.]"[141]

---

140 *Seasons of Our Joy*, Arthur Waskow, NY: Bantum Books, 1982. pp 2-3.
141 *The Book of Jewish Knowledge*, Nathan Ausubel, NY: Crown Publishers,
1977, pp 372-373.

The Present Jewish Calendar

In his book *Jewish Customs And Ceremonies*, Ben M. Edidin says, "*The present Jewish calendar was written down in the fourth century...by Hillel the Second some sixteen hundred years ago*" [142]

With this change that came some 1500 years after the feast was instituted, Yom Teruah lost its true meaning. Through this Babylonian distortion of the truth, some of the people of Israel began to be led astray—even as many of their brethren would later be led astray by the counterfeit claims of pagan Rome.

Following the Seasons of Our Joy

The God of all creation established the universe and all that is within it. He set the stars in the sky, sent the earth into orbit around the sun, and commanded the moon to circle the earth. It is He who instructed us that: *The head of My year is Abib*, the month of Passover (Leviticus 23:23-25). He is our creator and the Judge of all creation, and we should honor His instructions.

We must be careful about embracing a *civil* New Year observance that appears to be based on Babylonian practices.

While it is a given that the modern world bases its functions on various solar calendars, still, without being self-righteous or legalistic about this truth, we need to seek to honor our Father's agricultural calendar. We want to base our lives on His seasons of blessings, for they are to be the seasons of our joy.

---

142   *Jewish Customs And Ceremonies*, Ben M. Edidin, NY: Hebrew Publishing, 1978, pp 93,100.

Israel's Feasts and their Fullness

Twin Trumpets

T he Father told the sons of Israel how to commemorate Yom Teruah. He said: *"Make yourself two trumpets of silver, of hammered work you shall make them; you shall use them for summoning the congregation and for having the camps set out. When both are blown, all the congregation shall gather themselves to you at the doorway of the tent of meeting. If only one is blown, then the leaders, the heads of the divisions of Israel, shall assemble before you. When you blow an alarm, the camps...shall set out. ...When convening the assembly, however, you shall blow without sounding an alarm. The priestly sons of Aaron shall blow the trumpets; and this shall be for you a perpetual statute throughout your generations. When you go to war in your land against the adversary who attacks you, you shall sound an alarm with the trumpets, that you may be remembered before YHVH your God, and be saved from your enemies. Also in the day of your gladness and in your appointed feasts, and on the first days of your months, you shall blow the trumpets over your burnt offerings, and over the sacrifices of your peace offerings; and they shall be as a reminder of you before your God. I am YHVH your God"* (Numbers 10:1-10).

What is the truth about this day? Could this little-understood feast prove to be a most exceptional day for Believers? Could it be that as Messiah's Body, as Believers that are united in Him, *we* are called to fulfill this feast?

Our Messiah was born on Sukkot (Tabernacles), became our Sacrificial Lamb on Passover, was raised from the dead on the Day of First Fruits, then poured out His Spirit on Shavuot (Pentecost). Many believe He will return to rule and reign as Judge of the whole earth on Yom HaKippurim, Day of the Coverings (Atonement), and that He will forevermore Tabernacle here on Earth with His people Israel.

But what about Yom Teruah? How is *it* to be fulfilled? Could it be that it foretells the Father's reunited people declaring Yeshua's imminent return?

To answer, let us listen with the ears of the spirit to a brief outline of this feast.

The Father said that to honor this day, Israel must make *two* trumpets of silver hammered work. Priests were to blow these trumpets. Their *united* sound would be used to summon *all* Israel, and to have the camps set out. Two trumpets were to be sounded when going to war in the land —that we might be remembered before our God, and by Him, *be saved from our enemies*.

The two silver trumpets of Numbers chapter 10 were used to: Gather the assembly (vs. 2); move the camp (vs. 5); prepare for war (vs. 9); celebrate the feasts (vs. 10).

Two Trumpets—Two Witnesses

Yom Teruah calls for *two* trumpets to be sounded by priests, and trumpets depict voices (Revelation 1:10). "Cry loudly, do not hold back; raise your voice like a trumpet, and declare to My people their transgression and to the house of Jacob their sins" (Isaiah 58:1).

Historically, there have been only two people groups on the earth who have been giving voice to a testimony about the goodness of the "God of Abraham, Isaac, and Jacob." Those two groups are Christians and Jews. They are the only two major people groups to claim that He is "their God."

This is not to imply that everyone who says they belong to either group is acceptable to Him, but to say that both claim to believe in Him, and for many centuries both have been giving testimony about Him. In this way, we see these two groups as "two witnesses" for the God of Israel. As stated earlier, YHVH said of the sons of Israel, "You are My witnesses" (Isaiah 43:10), and He then divided the twelve tribes of Israel into the *two houses* of Ephraim/Israel and Judah (2 Chronicles 11:4).

In Israel, all things must be confirmed by "two or more" witnesses before a truth can be established, confirmed, or believed (Numbers 35:30; Deuteronomy 17:6; 19:15; John 8:17; 2 Corinthians 13:1). [143] And thus the Father has "two witnesses," but they have not sounded their voices in *unison*. Instead, they have been denying one another. Yet it is *only* their unified voice that will gather *all Israel*. And Yom Teruah foretells the day when two voices will speak in perfect harmony. It foretells "two witnesses" who will ultimately serve their true purpose: To *confirm* the Father's truth in the earth—Genesis to Revelation.

To call Ephraim and Judah two witnesses does not deny that there may be two actual latter-day witnesses whom the Father will raise up. It is merely to state that, historically,

---

143 This law reveals the *plurality* of the God of Israel, because execution demands a *plurality* of *witnesses*. Also, *one* is *echad*, which can mean a numeral, united, first, alike, alone, a man, only, other, together, same, single, each (*Strong's* # H259; TWOT # 61). This word is used to define our God in the *Shema*, the Deuteronomy 6:4 affirmation of faith: "Hear, O Israel...the Lord is one [*echad*]." *Echad* can mean both *alone*—as in *only*, or *together*—as in *one/united/same*. As for human witnesses, "echad" is taken in its "diversity within unity" meaning. Though our God is to be the "*One* and *Only* God" of an Israelite —it also is true that His *echad* claim must be understood in its "plural" form. For "Scripture cannot be broken" (John 10:35), and YHVH is depicted as a "witness" against the people of Israel (Mal 3:5; Lev 20:5; Deu 32:35; Psa 96:13). If He is "singular," and has been a "witness" against a man that leads to the death of that man, then He has broken Scripture. To be a proper "witness' against man, He must be understood in the "diversity within unity" sense of *echad*. And Scripture declares that He is "plural" with Messiah Yeshua—with Him Who ultimately will be both Judge and Jury (John 5:22-24,30-34: 12:48). Yeshua is the Living Word—His Word will one day judge all mankind (John 1:1; Heb 4:12). (House of David Herald, Vol. 8, Book 9, "One Witness?" by Batya Wootten and Judith Dennis.)

these two people groups *have been* "two witnesses" for the God of Abraham, Isaac, and Jacob, and that they now need to be two confirming witnesses for Him.

Hammered Until We Repent

The two trumpets of Teruah foreshadowed things to come. They were to be made of *one piece of hammered silver* (Numbers 10:2). Silver symbolizes refinement and redemption. Hammered trumpets tell of the Father molding us through affliction.

The Father says of His two witnesses: "Behold, I will refine them....in order to refine, purge, and make them pure, until the end time....I will...refine them as silver...and...they will call on My name, and I will answer them; I will say, 'They are My people,' and they will say, 'YHVH is my God' ....As a purifier of silver, He will purify...and refine...that they may present to YHVH offerings in righteousness" (Jeremiah 9:7; Daniel 11:35; Zechariah 13:9; Hosea 1:10; Malachi 3:3).

In hope, let us realize that the sons of Israel will not always be afflicted. A day will come when Messiah Yeshua will repay with affliction those who afflicted His followers. He will give relief to His afflicted ones when He is revealed from heaven with His mighty angels in flaming fire, when He comes to be glorified in His saints (Isaiah 64:12; 2 Thessalonians 1:1-10; Daniel 7:18,22; 12:10).

But first, these hammered sons must be taken to the wilderness. And there, the Almighty will deal with them "face to face" (Hosea 2:14; Ezekiel 20:35).

In seeing the face of the Holy One, these transformed people are forever changed. He seeks to purge them during this time of isolation of *all* that needs to be purged from their lives. When they come through this fire, they are a fully pardoned company of Jacob. "Through this Jacob's iniquity will be forgiven; and this will be the full price of the pardoning of his sin: When he makes all the altar stones like pulverized chalk stones; when Asherim and incense altars will not stand" (Isaiah 27:9).

Immutable Truths

To the extent that they would allow, the Father has been using the two houses to "hammer out" a twofold message— the twin truths of *Law* and *Grace*. As His two witnesses, we of Ephraim and Judah must come to a place of unity concerning these two immutable truths. For it is only in unity that we will be fully empowered to serve our true purpose—to confirm the entire Word of the God of Israel.

Despite our weaknesses the Holy One will continue to hammer us until we get it right. And there *will* be those who will get it right, for the Father always has "seven thousand" on whom He can rely (Romans 11:4).

Let us therefore willingly accept His rod of correction.

Tried as Silver

The trumpets of Teruah are made of silver, of *keh'sef.* This word comes from *kasaf*, a root word that can be translated as *longing*.[144] "My soul longed [*kasaf*] and even yearned for the courts of YHVH; My heart and my flesh sing for joy to the living God" (Psalm 84:2).

Those who step into the furnace of affliction, who long for deliverance from bondage, who yearn for the restoration of YHVH's Kingdom—they will yet sing a new song. For the Holy One has sworn: "I will gather those who grieve about the appointed feasts—They came from you, O Zion; the reproach of exile is a burden on them" (Zephaniah 3:18). Yes, the two witnesses will yet sing in unison "the song of Moses" and "the song of the Lamb" (Revelation 15:3).

One Trumpet Brings Only Leaders

For more than two millennia, most of Israel has heard only the sound of one trumpet. They have chosen to "hear" from only one of the two houses. But the Father set forth a rule concerning His two trumpets: "If only one is blown, then the leaders, the heads of the divisions of Israel, shall

---

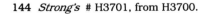

144 *Strong's* # H3701, from H3700.

assemble before you" (Numbers 10:4).

In other words, each house has *had* only one voice, and has chosen to *hear* only one voice, or one trumpet. Nevertheless, Scripture reveals that if only one trumpet is blown, only leaders respond—which is probably why we have far too many leaders in most churches and synagogues.

Although we have a tendency to elevate leaders, our Messiah called us to be *servants,* not leaders (Mark 9:35).

Let unified Israel be a people who are quick to repent of error. Let the unified servants of Israel gather together and call forth *all* Israel. Let the wicked shepherds who divide Israel's flock be put away. Let the good shepherds who will unite Israel's flock arise! (Ezekiel 34).

Time to Set Out!

The unified trumpets are to be sounded when it is time for the camps to set out" (Numbers 10:2). And it is time for Israel to "Move on beyond her ancient divisions!"

Sounded by Priests

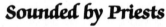

These trumpets must be sounded by priests: "The priestly sons of Aaron, moreover, shall blow the trumpets; and this shall be a perpetual statute throughout your generations" (Numbers 10:8).

We who are called by Yeshua are, "A chosen people, a royal priesthood, a holy nation, a people belonging to God, that you may declare the praises of him who called you out of darkness into his wonderful light" (1 Peter 2:9).

We are called to be like the priests of old who bore the stones of the twelve tribes on their breastplate. We must be a nation who feels we are not properly dressed unless all twelve tribes are present. The restoration of the twelve tribes must always be on our hearts. This is especially true of those who feel they are of tribe of Levi.

The Days of Elijah

Messiah is soon to return, and many are singing a popular song that tells of us entering into the "Days of Elijah." For it is written, "Behold, I am going to send you Elijah the prophet before the coming of the great and terrible day of the LORD" (Malachi 4:5).

In these latter-days, in the spirit of Elijah, we are to announce the return of our Messiah, Yeshua. He will then finish His assignment of ushering in a millennial, double-portion, seventh-day Sabbath rest for His followers (Luke 4:16-21; Isaiah 61:2-7).

In this vein, we liken Elijah's day to the sixth day and to the appointed time to gather the double portion. For Israel was told that on the day *prior* to the Sabbath, they were to gather *twice* as much manna (Exodus 16:22-29).

We also see that Elijah gave a firstborn double portion to Elisha,[145] and, having come in the spirit of Elijah, John the Baptist prophesied about the coming Firstborn One, Yeshua (Mark 1:4-11). Furthermore, Isaiah said the Messiah would give us a double portion (Luke 4:17-21; Isaiah 61:7). For we are His people, His "congregation of the firstborn" (Hebrews 12:23).

These are truly exciting times. But be warned: When the spirit of Elijah comes, so does the spirit of Jezebel...

Jezebel and the Great Day of Jezreel

Jezebel saw the God-given field of another and wanted it. She was even willing to kill for it (1 Kings 21). Those controlled by this spirit, man or woman, likewise see the fruit of others and want it for themselves. To obtain it, like Jezebel, they spread lies in order to steal, kill, or destroy the rightful owner of the field.

Jezebel wanted the field of "Naboth the Jezreelite." His

---

145 See 2 Kings 2:9: This probably refers to the law respecting the firstborn, who had a double portion of the property of his father. Elisha may have considered himself as the firstborn of Elijah, so he requested a double portion of his spiritual influence (Num 27:20 Deu 21:17 Zec 9:12 12:8 1Tim 5:17).

name might be said to mean "*fruitful returning one.*" Naboth is plural for *fruit*, and Jezreel refers to Ephraim's scattering and eventual *return* to sonship (Hosea 1:4,5; 2:22).[146] The Father calls His regathering of all the tribes of Israel, the *great day of Jezreel:* "The sons of Judah and the sons of Israel will be gathered together, And...**great will be the day of Jezreel**" (Hosea 1:11).

We are moving into a great day, but beware, because Jezebel sought to *steal and control* the fruit of the "Jezreelite." And this same controlling, prophet-hating, destructive spirit is remarkably active in these last days.

As stated in Revelation, Jezebel's reward is a bed of sickness. And those who commit adultery with her, those who encourage *thievery of the God-given giftings of others, through slander,* experience great tribulation—unless they repent (Revelation 2:20-22).

In Hebrew such slander is called *lashan hara—the evil tongue.* Slander, which is to ruin (kill) the reputation of another through falsehoods, is related to the sin of murder.

Let us not be a people who look for opportunity to steal the divinely-given fruit of others. Instead let us be a people who look for the fruit of repentance within ourselves.

A Saving Sound

The Father is restoring His fallen nation. He is calling forth His mighty army. Those from both houses who hear His voice must sound an alarm so we can be saved from our enemies. "When you go to war in your land against the adversary who attacks you, then you shall sound an alarm with the trumpets, that you may be remembered before YHVH your God, and be saved from your enemies" (Numbers 10:9).

Exciting and difficult times are upon us. In these days our enemies may even be "those of our own households" (Matthew 10:35). For if ever there were a message that could divide a household, it is the message of the restoration of both Ephraim and Judah.

---

146 *Strong's* # H5022 and H3157.

The two houses have been enemies in many ways and for many years. Each thinks their truth opposes the other. But this is not true. Each has been given charge over a truth and these truths do not oppose one another. They actually complement each other. Our disputes arise from errant interpretations by both houses. And so restoring the breach will be a difficult task. It is a task that can only be accomplished in the power of the Ruach HaKodesh.

But if we do not respond to the call, who will?

Rest assured, Israel's two olive tree witnesses *will* respond to His call. They will bring forth their fresh, golden oil. And it will be done as the Father says: "'Not by might nor by power, but by My Spirit,' says YHVH of hosts" (Zechariah 4:1-14; Revelation 11:4).

Our Reunited House Will Stand

Time is short, and while we are able, we *must* sound our united trumpet voices!

Let us determine that we will not be fearful in battle. Let us instead recall the truth that just as a house divided cannot stand, so a reunited Judah and Ephraim will be able to stand in power against the enemy (Luke 11:17; Obadiah 1:18; Zechariah 9:13; 1 Samuel 17:45; Isaiah 11:13-14.).

Let us make our unified voices heard. For, "when both [trumpets] are blown, all the congregation shall gather themselves to you at the doorway of the tent of meeting" (Numbers 10:3).

Now is the time to gather *all* Israel. For only if she stands together will she stand at all.

Sinless Israel

Our Father says of the destruction of Babylon: *"At that time...the sons of Israel will come, both they and the sons of Judah as well; they will go along weeping as they go, and it will be YHVH their God they will seek. They will ask for the way to Zion [The City of Truth], turning their faces in its direction; they will come that they may join themselves to YHVH in an everlasting covenant that will not be forgotten. In those days and at that time... search will be made for the iniquity of Israel, but there will be none; and for the sins of Judah, but they will not be found"* (Jeremiah 50:4-5,20).

Those who hear the sound of Yom Teruah are especially blessed: "How blessed are the people who know the joyful sound! O YHVH, they walk in the light of Your countenance [presence]" (Psalm 89:15,16). The *Tanakh* states this verse as: "Happy is the people who know the joyful shout." The *Revised Standard Version* calls this sound "the festal shout." And the *Amplified Bible* expands it to: "Blessed—happy, fortunate [to be envied]—are those who know the joyful sound [understand and appreciate the spiritual blessings symbolized by the feasts]."

The word translated *joyful sound,* or *festal shout,* is *teruah,* and *Brown-Driver-Briggs* defines the word as alarm, signal, sound of tempest, shout, war-cry, battle-cry, and a shout of joy.[147]

The sound of the Teruah Trumpets is a joyful sound that will cause us to be remembered by our Heavenly Father, they even bring us into His Holy Presence. "In the day of your gladness and in your appointed feasts, and on the first days of your months, you shall blow the trumpets over your burnt offerings, and over the sacrifices of your peace offerings; and they shall be as a reminder of you before your God. I am YHVH your God" (Numbers 10:10).

Let all Israel unite!
Let us proclaim the saving sound of Yom Teruah!

---

147 *BDB,* word #H8643.

Ten Rich Days

The final feast of Trumpets that occurs prior to Messiah Yeshua's return will once more mark the beginning of a ten day period.

It will begin a ten day period like no other.

In Hebrew, *ten* is *'eser*. Like the English number ten, it speaks of an accumulation of digits (such as "seven-teen"). This word comes from the same root as *'ashar*, which means to accumulate, or to make *rich*.[148]

Concerning riches, the apostle Paul foretold a day when Judah would no longer be blinded to the Messiah: "Now if their transgression is riches for the world and their failure is **riches** for the Gentiles, how much more will their fulfillment be" (Romans 11:12).

Israel's full restoration marks the beginning of a time of great richness. It is a richness of our Father's power and presence. For He said that one day, "*A fountain will be opened for the house of David and for the inhabitants of Jerusalem, for sin and for impurity....In that day...I will cut off the names of the idols from the land...and I will also remove the prophets and the unclean spirit from the land.*

---

148 *Strong's* s # H6235 and 6237 respectively.

And it will come about...that two parts in it will be cut off and perish; but the third will be left in it. And I will bring the third part through the fire, refine them as silver is refined, and test them as gold is tested. They will call on My name, And I will answer them; I will say, 'They are My people,' And they will say, 'YHVH is my God.' Behold, a day is coming for YHVH when the spoil taken from you will be divided among you" (Zechariah 13:1-14:1).

Riches will soon be poured out on reunited Israel. However...

Ten Days and Those Who Would Oppress

The phrase "ten days," is mentioned ten times in Scripture. We see it in Daniel's request that he and his friends be tested for ten days: "Test your servants for *ten days...*" he asked (Daniel 1:12-14).

Yeshua also used this phrase when He addressed the *ekklesia* of Smyrna: "Do not fear what you are about to suffer. Behold, the devil is about to cast some of you into prison, so that you will be tested, and you will have tribulation for *ten days*. Be faithful until death, and I will give you the crown of life" (Revelation 2:10).

Similarly, the Messiah said, "To the angel of the church in Smyrna write: The first and the last, who was dead, and has come to life, says this: 'I know your tribulation and your poverty (but you are rich), and the blasphemy by those who say they are Jews and are not, but are a synagogue of Satan'" (Revelation 2:8,9).

Those having their riches restored will have to battle some who claim to be "Jews," but in truth are of Satan himself (see Philippians 3:3). Therefore, in this hour we must watch for Roman *as well as* Babylonian snares, and for those who tout their errant teachings.

Exactly what is being depicted in these ten days of testing may not as yet be understood. However, this much we do know: Daniel and his friends passed the test, and were given knowledge and understanding that surpassed that of those around them (Daniel 1:17-20).

Moreover, Daniel was told to seal up his revealing "book until the end of time; [when] many will go back and forth, and knowledge will increase" (Daniel 12:4).

In the end, godly knowledge will again be increased in the Father's people, and they will perhaps again be tested for ten days.

A "Different" Feast

Yom Teruah is a feast that is set apart. It is *different* from the other feasts.

The Father said, "Speak unto the children of Israel, saying, In the seventh month, in the first day of the month, shall ye have a sabbath, a memorial of blowing of trumpets, an holy convocation..... And in the seventh month, on the first day of the month, ye shall have an holy convocation; ye shall do no servile work: it is a day of blowing the trumpets unto you" (Leviticus 23:23-25; Numbers 29:1, KJV).

Yom Teruah is the *only* feast that fell on the *first* of the month. It fell during the time of the *dark*, or first sliver of the new moon. All other feasts fell in the middle of the month, during the time of the *full* moon when it was *light*. In this way, Israel could celebrate in light. Such timing would be important to people who did not yet have the benefit of electricity. By the light of the moon they could travel to and from the feasts, and they could see in the evenings, so as to delight in the Lord of all Creation. But Yom Teruah was different. It fell on the first of the month on a moonless night, at a time when it was dark.

What does this signify?

Yom Teruah is not an agricultural feast. It is a Sabbath, a holy time, yet it speaks of *darkness.* Moreover, there is a day of judgment, or darkness, that is destined to come upon the rebels of this earth (Zephaniah 1:15; Acts 2:20). It is a time of darkness for the wicked, but those who have the Light of the world living in their hearts will have abundant light. Like our forefathers who lived through a

(margin handwritten note: Zikroòn)

dark night in Egypt, yet had light in Goshen, so we too will have the Father's light, protection, and provision.

Just as they had to live through ten days of judgment on the wicked, so we too may have to live through ten similar dark days (John 8:12; Exodus 8:22; 9:26; 10:23).

Receiving the Fathers's "Seal"

During this feast, we are instructed to have a *memorial*, a *zikroòn*, a time of *remembrance*. *Zikroòn* comes from *zaòkar*, which means to *mark*, so as to be recognized.[149]

With the ears of the Spirit we hear that we are to be *marked*, so as to be remembered on Yom Teruah.

John the apostle, while on Patmos, told of an angel who was "ascending from the rising of the sun, having the seal of the living God." John said this angel cried out with a loud voice to the angels to whom it was granted to harm the earth and the sea, "Do not harm the earth or the sea or the trees until we have sealed the bond-servants of our God on their foreheads."

(margin handwritten note: 144,000) John also said he heard the number of those who were sealed, "One hundred and forty-four thousand sealed from every tribe of the sons of Israel" (Revelation 7:2-4).

Yom Teruah is about marking, or sealing, the chosen of Israel, that they might be remembered, noted, and set apart from that which is about to come upon the earth.

In the Book of Ezekiel the prophet tells of a man clothed in linen who had a writing case at his loins. Ezekiel said YHVH told the man to, "Go through the midst of the city, even through the midst of Jerusalem, and put a mark on the foreheads of the men who sigh and groan over all the abominations which are being committed in its midst" (Ezekiel 9:3-4).

The above "mark" is the Hebrew letter *tav*, which symbolizes a signature, a mark, or an imprint.

According to the *Ryrie Study Bible* by Parsons Technology, in ancient Israel this last letter of the Hebrew

---

149 *Strong's* and *BDB word* #'s H2146 and 2142 respectively.

alphabet was written "like a cross." [150]

Those so marked would be spared.

Is this the mark that will be placed on the 144,000 during the tribulation period? (Revelation 7:3-4).

Some believe Israel's saving mark is the "sign" of the Sabbath, because the Father gave this perpetual sign, or distinguishing mark, to them: "You shall surely observe My sabbaths; for this is a sign between Me and you throughout your generations, that you may know that I am YHVH who sanctifies you" (Exodus 31:13; Ezekiel 20:12).

Many "signs" have been given by our Father. He gave the mark of Cain, that he might not be slain. He gave us His rainbow in the clouds, and the blood of the lamb on Passover doors. Both are signs that save us from disaster, plague and pestilence (Genesis 4:15; 9:13; Exodus 12:13). He has also given us the wisdom of His Torah, which reminds that with a powerful hand He brought us out of Egypt (Exodus 13:9). The sign of honoring Torah should be with us in all that we do and think (Exodus 13:16). In addition, we are given the sign of the virgin who gave birth to Immanuel (Isaiah 7:14). In this sign, in *Yeshua*, we have protection at all times (Hebrews 13:5-6).

Whatever the sign, we who are alive at that time want to be indelibly marked with it.

The Cloud is Moving...

Yom Teruah begins a time when Israelites are called to make peace with their brothers. It is decidedly a time for Ephraim and Judah to come together peacefully, but not at the price of compromising truth.

It is time for all Israel, both houses, to reexamine what has been presented to us as truth. To do so we must dig down to the *original* foundation. Both houses must stop building on faulty foundations.

It is time for the reunited camp of Israel to set out, to

---

150 *Strong's* #'s 8420; 8427.

move forward. As priests of the Most High God, we must encourage our Israelite brothers, we must call out to them even as did our forefathers when they were in the wilderness:

> *"It is time for the camps to set out!*
> *The cloud is moving and we must move with it!"*

Ten Days of Prayer

Speak to the sons of Israel, saying, "In the seventh month on the first of the month you shall have a rest, a reminder by blowing of trumpets, a holy convocation" (Leviticus 23:24).

Trumpets played an important part in ancient Israel. There were 120 trumpets sounded at the dedication of Solomon's Temple (2 Chronicles5).

How do we honor the feast of Yom Teruah?

When the people of Ezra's time celebrated this feast, Ezra read the Torah before the public assembly.

Having the Father's law written on our hearts by His Spirit is the very heart of His New Covenant promise to us. And we truly need to *reread* that law at this time in history. We need to hear the Father's Torah commands with the ears of the Sprit. Like our forefathers of old, we too need to weep and come to a place of true repentance and restoration (Nehemiah 7:73-8:2; Jeremiah 31:31-33; Hebrews 8:8-10).

Each year at the annual Messianic Israel Alliance Conferences, which occur just prior to Yom Teruah, we have honored this prophetic feast. First we read out loud from Numbers 10:1-10, just as Ezra read from the Torah. Then we have representatives of both Judah and Ephraim blow two 42 inch silver trumpets. With a clarion call we proclaim: *"Let the twin voices of Ephraim and Judah be heard in this place!"*

We also honor this feast in our congregations, and it is a stirring sight to behold. Something very precious in the spirit takes place when both the houses of Israel are properly honored, when they speak in unison.

Silver trumpets are available on the Internet.[151] If you cannot afford silver trumpets, go to a store that specializes in Christmas ornaments, buy an inexpensive pair of brass-plated trumpets, then spray paint them in a silver color.

At your celebration, have two men dressed in white read aloud Psalms 93-100, which are believed to have been composed especially for the feast of Trumpets.[152]

In Jewish tradition, Psalm 47 is read aloud seven times.

"O clap your hands, all ye people; shout unto God with the voice of triumph. For YHVH most high is terrible; he is a great King over all the earth. He shall subdue the people under us, and the nations under our feet. He shall choose our inheritance for us, the excellency of Jacob whom he loved. Selah. God is gone up with a shout, YHVH with the sound of a trumpet. Sing praises to God, sing praises: sing praises unto our King, sing praises" (Psalms 47:1-6).

Warring for Our Inheritance

It is exceedingly important that during this time we sound our united voices in prayer and intercession for all Israel, because it is a restored Israel who must sound the alarm for war against whatever would try to hinder the plans of the Holy One of Israel for these last days. We must war for our promised Land (Isaiah 11:13-14).

To do this, we need to realize that just as our forefathers were in bondage in Egypt, so we too are in bondage. We will only be freed from that bondage when we have a deep desire

---

151 See www.mim.net/marketplace.
152 *His Glory Revealed*, John Hagee, Nashville: Thomas Nelson Publishers, 1999, p 106.

for deliverance.

"Now it came about in the course of those many days that the king of Egypt died. And the sons of Israel sighed because of the bondage, and they cried out; and their cry for help because of their bondage rose up to YHVH. So YHVH heard their groaning, and He remembered His covenant with Abraham, Isaac, and Jacob. YHVH saw the sons of Israel, and He took notice of them" (Exodus 2:23-25).

We must *first* cry out for deliverance from the Egypt that binds us, then the Father will take notice and redeem us.

Ten Days of Prayer

In honor of the Ten Days of Awe, and because we believe in the Father's reunion plan for both the houses of Israel (Isaiah 11:13), we suggest the following "Ten Days of Prayer."

- ♦ **Day 1:** Pray that all Israel might come to true repentance, that they might be saved. Pray that they would put away all of their idols and be granted a new heart and a new spirit, that they might live and not die (Isa 30:15; Ezek 18:31-32). Pray that salvation in Yeshua will come to all Israel (Gen 48:19; Rom 11:25,26; Eph 4:15; Mat 1:21). Pray that the veil will be lifted from the eyes of both the houses of Israel so they will see the truth of Yeshua and cease to stumble over Him (Isa 8:14; Rom 11:25; John 2:22). Pray that as the "Standard," Yeshua be lifted up in all His glory and that the world may see Him in truth and not according to manmade religion (Isa 11:12).
- ♦ **Day 2:** Pray that Israel will see the truth about the "*melo hagoyim*" promised to Ephraim, and that the "fullness of Gentiles" will come into their fullness, or maturity. Pray that Ephraim will cease to be jealous of Judah, whether that jealousy is acted out in violence or in wishing they were Jewish. Pray that

Ephraim will make Judah jealous rather than being jealous of Judah, which causes Ephraim to lose his effectiveness (Rom 9:25,26; 10:19; 11:11; Hos 1:9,0; 2:23). Pray that Ephraim will learn to judge with righteous judgment, and that in their desire to be reunited with Judah they will not trade errant Christian ways for errant Jewish ways (Isa 11:13; Jer 31:21-25; John 7:24).

♦ **Day 3:** Pray that all whom the Father has chosen to "instruct" Ephraim in this time will arise, and that Ephraim will come to repentance and be "ashamed for the deeds of her youth" (Jer 31:18-19). Pray that she cease to be "like a silly dove without sense" and move beyond the "elementary things" and press on, to maturity (Hos 7:11; Heb 6:1-17). Pray that Ephraim repents of following man's commands and instead accepts Messiah's yoke of Torah (Hosea 4:6; 5:11-6:3). Pray that Ephraim will fulfill her divine mandate, which is to walk in a way that honors Torah and thus provokes Judah to want what she has (Romans 11).

♦ **Day 4:** Pray that all the sheep of Israel would be delivered from wicked shepherds who muddy the waters and feed themselves rather than the flock. Pray that the sheep be snatched out of the hands of shepherds who divide the flock of Israel. Pray that all wolves in sheep's clothing and all false prophets be exposed for who they are in truth (Ezek 34; Jer 23:1-3; Mat 7:15). Pray that the spirit of Jezebel be rooted out from among us and that Israel's prophets would not fear her; pray instead that the spirit of Elijah might be fully released on our day. Pray that the hearts of the fathers might be turned to their children and the hearts of the children to their fathers. Pray for godly families to be raised up in both the houses of Israel (1 Ki 21: Hos 1:4-5; 2:22; Rev 2:20-22; Mal 4:5-6).

♦ **Day 5:** Pray for the safety and well-being of those of Judah who have returned to the Promised Land; pray their hearts will be turned toward their fathers and that angels will be given charge over them (Isa 11:11; Luke 1:17; Psa 91:11). Pray that even as the Father has gathered for a "second time" the "dispersed of Judah," He will "restore their fortunes." Pray that the Father possess Judah as His portion in the holy land, and will again choose Jerusalem. Pray that He enter into judgment with those who "harass" Judah and Jerusalem (Isa 11:11-13; Joel 3:1-2; Zec 2:12).

♦ **Day 6:** Pray that the Father will use the tragic events of our time to bring His people to repentance and faith in Him through the shed blood of Messiah Yeshua (Obad 1:12; Jer 5:12-14; Luke 13:1-5). Pray that wisdom and discernment will be granted to those who have been granted influence over the nation of Israel in spiritual, political, and financial arenas (Dan 2:21; 4:32; 5:21; Rom 13:1). Pray that they realize that Ephraim is their brother, and that the only true answers are found in the gospel, in the sacrificial Lamb, and in He who paid the price for our sins (1 Cor 7:23; Mat 27:9).

♦ **Day 7:** Pray that the hearts of Ephraim and Judah might be circumcised with a love for each other. Pray that each will learn to give credit where it is due, and that each will learn to objectively see the role they have played as part of the people of Israel: Ephraim in declaring salvation through Messiah, who is the Living Torah; and Judah in declaring the feasts and the truths of the written Torah (Gen 48:19; Acts 1:8; Rom 4:15; 2 Chr 11:4; Ezek 37:15-28).

♦ **Day 8:** Pray that both houses quickly understand the Father's plan to have a pure, overcoming army, and that they give themselves fully to becoming that great army (Isa 11:11-14; 27:6-9; Zech 8:3,7,13;

9:13; 10:7-10; Hos 11:10; Obad 1:18; Jer 50:4,5,20; 3:14-18; Ezek 37:22-26). Pray that "the sons of Israel come, both they and the sons of Judah" and that they "go along weeping" in a true search for their God; pray they turn their faces toward Zion and truly be joined in covenant with Him (Jer 50:4-5; Hos 5:14-15). Pray that Ephraim would once again "be like a mighty man, with their heart glad as if from wine," and that "their children see it and be glad" and that "their heart rejoice in YHVH" (Zec 10:7). Pray that all Israel will seek to pay the full price for their pardon, and that all their pagan practices and idols will be made like "chalk stones," and so will be unable to stand (Isa 27:9). Pray that Israel's mighty ones will be equipped with the breath of the Spirit of the Most High (Ezekiel 37:10).

♦ Day 9: "Pray for the peace of Jerusalem, and that they who love her would prosper; that peace be within her walls and prosperity within her palaces" (Psa 122:6,7). Pray for Jerusalem to become the City of Truth, and to acknowledge Messiah Yeshua as her "King of Kings" (Psa 48:2; Zec 8:3; Mat 5:35; 23:37-39; Rev 17:14; 19:16).

♦ Day 10: Pray that the sons of Israel who are pursuing this work of the Kingdom will be strong and courageous. Pray that the spirit of Joshua and Caleb will be upon them, and that they will know that in the strength of the Holy One they will go in and possess the Land (Joshua 1:6-9,18; 10:25).

Yom HaKippurim

When the first ray of dawn crowned the horizon on the morning of Yom HaKippurim, a group of priests escorted Israel's high priest to the Temple laver. There he ceremonially washed himself ten times, and when dressed in gold trimmed garments, he stood before the altar of sacrifice. Gloriously arrayed, he had a golden diadem on his head, precious stones on his breastplate, and golden bells hanging from the hem of his robe of blue, purple and scarlet. In all his splendor, he offered the morning sacrifice for the faithful of Israel. With that sacrifice, His glory became blood spattered...

This picture of a Yom HaKippurim sacrifice during the time of Messiah, as painted by author John Hagee,[153] clearly depicts our Messiah. For Yeshua is royalty, and His blood sacrifice brought eternal redemption to all who would call upon His Name. He left Heaven itself, that He might pay the sacrificial price for our sins (Philippians 2:5-11).

Messiah Yeshua is the Apostle and High Priest of our confession. He entered a greater and more perfect Tabernacle. It is a Heavenly Tabernacle, not made with

---

153 *His Glory Revealed*, John Hagee, Thomas Nelson Publishers, Nashville, 1999, p 128.

mortal hands. The blood offered was His own precious blood and not that of mere goats and calves. With it He entered the holy place once for all, having obtained eternal redemption for us (Hebrews 3:1; 9:11-12; 1 Peter 1:18-19).

Yeshua's appearance in this Heavenly Temple as our High Priest tells of "the good things to come" (Hebrews 9:11).

Yom HaKippurim is both a day of blessing and a day of judgment. To those who need to fear Yeshua's coming (because all judgment has been given into His hand: John 5:22), it is a day of judgment. However, it is a blessed day for those who love Him and are covered by His blood.

The Removal of All Sin

Once the high priest of ancient Israel had offered the first sacrifice of Yom HaKippurim, he returned again to the golden laver, washed, and was dressed in white linen.[154] More sacrifices were made, and the priests cast lots to choose between two sacrificial goats. The one on which the lot fell was sacrificed on the altar, the other became the scapegoat, on which they laid all of Israel's sins, both *intentional and unintentional.*[155] This goat was then sent into the wilderness.

From this we see that on Yom HaKippurim (Day of the Coverings), *all* sin was covered, even sent away. As King David wrote: "As far as the east is from the west, so far has He removed our transgressions from us" (Psalm 103:12).

Both goats were sin offerings, one was slaughtered and one was taken away. Both depict Yeshua. He was both "cut off" from the land of the living, and He was taken outside the camp (Isaiah 53:4-9; Hebrews 13:11-12).

White Linen

On this day they had a special washing in preparation for the offerings (Leviticus 16:4,24). Aaron washed himself

---

154 *Ibid.*

155 Lev 4:2,13, 22,27; 5:15-18; 16:21; Num 15:24-31. See *Israel My Glory* magazine, "Yom Kippur" by Will Varner, Vol. 49, No. 4, Bellmawr, NJ, 1991.

and then he was dressed in white linen garments.

As priests of the Most High, we are to be washed with the water of the word, and we too are to be dressed in white linen. For it represents the righteous acts of the saints. [156]

Prayer and a Glorious Embrace

During this day of covering sacrifices, the high priest took the golden censer that was in the Temple and went behind the veil—he went into the Holy of Holies, there to stand in the presence of the Holy Ark of the Covenant and before the Mercy Seat.

This act depicts mediation through intercession. For it is prayer that will take us "behind the veil." It is in prayer that we find mercy. The smoke from the censer represents the prayers of our High Priest, Yeshua, who is ever interceding for us. It also tells of the prayers of the saints.[157]

On this golden Ark were seated two gold cherubim, each reaching out to the other. The *Shekinah* Glory of the Almighty dwelt in the midst of this embrace (Exodus 25:22). In its midst was found the Mercy Seat of the Holy One. The angelic embrace of these cherubim even served as a *covering* for the Mercy Seat.[158]

The *Shekinah Glory* will again be seen in the embrace of the two families of Israel (Jeremiah 33:24; 31:1). When Ephraim and Judah reach out and embrace each other in *mercy*, the greatness of the Glory of our God will truly begin to be revealed in the earth. Then we will know the final fulfillment of Yom HaKippurim.

Yom HaKippurim in Scripture

Yom Kippur means Day of Atonement. This day should

---

156 Psa 51:7; John 3:1-5; 15:3; 1 Cor 6:11; Eph 5:26-27; Titus 3:5; Heb 10:22; Rev 19:8,14.

157 Psa 141:2; Rom 8:34; 1 Tim 2:5; Heb 7:24-25; 9:4; 1 John 2:1; Rev 5:8; 8:1-5.

158 *Strong's* # H3727.

actually be called *Yom HaKippurim*, or "Day of the Coverings," because *coverings* is *plural*.[159] *Kippur* comes from *kaphar*, which means to cover, expiate, cancel, cleanse, forgive, pardon, to make reconciliation. This day is about Israel having her many sins, or *all* sins, covered, or pardoned, through the offering of sacrificial blood.

Leviticus 16 is entirely dedicated to the details of this sixth of the seven annual feasts. It also is mentioned in Leviticus 23:26-32 and 25:8-12.

Celebrated on Tishri 10, which corresponds to late September or early October, the feast of Yom HaKippurim is thought to be the most awesome day in the year. It is the supreme festival. It is often called simply, "The Great Day."

A Feast of Fasting

In Leviticus 23:32 we read: "It is to be a sabbath of complete rest to you, and you shall humble your souls; on the ninth of the month at evening, from evening until evening you shall keep your sabbath."

All work is forbidden on this day, it is a time to "humble your souls" (Leviticus 16:29-31). While a celebratory meal often is had *the day before*, just before Yom HaKippurim begins, most who honor this feast fast for twenty-four hours, from sunset to sunset.[160]

In Acts 27:9 this feast is called "the Fast." Fasting is an affliction of the flesh, and on this day, we are instructed to "humble our souls." *Humble* is translated from *'anah*, and means to abase, afflict, chasten.[161] Each of us should pray about what this should mean to us, because the Father said, "Any person who will not humble himself on this same day, he shall be cut off from his people" (Leviticus 23:29).

---

159 *Strong's* #'s 3725; 3722.

160 Fasting verses: Isa 58.Psa 35:13; 69:10; 109:24; Dan 9:3; Joel 2:12; Ezra 8:23; Neh 1:4; Mat 4:2; 9:14-15; Luke 2:37; Acts 13:2-3-4.

Some people avoid salt the day before Yom HaKippurim because it will make you thirsty the next day. Some use only a dry toothbrush on this day, so that the digestive system will not be activated in any way.

161 *Strong's* # H 6031.

Let us ask the Father how He would have us humble ourselves before Him. For He has sworn that in the end, after He has purged the world, He will leave among the people of Israel "a humble and lowly people" who take refuge in Him. He even says, "The remnant of Israel will do no wrong and tell no lies, nor will a deceitful tongue be found in their mouths..." (Zephaniah 3:12-13).

On Yom HaKippurim we are not to do "*any work*." For the Father says, "As for any person who does any work on this same day, that person I will destroy from among his people" (Leviticus 23:28-30).

The message in this day is that all of man's work is to cease. *All things end, they stop, on this most awesome day.* For this reason, many Messianic Believers anticipate that Messiah Yeshua will return to the earth on Yom Kippur.

Jewish Tradition

Destruction of the Temple in A.D. 70 brought an end to animal sacrifices, and with it changes in the way the Jewish people could observe this day. Its central focus had been its blood sacrifices, and Judah suddenly found itself without a sacrificial system. They were no longer covered by blood.[162]

Some customs that have begun over the ages include sacrificial prayers, avoiding washing oneself for pleasure and cohabitation, the wearing of leather shoes, anointing the body, and any pleasurable practices.

Many wear white on this holy day as a symbol of purity. The service in the synagogue begins at sundown with the *Kol Nidre* prayers (a Jewish service, in which all vows are cancelled), and it continues with much liturgy and prayer for forgiveness. Since those of Nineveh fasted and repented as a result of Jonah's preaching, the Book of Jonah is traditionally read at this time.

---

162 Those who followed the Messiah had, and His followers continue to have, an eternal Blood Sacrifice in and through Him.

Israel's Feasts and their Fullness

Repentance and Returning Tashlich and Teshuvah

The combined theme of Yom Teruah and Yom HaKippurim is that of repentance and returning. Therefore, in *the ten days prior to this day*, Jews are often seen gathered around a body of water, keeping a custom called *Tashlich*, in which pockets are symbolically emptied and stones (sins) are cast away into the water.[163] The tradition is based on Micah 7:19: "He will again have compassion on us; He will tread our iniquities under foot. Yes, You will cast [ve-tashlich][164] all their sins into the depths of the sea" (Micah 7:19).

Before one can return to the Father, one must repent, and repentance is the theme of Yom Teruah. Similarly, *teshuvah*, or returning, is an underlying theme of Yom HaKippurim. "Therefore the redeemed of YHVH shall return [shoov],[165] and come with singing unto Zion; and everlasting joy shall be upon their head: they shall obtain gladness and

---

163 Each stone cast represents a personal sin from which one wants to be delivered. See the *Jewish Book of Why*, Kolatch, p 233.

164 *Strong's* # H7993.

165 *Strong's* #H7725, "to turn back."

joy; and sorrow and mourning shall flee away" (Isaiah 51:11).

The Return of Faithless Israel

The Father told the prophet Jeremiah to, "Go and proclaim these words toward the north and say, 'Return, faithless Israel,' declares YHVH; 'I will not look upon you in anger. For I am gracious,' declares YHVH; 'I will not be angry forever'" (Jeremiah 3:12).

Ephraim lived in the *north* and was *faithless*, but on a coming Yom HaKippurim day, they will be fully returned to their land and to their God. In that day they will be both multiplied and blessed. For it is written that in the place where it is said to them, "'You are not My people,' it will be said to them, 'You are the sons of the living God'" (Jeremiah 3:6-12; Hosea 1:10).

Jubilee

Jubilee provides a picture of *atonement* as bringing freedom, restoration, and return.

The Father commanded that in the year of Jubilee, "Each of you shall return to his own property and each of you shall return to his family" (Leviticus 25:10).

Jubilee comes from *yabal*, meaning to flow (like a stream of water), to bring, carry, conduct, bear along.[166]

We who understand the Father's plan for His coming Jubilee need to help carry forth His divine plan. To do so, we must flow in *streams of living water.* As Yeshua said, "He who believes in Me, as the Scripture said, 'From his innermost being will flow rivers of living water'" John 7:38).

Most believe Yeshua will return *during a Jubilee year,* and the year of Jubilee begins on Yom HaKippurim.[167]

Surely Messiah Yeshua's return cannot be far from us. If so, the prospect that we will be part of the "Jubilee Generation" that will see His return should inspire us, for it

---

166 *Strong's* and *BDB* word #'s H3104 and 2986 respectively.

167 See *Restoring Israel's Kingdom,* by Angus Wootten, and *When Will The Messiah Return?* by John K. McKee both from Key of David Publishing.

signifies that we will have the honor of proclaiming freedom to our brethren!

The Roles of the Trumpets and the Shofar

Some claim that it is not clear from Scripture that the silver trumpets are to be used to announce Yom Teruah, but that the ram's horn, or shofar, instead should be used.

The rules for sounding, or blowing (teruah) before our feasts and sacrifices may appear to be shadowy, but since Yom Teruah falls on the first of the month and at the time of the new moon, we know for certain that two silver trumpets are to be blown on this particular day (Numbers 10:2,10).

"On the **first day** of the seventh month hold a sacred assembly and do no regular work. It is a day for you to sound the **trumpets**" (Numbers 29:1, KJV).

The word translated *trumpets*, is *teruah*. *Strong's* defines it as a "clangor of trumpets." *Brown-Driver-Briggs* calls it a "signal, shout, blast of war, alarm, or joy." The word comes from *roo-ah'*, which means to cry out in distress, joy, or triumph—or to give a war-cry, a battle alarm. [168]

Yom Teruah begins with the sound of the silver trumpets, but Jubilee begins with the blowing of the *shofar*. Every fifty years there is a Jubilee year, and it always begins on Yom HaKippurim; therefore, we assume that this feast also begins with the sound of the shofar.

Perhaps the shofar is to be used for these occasions because the focus of Yom HaKippurim and Jubilee is *not* on a declaration being made by confirming voices, but on the *finished work of the Sacrifice Lamb*.

It is appropriate that a *ram's horn* is used to begin Yom HaKippurim and the year of Jubilee. Its haunting sound heralds the time when the bond-servant is able to return to his land and his family. Its prophetic cry announces

---

168 *Strong's* and *BDB* #'s H8643; H7321.

Archeological renderings of these trumpets can be seen on the Arch of Titus, which commemorated the destruction of Jerusalem in A.D. 70 and on silver coins minted during the Simon bar Kochba revolt (A.D. 132-135). Recently like trumpets have been recreated by the Temple Institute in Jerusalem.

freedom, deliverance, and equality for all Israel.

It is written that we are to "sound a **ram's horn**[169] **abroad on the tenth day of the seventh month; on the day of atonement** you shall sound a horn all through your land."

This command is given in the midst of the instructions for commemorating, or announcing, the year of Jubilee: *"You are to count off seven sabbaths of years for yourself, seven times seven years, so that you have the time of the seven sabbaths of years, namely, forty-nine years. You shall then sound a ram's horn abroad on the tenth day of the seventh month; on the day of atonement you shall sound a horn all through your land. You shall thus consecrate the fiftieth year and proclaim a release through the land to all its inhabitants. It shall be a jubilee for you, and each of you shall return to his own property, and each of you shall return to his family"* (Leviticus 25:8-10).

The Sound of the Shofar

The sound of the shofar is distinct, it is even haunting. It is a sound that Judah has used exclusively to announce the feasts to their people.

After the destruction of the Temple, the rabbis debated about how to blow the shofar and how many times to blow it. They settled on three distinctive sounds that they named: the *tekiah*, a long, unwavering blast; the *shevarim*, three short, broken blasts; and the *teruah*, a nine-part staccato blast (reminiscent of the sound of sobbing).[170]

They also developed the following collective pattern for blowing the shofar:

- *Tekiah:* One long clear and consistent blast
- *Shevarim:* Three short, broken calls
- *Teruah:* Nine rapid, staccato notes of alarm
- *Tekiah Gedolah* (The Great Tekiah): One long clear and consistent blast held as long as possible

---

169 *Strong's* and *BDB* #H7782, *shofar.*

170 *The Shofar: From Genesis to Revelation*, Tony Fadely. Whole Loaf Worship Center. Cocoa, FL. 2001.

Though used extensively by the people of Judah to announce the feasts, the shofar is mentioned only four times in the Torah: three times it was sounded at Mount Sinai, and as noted, it is mentioned once in the instructions about announcing the year of Jubilee (Exodus 19:16,19; 20:18; Leviticus 25:9).[171]

However, the shofar is mentioned repeatedly in the Book of Joshua. There we see it used to emit a powerful divine sound that caused walls to fall down flat (Joshua 6:4-20).

When Will Yeshua Return?

Will Yeshua return on Yom HaKippurim?

Author John K. McKee, in his forthcoming book, *When Will the Messiah Return?* explains that many post-tribulational prophecy teachers believe Yeshua will return on Yom Teruah, because they believe that a shofar is to be blown on that feast.

In rebuttal to this theory, McKee compares the way the Yom Teruah commands are rendered in the Hebrew Tenach versus the Greek Septuagint.[172] The Greek translators have so influenced Christian theologians in their handling of New Covenant passages about the Messiah's Second Coming that they have often drawn wrong conclusions. McKee concludes that Numbers 10:2,10 instructs us to use the *silver trumpets* of Yom Teruah, not the shofar.

McKee further argues that Messiah Yeshua probably will return on Yom HaKippurim. He gives several reasons: Yeshua's return marks the beginning of a year of Jubilee, and a shofar is blown at that time. Moreover, there are several verses that speak of the shofar (Greek *salpigx:* σάλπιγξ) being sounded at the time of Messiah Yeshua's return (Matthew 24:29-31; 1 Corinthians 15:51-52; 1 Thessalonians 4:16-17; Zechariah 9:14).

---

171 Shofar: BDB #H7782, horn, ram's horn, in the original sense of incising. Total occurrences, 72, translated as trumpet, 48x, trumpets, 20x, cornet, 3x.

172 Greek translation of the Hebrew Scriptures completed 200 years before Messiah's birth.

McKee states that Yom Kippur is a most solemn feast and that Yeshua's return will be a day of great *mourning* —especially for those who fear His judgement.[173]

"It will come about in that day that I will set about to destroy all the nations that come against Jerusalem. And I will pour out on the house of David and on the inhabitants of Jerusalem, the Spirit of grace and of supplication, so that they will look on Me whom they have pierced; and they will mourn for Him, as one mourns for an only son, and they will weep bitterly over Him, like the bitter weeping over a firstborn. In that day there will be great mourning in Jerusalem, like the mourning of Hadadrimmon in the plain of Megiddo" (Zechariah 12:9-11).

Looking On Him Whom We Pierced

The Apostle John mentions the above verse in relation to Yeshua's crucifixion. He says, "These things came to pass to fulfill the Scripture, 'Not a bone of Him shall be broken.' And again another Scripture says, **'They shall look on Him whom they pierced'**" (John 19:36-37).

From John's comment, we see that the Zechariah verse knew some fulfillment when Yeshua's followers looked on Him as He hung on a cross, dying, pierced for their own transgressions.

Even so, a day will come when each of us will meet the Messiah face to face. At that time we will look on His nail-scarred hands—knowing that our own personal sins helped produce those scars. On that day we will surely mourn.

Fire That Burns—
Fire That Brings Release

Concerning Messiah Yeshua's return, we must not look on it as a day from which we want to escape, or be

---

173 *When Will the Messiah Return?*, John K. McKee, Saint Cloud, FL: Key of David Publishing, Fall, 2002.

Coming judgement by Messiah Yeshua: See John 12:48; Heb 4:12; Rev 1:16; 2:16; 19:15,21.

"raptured." Instead, we must see the days prior to His return as an exciting time when we will experience the Father's protection and provision, a time when we will actually be used to help restore His Kingdom on earth.[174]

Just as the ancient flood waters drowned the many, those same waters buoyed up Noah and his family, ultimately carrying them to safety. Just as there was darkness in Egypt during the time of the Father's judgment, so there was light in Goshen. The cloud and fire that gave protection and guidance to the sons of Israel is the same cloud and fire that confounded the pursuing Egyptians. The fire that burned Nebuchadnezzer's mighty men also burned the bonds of Shadrach, Meshach, and Abednego.[175]

Saints of the Almighty are often called to go through fire. They are even to be "baptized with fire" (Luke 3:16-17). The Father's fire should be a welcome thing to those who love Him, as it purges the dross from us. However, His fire is a terror to those who do not know and love Him.

Entering into Jubilee

As previously noted, the Jubilee year begins on Yom HaKippurim, and it is believed that our Messiah's return will mark the beginning of a Jubilee.

Surely Yeshua described a time of Jubilee when He read from the scroll of Isaiah that day in Nazareth (Luke 4:16-21). When He stood up to read in the synagogue, He announced that He was the Anointed One (Messiah) spoken of by Isaiah the prophet: "The Spirit of YHVH is on me, because he has anointed me to preach good news to the poor. He has sent me to proclaim freedom for the prisoners and recovery of

---

174 Dan 7:18; Micah 4:8; Mat 6:10; 12:28.
Our Messiah's kingdom is not of this world, and it *must first be established in our own hearts* (2 Cor 10:5; John 18:36; Mat 7:3-5). His kingdom is now, and it is yet to come in its fullness: Exo 19:6; 2 Sam 7:12-16; Luke 1:32-33; Dan 7:22; Luke 12:32; Rev 5:9-10; 20:6:1 Peter 1:1; 2:5-10; Heb 1:3; 8:1; 3:6; 10:19.
175 *The Feasts of the Lord*, Robert Thompson, Medford, OR: Omega Publications, 1975, pp 138-139.

sight for the blind, to release the oppressed, to proclaim the year of YHVH's favor" (Luke 4:17-19).

Yeshua stopped reading before He reached the end of Isaiah's Messianic declaration because He knew He would return again to fulfill the remainder of Isaiah's prophecy.

Isaiah said a day would come when the Messiah would "Comfort all who mourn...giving them...the oil of gladness ....the mantle of praise....so they will be called....the priests of YHVH....Instead of shame they will have a double portion...they will shout for joy over their portion...they will possess a double portion in their land, everlasting joy will be theirs" (Isaiah 61:2-7).

In the coming eternal Jubilee year we will return to our promised land. At that time we will have freedom and restoration, we will have release and everlasting joy!

May We Be Counted Worthy...

Whenever our Messiah returns—whether on Yom HaKippurim or on any other day—the most important point for each of us must be that He finds us worthy to enter into His Eternal Jubilee.

Even so, come quickly, Lord Yeshua!

Tabernacles

Tabernacles is the seventh of the Father's feasts. It falls in the seventh month and lasts for seven days. Seven is the number of perfection and of completion. Thus, Tabernacles is thought to be *the feast of all feasts.*

Among its many names, this feast is called Tabernacles, Booths, *Sukkot,* and Ingathering (Leviticus 23:34,39; 1 Kings 8:2). It is also known as the "Season of Our Joy." This feast is so popular among the people that many simply call it "*The* Feast."

For ancient Israel, the much anticipated week-long celebration of Sukkot began on Tishri 15 after the fall fruit harvest. It was one of their three great pilgrimage festivals, called a *Shalosh Regalim* in Hebrew. After the somber times of Yom Teruah and Yom HaKippurim, this autumn feast, which came only five days later, was literally bursting with joy and was greeted with much celebration and rejoicing!

People came from far and wide for this convocation more than they did for any of the others, because the farming year was over and they could truly relax and enjoy the festival.

Israelites flocked to Jerusalem, bearing offerings of grains, fruits, oils, and animals. Happy travelers walked hot dusty roads, singing songs of ascent, as they made their way up to Jerusalem, up to the Sanctuary of their God: *"How lovely are Your dwelling places, O YHVH of hosts! My soul longed and even yearned for the courts of the YHVH; My heart and my flesh sing for joy to the living God....How blessed are those who dwell in Your house! They are ever praising You. How blessed is the man whose strength is in You, in whose heart are the highways to Zion! ....They go from strength to strength, every one of them appears before God in Zion" (Psalm 84:1-7).*

Such shouts of praises to the Holy One of Israel increased as great throngs of worshipers ascended the holy hill of Zion.

Temporary Sanctuaries

The people of ancient Jerusalem made tabernacles of leafy branches. These booths were built everywhere—against walls, buildings, in open courtyards, on rooftops, or anywhere there was room (Nehemiah 8:16).

The Father commanded that the Israelites celebrate this feast by dwelling in *sukkahs*, or booths, for seven days. He wanted them to remember that their ancestors had to dwell in booths made from tree branches after they left Egypt (Leviticus 23:41-43).

These temporary dwellings were open to the elements, which reminded Israel that the Almighty is their only true source of protection. Today they remind us of our wilderness sojourn on this earth, for our lives are temporary in these earthly bodies.

Tabernacles in Torah

Again YHVH spoke to Moses, saying, *"Speak to the sons of Israel, saying, 'On the fifteenth of this seventh month is the Feast of Booths for seven days to YHVH. 'On the first day is a holy convocation; you shall do no laborious work of any kind. For seven days you shall present an offering by fire to YHVH. On the eighth day you shall have a holy convocation and present an offering by fire to YHVH; it is an assembly. You shall do no laborious work. These are the appointed times of YHVH which you shall proclaim as holy convocations, to present offerings by fire to YHVH—burnt offerings and grain offerings, sacrifices and drink offerings, each day's matter on its own day—besides those of the sabbaths of YHVH, and besides your gifts and besides all your votive and freewill offerings, which you give to YHVH. On exactly the fifteenth day of the seventh month, when you have gathered in the crops of the land, you shall celebrate the feast of YHVH for seven days, with a rest on the first day and a rest on the eighth day. 'Now on the first day you shall take for yourselves the foliage of beautiful trees, palm branches and boughs of leafy trees and willows of the brook, and you shall rejoice before YHVH your God for seven days. You shall thus celebrate it as a feast to YHVH for seven days in the year. It shall be a perpetual statute throughout your generations; you shall celebrate it in the seventh month. You shall live in booths for seven days; all the native-born in Israel shall live in booths, so that your generations may know that I had the sons of Israel live in booths when I brought them out from the land of Egypt. I am YHVH your God....You shall celebrate the Feast of Weeks, that is, the first fruits of the wheat harvest, and the Feast of Ingathering at the turn of the year" (Leviticus 23:33-43; Exodus 34:22).*

Solomon, Ezra, and Tabernacles

King Solomon, son of David, built the first Temple and appropriately consecrated it on Sukkot, asking the Father to "dwell" among them. Surely this feast was chosen because it is a season of rejoicing, and there was great joy associated with that momentous event.

After Solomon's death the two houses of Israel were dispersed in two different directions. There was a difference of many years in their separate dispersions. Then, when some from Judah returned to the Land after their exile in Babylon, they came to repentance and began to honor the Father's set times—they then celebrated the feast of Tabernacles.

"They found written in the Torah how YHVH had commanded through Moses that the sons of Israel should live in booths during the feast of the seventh month. So they proclaimed and circulated a proclamation in all their cities and in Jerusalem, saying, 'Go out to the hills, and bring olive branches and wild olive branches, myrtle branches, palm branches and branches of other leafy trees, to make booths, as it is written.' So the people went out and brought them and made booths for themselves, each on his roof, and in their courts and in the courts of the house of God, and in the square at the Water Gate and in the square at the Gate of Ephraim. The entire assembly of those who had returned from the captivity made booths and lived in them. The sons of Israel had indeed not done so from the days of Joshua the son of Nun to that day. And there was great rejoicing. He read from the book of the law of God daily, from the first day to the last day. And they celebrated the feast seven days, and on the eighth day there was a solemn assembly according to the ordinance" (Nehemiah 8:14-18).

Zechariah and Tabernacles

This feast is sometimes called the "Feast of the Nations" because of what Zechariah prophesied about its restoration. However, we must remember that Zechariah wrote about the nations who *went up against* Jerusalem.

We want to be among those who return to the Feast of Booths because of our love for the Father's ways. We certainly do not want to be counted among those who went against His divine plan and were then forced to comply with this feast. That is what Zechariah's prophecy was about. "Then it will come about that any who are left of all the nations that went against Jerusalem will go up from year to year to worship the King, YHVH of hosts, and to celebrate the Feast of Booths" (Zechariah 14:16).

Ancient Traditions

Tabernacles is sometimes called the "Feast of Lights," in commemoration of the pillar of fire that led the people of Israel by night. It is also given this name because of an ancient tradition. Great festivities took place every night during this feast in the women's courtyard. Huge lighted golden menorahs were said to have shed enough light to illuminate every courtyard in Jerusalem. These menorahs had enormous wicks made of braided holy garments worn by the priests during the previous year.[176]

Levites played music on harps, lyres, cymbals and trumpets during this festive time. The Talmud says of this celebration, "He who has not seen the joy of the water-drawing celebration has never seen joy in his life." [177]

It was during this feast that Messiah Yeshua made His declaration, "*I AM the light of the world*" (John 9:5).

The Talmud described an ancient Tabernacles tradition called *Simchat Beit Hashoeivah*, the water-drawing celebration. This ceremonial event commemorated the drawing of water from the rock at Horeb (Exodus 17:1-7).

It was also a prayerful appeal for winter rains that would water the crops and provide for a plentiful spring harvest. Water was drawn from Jerusalem's chief spring, and with great ceremony a priest carried a large golden ewer from the Temple mount down to

---

176 Being blood-spattered would necessitate discarding such garments. See Rabbi Chaim Richman, www.lttn.org/R5_Article2_TemplePriestlyGarments.htm. Also see *His Glory Revealed*, John Hagee, Nashville: Thomas Nelson Publishers, 1999, pp 146-147; *The Temple* by Alfred Edersheim, Grand Rapids: Kregal Publications, 1997.

177 *In the Jewish Tradition, A Year of Food and Festivities*, Judith Fellner, Middle Village, NY: Jonathan David Publishers, 1995, pp 41-42.

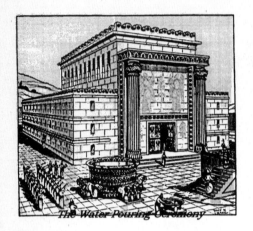

The Water Pouring Ceremony

the Pool of *Siloam*, which means *sent* (John 9:7). The priest drew water from the well, then ceremoniously returned to the Temple.

Jubilant worshipers lined the way as the priest paraded through the Water Gate, so named because of this ceremony. Crowds cheered and priests sounded the ceremonial silver trumpets.

The priest drew one jar of water for each day of the feast until the seventh day, when seven priests drew seven jars of water. During this ceremony palm branches were waved and silvery notes were played by the priests, and Psalms were recited.

As the water was poured out on the Temple altar, priests chanted the prophetic, yet little understood words of Isaiah: "Behold, God is my salvation, I will trust and not be afraid; For the LORD God[178] is my strength and song, and He has become my salvation. Therefore you will joyously draw water from the springs of salvation" (Isaiah 12:2-3).

Living Waters

Messiah Yeshua, the "Sent One," [179] He whose very name means Salvation, saw this inspiring ceremony many times throughout His lifetime. During this feast He made another revealing declaration to the sons of Israel.

The seventh day of this feast, is known as the "Hoshanah Rabbah (The Great Hosanna)." The name speaks of a request for mercy. It means, "Save us Now!"

---

178 Actually reads, "Yah YHVH." See *Strong's* #'s 3050; 3068.
179 Luke 4:43; John 3:34; 6:29; 8:42; 17:3.

It is taken from the Psalms: "O YHVH, do save, we beseech You..." (Psalms 118:25), and in ancient Israel, on the seventh day of Tabernacles, the people circled the altar seven times, and they repeated this cry seven times.

As they called out for salvation on this day during the water pouring ceremony, Yeshua, who is Salvation Himself, cried out, "If anyone is thirsty, let him come to Me and drink. He who believes in Me, as the Scripture said, 'From his innermost being will flow rivers of living water'" (John 7:37-38).[180]

This is not the only time Yeshua referred to Himself in this way. It is written in Isaiah, "I will pour out water on the thirsty land and streams on the dry ground; I will pour out My Spirit on your offspring and My blessing on your descendants" (Isaiah 44:3). When Yeshua told the Samaritan woman at the well about His "living water" He said to her, "Everyone who drinks of this water will thirst again; but whoever drinks of the water that I will give him shall never thirst; but the water that I will give him will become in him a well of water springing up to eternal life" (John 4:7-14).

Traditions of Today

Since the time of the Second Temple, Judah has celebrated this feast by waving something called the lulav and the etrog.

The etrog is about the size of a lemon but is not as sour. A lulav is created from palm, myrtle, and willow branches.

Together, these two elements are called the "four species." Use of these elements in this tradition is based on Leviticus 23:40:

"On the first day [of the feast] you shall take for yourselves the foliage of beautiful trees, palm branches and boughs of leafy trees and willows of the brook, and you shall rejoice before the Lord your God for seven days."

The lulav is traditionally held in the right hand and the

---

180 Note: YHVH Himself is the Living Water: Jer 2:13; 17:13.

citron in the left. They are then waved up and down in the four directions: north, south, east, and west, as Psalms 113-118 are recited.

Judaism has ascribed various meanings to this ritual. The four species are said to typify various things. One tradition says they symbolize the four patriarchs: Abraham, Isaac, Jacob, and Joseph, another says they represent the four Hebrew letters that make up the name of YHVH.

Probably the best known tradition shows them as symbolizing four classes of Jews. The fragrant and tasty citron is said to depict the Jew who knows Torah and does good deeds. The palm date has taste but no smell, and thus represents the Jew who knows Torah but does not do good deeds. The myrtle has aroma but no smell, and therefore symbolizes Jews who do good deeds but do not know Torah. The willow has neither taste nor smell, and stands for the Jew who neither knows Torah nor does good deeds.

Celebrating in the Sukkah

Jewish families try to eat as many meals as possible in their sukkahs during Sukkot. These picnic-type meals are meant to be relaxed and happy times of rejoicing.

Following the traditional blessing over the bread and wine, a special blessing is said for Sukkot:

"Blessed art Thou, O Lord our God, who has command-ed us to celebrate in the sukkah."

As it is with all the feasts, Sukkot is a time of giving. It is a time to bless those who are like priests to you, and to bless the widow, the orphan, and the stranger.

It is a Tabernacles tradition to invite others into your sukkah to share in the celebration. These relaxed gatherings provide an opportunity to share your faith, and to enjoy fellowship with others.

Building Materials and their Meaning

Leviticus 23:40 says of the sukkah: "On the first day

you are to take choice fruit from the trees, and palm fronds, leafy branches and poplars, and rejoice before the Lord your God for seven days" (NIV). "Ye shall take you on the first day the boughs of goodly trees, branches of palm trees, and the boughs of thick trees, and willows of the brook; and ye shall rejoice before the Lord your God seven days" (KJV).

The prophet Nehemiah tells us that the celebrants in ancient Israel, "proclaimed and circulated a proclamation in all their cities and in Jerusalem, saying, 'Go out to the hills, and bring olive branches and wild olive branches, myrtle branches, palm branches and branches of other leafy trees, to make booths, as it is written'" (Nehemiah 8:15, NIV).

The palm tree is said to symbolize victory, the willow, weeping, the myrtle, joy, and the olive branches, be they natural or wild, symbolize anointing and peace. [181] For a repentant and thus victorious Israel is to build anointed sukkahs of joy and peacefully dwell in them.

Decorating Our Sukkahs

Gather family and friends to help search for usable tree branches. As you build your sukkah, be sure that you can see the stars through the roof. Your sukkah does not have to be elaborate, but it does have to be fun! For it is written, "You shall rejoice before YHVH your God for seven days."

Let Sukkot be a wonderful family time. Regardless of how young or old your children may be you can involve them in the project.

This is an excellent time to explain your faith to your family. Little ones can draw special pictures and make construction paper chains to hang on sukkah walls with paper clips. You can also decorate the tabernacle with fruits and flowers and weave in twinkle lights on a string for evening outings. Put a small table in the center for mealtimes and decorate it with your favorite things.

For this special feast, gather your family and read the

---

181 The *Feasts of Israel* by Kevin J. Conner, Portland: City Bible Publishing, 1980, p 69.

Israel's Feasts and their Fullness

Scriptures pertaining to Tabernacles (Leviticus 23:33-43; Exodus 34:22; Nehemiah 8:18.). Have a group act out a water pouring ceremony. Wave your lulav and etrog, and give thanks to the wonderful God of Israel. Above all remember to celebrate and rejoice!

He Came To Tabernacle Among Us

Our God tabernacled among us in the days of old. His only begotten Son also came to tabernacle among us. It is written in the *Brit HaDoshah*, the New Covenant, that "the Word became flesh, and **dwelt** among us, and we saw His glory, glory as of the only begotten from the Father, full of grace and truth" (John 1:14).

The word "dwelt" is translated from the Greek *skenoo* (skay-no'-o), meaning to tent or encamp, to occupy or reside, just as our God encamped in the Tabernacle in the wilderness. This comes from a word that means "hut" or "temporary residence." It speaks figuratively of the human body being the *abode* of the spirit. In other words, dwelt, or *skenoo*, means to *tabernacle*. [182]

The living Word of God, Yeshua, became flesh and tabernacled among us, just as it was foretold in the Torah and the Prophets. The evidence is that He came to dwell among us on the feast of Tabernacles.

---

182 *Strong's* #'s G4637; 4636; 4633.

Evidence from the Gospels

- Tabernacles is especially known as the "Season of Our Joy." When the angels announced to the shepherds the birth of our Messiah, they said, "Do not be afraid; for behold, I bring you good news of great joy which will be for all the people" (Luke 2:10).
- According to Jewish tradition, a prayer was recited on the first day of the feast that says, "Glory to God in the Heavens and on the earth peace and good will towards the earth." [183] This clearly is similar to the passage in Luke that describes the angels proclaiming, "Glory to God in the highest, and on earth peace among men with whom He is pleased" (Luke 2:14).
- On the feast of Tabernacles devout Jews from all the nations were commanded to come to Jerusalem for the feast. The inns and dwelling places were over-crowded with multitudes. Since Bethlehem was so close to Jerusalem, it absorbed the overflow. As the Scripture says, "and she wrapped Him in cloths, and laid Him in a manger, **because there was no room for them in the inn**" (Luke 2:7).
- The Gospel accounts tell us that the shepherds were in the fields tending their flocks. However, shepherds do not tend flocks outside in the cold of a Bethlehem winter. Their flocks were brought in and were sheltered in caves during the winter months.
- Jewish tradition states that the sheep to be sacrificed at Tabernacles were kept in the fields for seven days and sacrificed on the eighth day. It is only on the Feast of Tabernacles that the flocks were commanded to stay out all night, the rest of the time the sheep were brought in at night. [184]

---

183 *Birth of the Messiah*, David Yaniv, Lynnwood, WA: New West Press, 1997. p. 10.

184 John Hagee, *His Glory Revealed*, Nashville: Thomas Nelson, 1999 p. 152.

Further Evidence for When He Came

We know from the Gospel accounts that Joseph and Mary went to Bethlehem because of the census. Historical records show that the Romans would generally conduct a census sometime between August and October. This was an ideal time because the crops had been harvested and the people were finished with their usual duties. They were free to celebrate the feast of Tabernacles, and many were already traveling. Shepherds were in the fields watching their birthing flocks.

The Book of Luke recounts the story of a priest named Zacharias who was ministering in the Temple, and who had a wife from the daughters of Aaron, named Elizabeth. Zechariah was "of the division of Abijah," and he was "performing his priestly service before God in the appointed order of his division." This order is outlined in 1 Chronicles 24:10. Thus, we know that Zechariah served in the Temple from approximately June 1 to June 8 (Luke 1:5-25).

An angel of God named Gabriel appeared to Zechariah and told him his wife would have a son. Although he and his wife were both very old, after his priestly service Elizabeth became pregnant. It can be calculated from this information that their son, John the Baptist, was born at Passover.

In Elizabeth's sixth month of pregnancy (Luke 1.36), the angel Gabriel told a virgin named Miriam that she would be the mother of the Messiah when the Holy spirit came upon her. This would have been in December, and then, nine months later, in September, she gave birth to a baby named Yeshua. Scriptural evidence shows that John was born at Passover, and Yeshua's birth six months later would have been around the time of Tabernacles.

That is why the Gospel of John tells us "the Word was made flesh and dwelt [tabernacled] among us" (John 1:14). Therefore, the Feast of Tabernacles fittingly symbolizes God dwelling among us as a man.

Born in Bethlehem

Luke tells us, *"It came about in those days that a decree went out from Caesar Augustus, that a census be taken of all the inhabited earth. This was the first census taken while Careens was governor of Syria. And all were proceeding to register for the census, everyone to his own city. And Joseph also went up from Galilee, from the city of Nazareth, to Judea, to the city of David, which is called Bethlehem, because he was of the house and family of David, in order to register, along with Mary, who was engaged to him, and was with child. And it came about that while they were there, the days were completed for her to give birth. And she gave birth to her firstborn son; and she wrapped Him in cloths, and laid Him in a manger, because there was no room for them in the inn. And in the same region there were some shepherds staying out in the fields, and keeping watch over their flock by night"* (Luke 2:1-8).

It is written of the city where our Messiah was born, "But as for you, Bethlehem Ephrathah, too little to be among the clans of Judah, from you One will go forth for Me to be ruler in Israel. His goings forth are from long ago, from the days of eternity" (Micah 5:2).

He whom Daniel calls the "Ancient of Days" and whom we call Yeshua, or Salvation, was born in Bethlehem.[185]

During the time of Messiah Yeshua's earthly sojourn, among the many who made their way up to Jerusalem for Sukkot, precious few realized that God Himself was tabernacling among them.

Evidence in the Skies—the Stars for a Sign

According to Genesis 1:14, the Father gave us the stars for a *sign*. This means that in their positioning there is a *pictorial* account of His *plan of salvation* for mankind.[186]

---

185 Dan 7:9,13,22; Mat 19:28; 25:31; Luke 1:32-33; Rev 1:13-14.

186 *The Witness of the Stars*, E. W. Bullinger, Grand Rapids: Kregal, 1981; *The Heavens Declare*, William D. Banks, Kickwood, MO: Impact Books, 1985.

We must not confuse this with astrology, which the Almighty says is an abomination to Him. [187]

For ages astronomers (not astrologers) have been proclaiming the gospel message through the signs pictured in the stars.

According to Jewish astronomical tradition, Messiah's appearance would occur in conjunction with the appearance of Jupiter and Saturn in the constellation Pisces, which was thought to be the constellation of God's people because it concurs with Abib, the month of redemption (Passover).

Saturn was associated with the Sabbath and signified the "Most High." Jupiter, the royal planet, was said to be the "Star of the Messiah." Jupiter's conjunction with Saturn was thought to symbolize the transfer of royal power from the Most High to his Messianic King, the One who would bring redemption to God's people.[188]

In the 1600's, the German astronomer Johannes Kepler suggested that Messiah was born in 7 B.C., and many agree that a remarkable conjunction of the planets Jupiter and Saturn took place in the constellation Pisces in the fall of that year.[189] However, Bob Wadsworth, Biblical astronomer, and author of the book, *A Voice Crying in the Heavens*, says:

"There were three conjunctions of these planets in 7 BC. A triple conjunction of Jupiter and Saturn occurs in Pisces about every 600 years which makes this a rare event. Following this triple conjunction in 7 BC was an even rarer event which was the massing of Jupiter, Mars, and Saturn in Pisces in late February 6 BC. The massing of these three planets in Pisces occurs about every 800 years, on the average. These were four events in a series of many celestial events which occurred between 7 BC and 2 BC marking the

---

187 Gen 40:8; Duet 13:1-11; 17:2-5; 18:10-14; 1Sam 15:23; Dan 1:20; 2:28; Isa 8:19,20; 47:13,14; 65:11,12; Ezek 13:3-9; Amos 5:26.

188 See *NIVSB* Study Notes, Matt 2:1-2; *The Witness of the Stars*, by E.W. Bullinger, Grand Rapids: Kregal, 1981, p 39; *The Star of David* by Batya Wootten, Saint Cloud, FL: Key of David, 2002.

189 Star of Bethlehem, *The Interpreters Dictionary of the Bible, Supplementary Volume*, Nashville: Abingdon, 1976, p 842.

season of the birth of Messiah." [190]

Most astronomers agree that Yeshua was born during this approximate time frame, and that the massing of these planets would have presented a brilliant spectacle in the night sky, one that would not have gone unheeded.

Perhaps the brilliance was from more than a collection of stars. Perhaps it was...

The Shekinah Glory—
God Dwelling with His People

The brilliance in the sky at the time of Yeshua's birth was probably the Shekinah glory of God. The word "Shekinah" means that which dwells. It indicates the presence of YHVH's Glory. It expresses His nearness to His people.[191] The Shekinah led the people of Israel in the wilderness. It symbolized His presence in the Tabernacle, which had not been seen since the destruction of Soloman's temple, yet now it was present again for the people of Israel. It led the magi to Yeshua, and it announced to all Israel that the Holy One was now present in their Messiah!

Once more the Holy One of Israel had come to tabernacle among His people.

His Star—A Guiding Light

At the birth of Yeshua a brilliant star lit the night sky. "Now after Yeshua was born in Bethlehem of Judea in the days of Herod the king, behold, magi from the east arrived in Jerusalem, saying, 'Where is He who has been born King of the Jews? For we saw His star in the east, and have come to worship Him'" (Matthew 2:1-2).

These wise men were probably from Persia, or Chaldea (Babylon), where knowledge of the stars was a deeply rooted

---

190 *A Voice Crying in the Heavens* (second edition), Bob Wadsworth, Biblical Astronomy, Oregon City, OR. 1997. www.atlbible.org/astronomy.htm

191 See "Shekinah," *Interpreters Dictionary of the Bible, Volume 4*, Nashville: Abingdon, 1976, pp 317-319; also see Exo 16:10; 24:16-17; 33:22; 40:34.

science. Some scholars suggest they may have been Jewish rabbis who were still living in Babylon, and who studied the Torah and knew the Messiah was coming. Others say they may have been proselytes.[192]

Regardless of their identity, they surely learned the "Gospel of the Stars" from Daniel, who was the *rab-mag,* or chief of the magi in Babylon (Daniel 2:48; 5:11). Though Daniel was sent to Babylon, he was nevertheless a prophet of Israel, and he had foretold the timing of the coming of the Messiah in his writings (Daniel 9:24-27).

The magi would have eagerly looked for the birth of the Jewish King. First, because they were awaiting the coming Messiah, and second, because it was their duty to elect the King of the realm. They would have readily accepted a Jewish King, as their history was studded with Jewish nobles. Since the Shekinah glory had guided the people of Israel in the desert, the magi would have had no difficulty believing that this same glory was guiding them to the Messianic King.

The magi probably followed this star for two years, because it is written that Herod, "slew all the male children who were in Bethlehem and in all its environs, from **two years old and under,** according to the time which he had ascertained from the magi" (Matthew 2:16).

The Glory of Israel—A Light to the Nations

When Mary and Joseph presented the baby Yeshua in the Temple to complete the custom of the Law, Simon, a righteous man, prophesied that He was: "A light of revelation to the Gentiles, and the glory of Thy people Israel" (Luke 2:32).

After a night of darkness, the morning star appears and begins to drive away darkness. Darkness is symbolic of sin and light is symbolic of YHVH's glory, of knowledge, and understanding. Gentiles were pagans, heathens, people

---

192 See "Magi," *Zondervan Pictorial Encyclopedia of the Bible,* 5 Volumes, Grand Rapids: Zondervan, 1976, pp 33-34.

without light. Thus, they were considered "foreign" to the God of Israel. However, through the Father's mercy and grace, the light of Israel's Star was about to shine upon them. Soon they too could know the Messiah of Israel.

Dwelling Among Us

Sukkot depicts Yeshua's first appearing as a babe in Bethlehem, and it points us toward His return and reign as the King of Kings and Lord of Lords.

If we are to celebrate His birth, then it must be celebrated at this time. For Sukkot is all about the Holy One dwelling, or tabernacling, with His people.

The Roots of Christmas

For untold decades on the Julian calendar of Rome, December 25 was known as a day of obscene revelry. To oversimplify the pagan beliefs of the day, it was generally believed that a woman called the Great Mother, or the Queen of Heaven, also known as Ishtar, Isis, Astarte, Ashtoreth, Venus, Dianna, Semeramis, Cybelle, and Rhea—was found with a consort. He was known as Baal, Molech, Milcom, and various other names, and she, or they, had a child (the consort was sometimes reborn as her child). This child was variously named Zoroaster, Tammuz, Tamus, Osiris, Bacchus, Deoius, and so on, and was called the undefeated sun-god, a title given to him after his supposed meritorious death and reincarnation.[193] The birth of this son, this false god of paganism, was celebrated with pagan revelry on December 25, the day of the ancient winter solstice.

How did Christianity come to celebrate the birth of Jesus Christ on this same day? Is it possible that the Early Christians created *their* version of this holiday so they could *avoid* participating in these pagan celebrations?

---

193 Verses that mention false gods: 1Ki 11:5,33; 16:33; 18:19; 2Ki 21:3-7; 23:4-7,13,15; 1 Sam 7:4; 31:10; 2Chr 33:7; Judg 2:13; 6:25-30; Jer 7:18; 44:17-28; Ezek 8:14; Acts 19:29.

For centuries before the birth of Messiah, the last week of December was a time of idolatrous festivals. It was the time of the winter solstice, the day when the sun is farthest south in the sky and when the days are the shortest. (On the present Gregorian calendar the day of the winter solstice is December 21 or 22).

Boisterous Roman celebrations were held at this time. But because the Christians were outlaws in Rome and forbidden to worship, they used these times as a disguise for their own rites. History indicates there were pagan customs of gift-giving and decorating of doorways with evergreens. These customs were incorporated by the Christians and a form of Christmas was born.

A form of Christmas may have been born on this day, but was Yeshua born on this day?

Time to be Taxed

Joseph and Mary had to return to his hometown to be taxed, so Yeshua was born in Bethlehem (Luke 2:4).

The question is, *when* did they go there and *when* was He born?

As previously noted, the shepherds spoken of in Scripture would not have been out in the fields at night with their flocks in the dead of winter (Luke 2:8). December is the cold and rainy season of *Eretz Yisrael*.[194] Yeshua even said of this season, "Pray that your flight be not in **winter**" (Matthew 24:20).

However, shepherds would have been in the fields tending their many flocks destined for sacrifice during the milder month of Tishri when Sukkot occurs.

Winter was not a good time for travel. Additionally, during the time of Sukkot the agricultural people of Israel had finished their yearly harvests and would have had more money than in the winter. The Roman governors knew this and timed their taxation accordingly.

---

194 *Eretz Yisrael* means Land of Israel.

So how did it happen? How did Christians come to celebrate the birth of the Savior on December 25?

The Son of God—The Sun of Righteousness

The apostle Paul declared the Good News to those living in pagan Rome. Many accepted Yeshua as their Messiah and were circumcised of heart by His Holy Spirit. However, unless these converts were first circumcised in the flesh they were not welcome in the Jewish synagogues. When the Jewish leadership rejected the non-Jews over this and other issues, the non-Jews responded with anti-Jewish actions. It was their *rejection* that caused their angry reaction, and it continues to be a common problem in much of the Body of Messiah today.

Persecuted by mighty Rome and rejected by the Jewish leaders of their day, it appears that the Roman Christians made use of the pagan holiday in which the false sun god was worshiped—they instead worshiped the *Son of God*.

Like Judah did when in Babylon, these Early Believers lived in a land in which an unredeemed majority ruled.[195]

Can it be that this is how compromise slowly crept into the Church? Like the people of Judah with their celebration of Rosh HaShanah, did the Roman Christians also begin to weave and twirl, attempting to embroider a richer fabric of renewal? Did they slowly borrow and try to transform traditions? [196] Did they take a crown from the sun god and place it on the head of the Son of God? In the end, did they, like Judah, create a holiday that was tainted by heathenism, this time by a pagan *Roman* tradition?

A Day that Marks an Increase in "Light"

While we do *not* want to try to justify errant traditions, we nonetheless must ask, did the Father especially use the

---

195 We do not mean to imply that these Believers fully understood the Jewish Messiah, nor that they did not err in their decisions, for history proves other wise.

196 See "Yom Teruah," chapter 25, "Babylon and the New Year."

winter solstice to mark a certain preplanned event?

It is a scientific fact that the winter solstice marks the end of the shortening winter days and the lengthening winter nights. This day marks the end of the increase in darkness, and the beginning of an *increase in light*.

Malachi speaks of the "sun of righteousness [that] will rise with healing in its wings" (vs 4:2). Could it be that this Messianic prophecy refers to a time when, *with the rising of the sun*, comes the beginning of healing of the Father's people? Does this verse refer to the time of Messiah Yeshua's conception? Was Yeshua conceived at the exact point in time when light overtook darkness?

It would certainly be an appropriate moment for His conception to occur. It would even be a poetic moment.

Hanukkah: Festival of Lights

Some associate Yeshua's conception with the Jewish festival of Hanukkah, which was a post-Torah event that occurred over a hundred years before Yeshua's birth.

Hanukkah means dedication. It is an eight-day festival that commemorates Judah's victory over the Syrian tyrant, Antiochus, who had shown his contempt for the God of Israel by sacrificing a pig on the altar of the temple after he defeated Jerusalem in 165 B.C. He also put to death any Jewish people who dared to observe the Laws of Torah.

Judah Maccabee, son of the Hasmonean priest Mattathias, led a revolt against this heathen oppression. He led an outnumbered and unskilled guerilla army to a decided victory over superior Syrian forces. Then, upon entering Jerusalem, he cleansed and rededicated the Temple.

When the Maccabees gained control of the desecrated Temple, they found only one undefiled cruse of oil with which they could light the Temple menorah. According to tradition, that one day supply of oil lasted a full eight days, thus keeping the menorah lit while allowing them time to consecrate more oil (Exodus 31:11).

Called "the Festival of Lights," this special occasion is commemorated on the twenty-fifth day of the winter month of Kislev. Today, Jewish people light the lamps on a specially created eight or nine branched candelabra, called a *hanukkia* (plural: *hanukkiot*).[197] These lamps are lit by the ninth light, called the *shammas* (helper, servant).

On the first night of Hanukkah, the shammas is lit and it is used to light one light. The second night the shammas is lit and used to light two lights, and so on until, on the eighth night, all the lights plus the shammas are lit.

Lighting the Hanukkia

According to *The Encyclopedia of Jewish Symbols*, "In Israel today, Hanukkah has become a symbol of national liberation and the triumphant Jewish spirit." [198]

The victory of the Maccabees is an event that is worthy of honor. However, the Father allowed the Temple, once cleansed by the Maccabees, to ultimately be completely destroyed, and He allowed the people to again be scattered.

But before that scattering, He sent them a Temple that needed no cleansing. He sent Messiah Yeshua.[199]

Again, some people associate Yeshua's conception with Hanukkah, which occurs frequently at the time of the winter solstice. Biblical Astronomer Bob Wadsworth believes Yeshua was conceived in 4 BC. In that year, if the end of the 29th day of the 8th month had been hazy or cloudy

---

197 Note: The Temple menorah had *seven* branches, not eight or nine. The nine branched hanukkia was created much later as the hunakkah tradition grew.

198 *The Encyclopedia of Jewish Symbols*, Ellen Frankel and Betsy Platkin Teutsch, Northvale, NJ: Jason Aronson Inc., 1992.

199 See Isaiah 8:14; John 2:19-22.

enough so that the first crescent of the new moon was not seen visually from Jerusalem, then by default, the month of Kislev would have begun a day later, and the eighth day of Hanukkah would have occurred on the same day as the winter solstice.

Human Gestation

The period of human gestation takes approximately 280 days, or about nine months. If we count forward nine months from the winter solstice, we come to the time of Tabernacles, to the time when Scripture tells us that the Son of God came to *dwell*, to tabernacle, among men.

We also note that in the Eastern mind, the day of one's conception is regarded as their "birthday." Since Messiah Yeshua was born in the Middle East, perhaps this tradition played a small part in the decision of some people who began to celebrate his birth around the winter solstice.

Rising of the Light

Yeshua is called "the Dayspring from on high," and "the morning star...[that] arises in our hearts" (Luke 1:78; 2 Peter 1:19). These verses define Yeshua in terms of a *rising of light.* Did His conception occur at the time of the greatest light of Hanukkah—at the moment of the rising of the first star after the longest of dark nights? Certainly it occurred at some moment in time, and the world was in the darkness of sin. Then came "The glory of Israel," He who is "a light of revelation to the nations" (Luke 2:32).

Prior to Messiah Yeshua's return, some things simply will not be settled among men. The exact timing of Yeshua's conception falls in that category. We must realize this and not be legalistic about such issues. Therefore, our ideas about the timing of Yeshua's birth are put forth as suggestions for consideration. Moreover, as we try to reunite the two houses of Israel, we would do well to be aware of the tactics of the enemy...

An Original Counterfeit?

A counterfeiter can never create a real dollar bill. If his bill were an *original design*, it would be different from the real dollar bill and he could not deceive people with it. The motivation of a counterfeiter is to deceive. The way they do it is to copy an original. Therefore, the appearance of a counterfeit indicates that an original exists.

The ideas of a "day of judgment" and "a resurrected Son of God who redeems the people," are thoughts that originated with the Almighty, and were copied by Satan himself, the chief counterfeiter. His counterfeit copies can even appear first, since he knows the plans of YHVH. Thus, we can have a counterfeit "Babylonian day of judgment," [200] and a counterfeit pagan "sun-god," who supposedly redeems.

We must consider this when we speak of these things. We should be careful in our criticisms. When we share our understanding of the Father's feasts, if we appear to be judgmental, condescending, critical, or self-righteous toward others—we will only add to the problem.

Judah is correct, even as their traditions teach, there is a "day of judgment" and there is a "Book of Life." And we all should want to have our names written in it.[201]

We also must realize that the conception and birth of the Messiah of Israel are events that changed the entire world. The birth of Messiah Yeshua is an event that is surely worthy of recognition. However, if we choose to recognize it, let us do so at the proper time.

Equal Weights and Measures

Should we celebrate Messiah Yeshua's birth?

If we do as some, and say that celebration of His birth is "not commanded in Scripture," then we must use the same standard for Hanukkah, because we are commanded

---

200 See chapter 25, *Yom Teruah*, "Rosh HaShanah—The Jewish New Year."
201 Luke 22:30; John 5:22; 5:24,27,30; 12:47-48; 16:8; Acts 17:31; Rev 20:4; 20:12-13.

to use equal weights and measures. [202] And celebration of Hanukkah likewise is not commanded in Scripture.

Yeshua's birth is given far more mention in Scripture than is the one time that we read of Hanukkah: "At that time the Feast of the Dedication took place at Jerusalem; it was winter, and Yeshua was walking in the temple in the portico of Solomon" (John 10:22-23).

For the sake of those who would say that Hanukkah is more important, or more scriptural, than is a celebration of the birth of the Messiah, we say: The Father is very careful about the words used in Scripture, and this verse does not indicate that Yeshua was "participating" in this event. It says He was "walking" around in "Solomon's Porch."

Yeshua may have had reservations about lifting up this celebration because He knew that He was the true "Temple" (Isaiah 8:14; John 2:19-22), and that the Jerusalem Temple being honored was destined to be destroyed. He even said: *"O Jerusalem, Jerusalem, the city that kills the prophets and stones those sent to her! How often I wanted to gather your children together, just as a hen gathers her brood under her wings, and you would not have it! Behold, your house is left to you desolate; and I say to you, you will not see Me until the time comes when you say, 'Blessed is He who comes in the name of the Lord!'" (Luke 13:3435).*

Wise Men Were Rejoicing

When we read in Scripture of Messiah Yeshua's conception and birth, we see that angels, shepherds, and wise men were rejoicing—at the appropriate time.

Both Hanukkah and the winter solstice can be said to represent Yeshua's time of *conception*. But since Yeshua is a Temple that needs no cleansing, between Hanukkah's feast of Lights, and the point in time when light overtakes darkness, the latter better represents who He is to us. It is the more pure of the two symbolisms.

---

202 Deu 25:13-16; Pro 20:10.

When was Yeshua born?

It would be out of character for He who so poignantly fulfilled the Passover-related feasts, to come to dwell among men at any time other than the feast of Tabernacles. Moreover, to celebrate His birth on December 25 is to celebrate based on the traditions of men, and Yeshua clearly spoke *against* the traditions of men (Mark 7:8,13).

Even if we assume that Yeshua was *conceived* around this time, we would not want to participate in the crass commercialization connected with this day. Nor can our conclusions about Yeshua's conception be construed as an endorsement of the cult of Santa Claus, the all-knowing one who gives rewards to good little children.

Telling Tales to Little Israelites

The fable of Santa Claus and his reindeer is not true. Neither is it true that a tooth fairy takes the lost teeth of little people and leaves money in their place. Nor is the tale true that an Easter Bunny lays eggs and leaves baskets of goodies for little children. Most importantly, we are told to "lay aside falsehood," and to "speak truth each one to his neighbor" (Ephesians 4:25).

These are not innocent little fables. The tales told about an all-knowing Santa Claus rob children of the ability to focus on an all-knowing Yeshua, the one who truly loves the little children. When we lift up an Easter Bunny that brings candy, we detract from a Savior who was lifted up on a cross, that He might offer the sweetness of life eternal.

We must not tell our children these lies. We must tell them that some people like to "pretend" that these things are so, but that they are not true.

Let us instead tell our little ones about the Messiah of Israel. Then we will not cause them to stumble, and we will not have to repent for leading them away from the truth. And perhaps, just perhaps, if we tell them the truth when they are little Israelites, they will be more likely to believe us when they are big Israelites.

A Source of Shame

Commemorating the feasts serves as a sign that we belong to the God of Israel, yet for many centuries most Believers have failed to honor them. Though the truth of the feasts is clearly contained in Scripture, most previously blinded shepherds have not taught them to their hungry flocks. Instead, as partially blinded shepherds,[203] they have emphasized a celebration centered on Santa Claus' bag of toys and Easter's basket of goodies. They have missed the true joy of celebrating the feasts of the God of Israel.

To many Believers, these errant celebrations are a source of shame. Furthermore, if they try to tell their families they prefer not to participate in these traditions, then reproach and disdain are often heaped on the one who wants to return to the feasts.

Despite the great price that often has to be paid, numerous Believers are now forsaking worldly celebrations and choosing to follow a new, yet ancient pathway. However, as we make this transition, each of us must ask a difficult question: *How do we behave toward the loved ones we leave behind?*

Ministering to Those Who Do Not Yet See

Some people describe Christian holidays and traditions as "pagan celebrations," but such statements can be very offensive to those who still celebrate these traditions. This is especially so if the person truly is a Believer in the Messiah, but is misinformed about these issues.

Although it is true that many "Christian" traditions are rooted in paganism, we must be careful how we express ourselves. The Father will hold us accountable for injuries to others if we cause them to stumble because we are hardhearted in our appraisal and in our words.

Yeshua will require an accounting of all careless words. He warned us: "I tell you that every careless word that

---

203 Gen 48:19; Isa 8:14; Rom 11:25.

people speak, they shall give an accounting for it in the day of judgment" (Matthew 12:36).

We must hold fast to the truth and yet be merciful to those who are still blinded. Nonetheless, decorating trees to celebrate the Messiah's birth obviously gives detractors ammunition to fire at the beguiled.

Concerning decorated trees, Jeremiah warned:

"Hear ye the word which YHVH speaks to you, O house of Israel: Thus saith YHVH, Learn not the way of the heathen....For the customs of the people are vain: for one cutteth a tree out of the forest, the work of the hands of the workman, with the ax. They deck it with silver and with gold; they fasten it with nails and with hammers, that it move not" (Jeremiah 10:1-4, KJV).

An elementary investigation of the customs of Christmas reveals roots that do not bring honor to the Holy One. But if we allow ourselves to be among those who speak against these things without mercy, we will not bring about a change, and may even cause further divisions.

We must remember that the Father is always looking on the thoughts and intents of a man's heart. He knows exactly *why* an individual is celebrating Christmas, and He also knows *why* someone is being critical of that celebration.

If the Holy One is going to use us to bring change to others, then we must try to hear the heart intent of those around us. When correcting error, we must remember that we have all received mercy and grace, and without compromising the truth, we in turn must sow seeds of mercy and grace to those who do not yet understand (James 2:13).

Sukkot and The Shekhinah

Messiah Yeshua fulfilled Sukkot in yet another way. The event is often overlooked because it has not been generally viewed from a Hebraic perspective. Yet when we see with Hebraic eyes we are inspired with new understanding about the Shekhinah Glory and the meaning of Sukkot.

The following is excerpted from an article written by friends, Toby and Shannon Janicki. The article, called "Sukkot, The Shekhinah, and Yeshua," appeared in the Messianic Israel Herald Magazine.[204]

In Leviticus 23 we read of the *mo'edim*, the appointed times of Yahveh. These are times when He desires to meet personally with the children of Israel to celebrate and focus on certain themes. In verses 39-43 we read of Sukkot (also see 1 Kings 8:2; Ezekiel 45:25).

When we look at Yeshua's life we see that He indeed celebrated Sukkot and made the required pilgrimage to the Temple in Jerusalem. Much has been written about John

---

204 Volume 2, Issue 3.
Toby and Shannon Janicki live in Loveland, Colorado, where they lead the Messianic Israel congregation, Kehilat Y'shua.

7:37-39 and Yeshua's role at the "Rejoicing of the Water Pouring" ceremony. Also we learn of the great menorahs that would have been present on the eighth day of the feast, *Shemini Atseret*, and of Yeshua's declaration, "I am the light of the world!" (John 8:12). But there is another story in the Gospels that probably took place around the time of Sukkot. It is the story of Yeshua's transfiguration.

We find this story in all of the synoptic Gospels (Matthew 17:1-8; Mark 9:2-8; Luke 9:28-36). Yeshua and his three closest disciples, Simon Peter, John, and James went up on a high mountain where Yeshua was "transfigured." Then Moses and Elijah appeared. And seemingly out of the blue, Peter, stumbling for words, suggested building *booths* for all three of them. Then a voice was heard from heaven and as quickly as it all began, the transfiguration ended.

What were Moses and Elijah doing there and why did Yeshua tell them afterwards to mention this episode to no one? What does it mean that Yeshua was "transfigured," and why did Shimon wish to build "booths"?

The answers tie into the theme of Sukkot.

First, let us address the Transfiguration. The Greek word used here is *metamorphoo*, which means to change into another form.

What form did Yeshua change into?

The passage tells us that "His face shone like the sun" and "His garment became white as light." The idea that "His face shone like the sun is expressed in Inter-Testimental literature in a Hebrew phrase *ziv haShekinah*. In other words, Yeshua's face was like the *Shekinah* glory of Yahveh. That His garments were "white as light" is more imagery of the reflection of glory of Yahveh upon Yeshua. He became visible as the Shekhinah.

The word *Shekinah* is a post biblical word derived from the Hebrew verb *shekhan*, to *dwell* (Exodus 25:8). This word is used when Yahveh describes the purpose for the building of the Tabernacle. In fact the word for *tabernacle* in Hebrew is *mishkan*, which derives again from the Hebrew word *shekhan*, meaning to dwell. The word Shekinah became the word used to describe Yahveh's visible presence on earth. For example in Exodus 24:16, we read of the "Presence of Yahveh" resting on the Mountain. In Exodus 13:21-22 we read of the "pillar of cloud" and "pillar of fire" that guided the Israelites out of Egypt. Both are examples of the Shekhinah, the visible presence of Yahveh on earth. While no man could see the face of Yahveh and live (Exodus 33:20), one could see His Shekhinah.

What better way to describe Yeshua on earth than with the word Shekhinah? In John 1:14 we read, "the Word was made flesh and dwelt among us." This is reminiscent of the language of Exodus 25:8, where Yahveh says He wishes to dwell among us. How does He accomplish this? Through His Shekhinah, through Yeshua.

We read of "a bright cloud" that overshadowed the disciples on the mount of Transfiguration. This cloud is reminiscent of the cloud mentioned in Exodus 13:21-22, the cloud that led the Israelites through the wilderness—the Shekhinah.

The Greek word used for *overshadowed*, is *episkiazo*. It is sometimes used in the Septuagint to translate the Hebrew word Shekhan, to cover or overshadow (Exodus 40:35). Again this is imagery of the wilderness journey where Yahveh's visible presence was seen in the cloud and the pillar of fire leading and protecting them in the wilderness. It is a perfect example of the Shekhinah.

Before we answer the question about the "booths," we ask: What does the Shekhinah specifically have to do with Sukkot?

One of the major themes of Sukkot is that Yahveh provided for the Israelites in the wilderness and kept them safe. In Leviticus 23:42 we are told to build/dwell in a sukkah (booth) for seven days. Being out in the sukkah reminds us of being in the wilderness forty years and having Yahveh provide for us. But not only did the Israelites have just the physical booths to protect them, more importantly, they had the cloud of glory, the Shekinah to protect them. The famous commentator, Rashi, speaking on Leviticus 23:43, says he believes the booths spoken of here by Yahveh were actually the "Clouds of Glory."

The Millennial Kingdom also is spoken of in the context of Sukkot. During that time all the nations shall go up to Jerusalem to celebrate Sukkot (Zechariah 14:16-19). There is also a promise in the prophets that the sukkah/booth of the "Clouds of Glory" that protected the Israelites in the wilderness will appear to protect and keep Israel once again.

"And Yahveh will create upon every dwelling place of mount Zion, and upon her assembly, a cloud and smoke by day and the shining of a flaming fire by night for upon all the glory shall be a covering. And there shall be a Tabernacle (sukkah) for a shadow in the daytime from the heat, and for a cover from storm and rain" (Isaiah 4:5-6).

This is the same cloud that was there in the wilderness. Yeshua is that cloud, the Shekinah glory of Yahveh that will protect us in days to come.

The idea of Yeshua appearing as the Shekinah, the visible presence of Yahveh, fits perfectly into the theme of Sukkot. He dwelt among us and still does as we carry the theme of Sukkot with us all year round. The festivals are a time when we learn certain concepts to carry with us year round. Each year, because as humans we are prone to forget, we learn these concepts over again. Sukkot is a time to focus on the dwelling of Yahveh among us and in us.

Why was Yeshua transfigured?

To show His most intimate disciples that he indeed was Yahveh in the flesh, to show them that He was indeed the Shekhinah glory that was seen in the Torah.

Our second question is, why did this make Peter want to build booths?

The word for *booths* in Greek is *skene*. It is used at times in the Septuagint to translate the Hebrew word *sukkah*, booth. Peter was most likely so overwhelmed by seeing the Shekhinah glory that the first thing that came to mind was Sukkot, and the role that the Shekhinah plays in it. So he suggested building the booths, which is the primary act of Sukkot. This event probably took place around the time of Sukkot and so we see Yeshua fulfilling yet another aspect of the feasts of Israel.

Sukkot is a wonderful time of rejoicing and celebrating. It is a time to head outdoors when most of the world is going indoors. It is a time to focus on Yahveh/Yeshua and His presence among us.

As we celebrate this feast, let us keep in mind the thought of Yahveh's Shekhinah dwelling among us and the promise that a "Shekhinah sukkah" will appear again in the end of days.

The Eighth Day

*O*n the first day of Tabernacles you shall have a
*holy convocation and do no laborious work. For
seven days you shall present an offering by fire to YHVH.
On the eighth day you shall have a holy convocation and
present an offering by fire to YHVH; it is an assembly. You
shall do no laborious work (see Leviticus 23:35-36).*

The *Eighth Day* of Tabernacles, or *Shemini Atzeret*, both
is and is not connected to Tabernacles.

We say this because the seven days of Sukkot speak of
the perfect Messianic Age, and the Eighth Day speaks of
eternity—it foretells the Father's invitation for Israel to
remain in that state with Him for an eternity. The
Messianic Age is a definitive period of time, but *Shemini
Atzeret* represents a Day that is "beyond time." [205]

In Hebrew, the word for eight, or *shemini*, comes from
shemoneh, which indicates the idea of *plumpness*, as if it is
a surplus above the "perfect" seven. [206]

The perfect Millennial Kingdom will be rounded out with
the fullness of the Eighth Day, when the new Jerusalem

---

205 From a personal letter from Rabbi Mordechai Silver dated 6/27/02.
Thanks to Rabbi Silver for clarifying several points in this chapter.
206 *Strong's* #'s H8066; 8083; 8082.

comes down, and the Father will forevermore dwell among us (Revelation 3:12; 21:2; 1 Corinthians 15:24-28).

Orthodox Jews view *Shemini Atzeret* as a separate feast, because the command to dwell in the sukkah and to wave the four species was for the first seven days (Leviticus 23:40-42). However, its scriptural name, "the Eighth Day" connects it to Tabernacles, for we have only *seven* days in our weeks and no eighth day. To be an "eighth" day it must be connected to the other seven days. Thus our statement, "The *Eighth Day* of Tabernacles, or *Shemini Atzeret*, both is and is not connected to Tabernacles."

Celebrating the Torah

In Israel, groups of men who have gathered from all over the world can be found in the park dressed in colorful native costumes and dancing with their beloved Torah. To them Torah is a liberating yoke, comprised of fetters of freedom. Their unfettered dance is an encouraging sight to behold.

Judaism has divided the Torah, and most of the words of the prophets, into weekly "portions," called "*parasha*," (plural: *parashot*) so that everyone is reading and discussing the same group of texts at the same time. [207] On the Eighth Day of Sukkot, the last parasha of Deuteronomy and the first portion of Genesis are read. In this way, they are never "finished" with the Torah. This event is celebrated in a ceremony called *Simchat Torah, Rejoicing in the Torah*. Beloved Torah scrolls are joyously carried around in ceremonious procession. (Some Jews in the Diaspora celebrate *Simchat Torah* on the following day.)

Eighth Day Circumcision

There are many commands concerning the "eighth day" in Scripture. For example, it was the custom to circumcise children on the eighth day of their lives (Leviticus 12:3). And we read about Messiah Yeshua, "On the eighth day, when it was time to circumcise him, he was named Yeshua,

---

[207] See <mim.net.torahportions>.

the name the angel had given him before he had been conceived" (Luke 2:21, NIV). Yeshua's parents performed everything according to the Father's Law. Even as were the Patriarchs, John the Baptist, and Paul the apostle, Messiah Yeshua too was circumcised on the eighth day (Acts 7:8; Luke 2:27,39; 1:59; Philippians 3:5).

Assuming Yeshua was born on the first day of Tabernacles, then "the eighth day" mentioned above is "The Eighth Day," the final day of the feast of Tabernacles.

Eighth Day Hallmarks

Concerning the eighth day, we are told that:

♦ Oxen and sheep had to be with their mothers for seven days, and on the *eighth day* they could be offered to the Holy One (Exodus 22:30; Leviticus 22:27).

♦ In this example we see that the seven days that culminate in an "eighth day" presentation represent a time of nurturing.

♦ Altars were dedicated on the eighth day.

♦ Priests had to be consecrated for seven days, because they were unfit to minister before being presented on the eighth day.

♦ All creatures, for the most part, were considered as in a state of uncleanness and imperfection for seven days, and were perfected on the eighth.

♦ Lepers and lambs alike were presented on this day.[208]

The Ancient Water Pouring Ceremony

The Eighth Day of Sukkot was to be a Sabbath day of joyous convocation and fewer sacrifices were offered (Leviticus 23:36,39; Numbers 29:35). Little is said about this day. However, we do know that it was *preceded* by the extraordinary water pouring ceremony from the pool of Siloam.

---

208 Exo 12:2,3; 14:8-10; 15:13,14; 22:27; Lev 8:33; 14:10,23; 15:14,29; 22:27; Num 6:9-10; 2 Chr 7:9; 29:17; Eze 43:26,27; Mat 28:1.

They poured this water mixed with wine on the sacrifice as it lay on the altar. One might say that this poured out water and wine washed away the stain of sin.

This ceremony was done with such expression of joy that it became a common proverb, "He that never saw the rejoicing of drawing of water, never saw rejoicing." The custom was based on Isaiah 12:3: "With joy shall ye draw water out of the wells of salvation."

On this day Yeshua stood and cried out, saying, "If any man thirst, let him come unto me, and drink: he that believeth on me, as the Scripture saith, out of his belly shall flow rivers of living water" (John 7:37-38:).

Yeshua cried out in this way that He might call the people up to a higher realm. He was calling them to seek His spiritual and eternal refreshment (Leviticus 23:36; Revelation 7:9-17). He was calling for holy altars of sacrifice, for true consecration on the part of His priesthood, that we might be presented to the Holy One, and that we might be fit to offer Him sacrifices of praise.

When we are truly consecrated, then we are accepted (Ezekiel 43:27). That is what Tabernacles must mean to those who wish to see the Kingdom of our Messiah restored. That is what it must mean to those who truly want to enter into its glorious and final Eighth Day.

Crying Out

Just as our Messiah cried out, so we must lift up our voices in the square and cry out in the gates. Though we may feel like a voice in the wilderness, we must nonetheless call out, "Ho! Every one who thirsts, come to the waters; and you who have no money come, buy and eat. Come, buy wine and milk without money and without cost" (Proverbs 1:20; 8:3; Isaiah 40:6; 55:1).

We also must speak out against hypocrisy and declare the truth. "Cry loudly, do not hold back; raise your voice like a trumpet, and declare to My people their transgression and to the house of Jacob their sins" (Isaiah 58:1).

Yes, the Eighth day of Tabernacles is coming! It is a day of great rejoicing, but if we desire to be ministering priests on that day, we must first be consecrated.

The Coming Heavenly Water

There is coming a "water pouring ceremony" that will be greater than anything man has ever seen. For our High Priest, Messiah Yeshua, promises a river of living water that is without cost (Revelation 7:17; 21:6; 22:17).

Ezekiel saw a coming Tabernacles-type "river of living water." He said of his vision, *"Behold, water was flowing from under the threshold of the house toward the east, for the house faced east. And the water was flowing down from under, from the right side of the house, from south of the altar. He brought me out by way of the north gate and led me around on the outside to the outer gate by way of the gate that faces east. And behold, water was trickling from the south side. When the man went out toward the east with a line in his hand, he measured a thousand cubits, and he led me through the water, water reaching the ankles. Again he measured a thousand and led me through the water, water reaching the knees. Again he measured a thousand and led me through the water, water reaching the loins. Again he measured a thousand; and it was a river that I could not ford, for the water had risen, enough water to swim in, a river that could not be forded. He said to me, 'Son of man, have you seen this?' Then he brought me back to the bank of the river. Now when I had returned, behold, on the bank of the river there were very many trees on the one side and on the other. Then he said to me, 'These waters go out toward the eastern region and go down into the Arabah; then they go toward the sea, being made to flow into the sea, and the waters of the sea become fresh. It will come about that every living creature which swarms in every place where the river goes, will live. And there will be very many fish, for these waters go there and the others become fresh; so everything will live where the river goes.*

And it will come about that fishermen will stand beside it; from Engedi to Eneglaim there will be a place for the spreading of nets. Their fish will be according to their kinds, like the fish of the Great Sea, very many. But its swamps and marshes will not become fresh; they will be left for salt. By the river on its bank, on one side and on the other, will grow all kinds of trees for food. Their leaves will not wither and their fruit will not fail. They will bear every month because their water flows from the sanctuary, and their fruit will be for food and their leaves for healing.

"Thus says the Lord YHVH, 'This shall...fall to you as an inheritance" (Ezekiel 47:1-14).

The apostle John likewise saw this coming river. He said the angel who took him up into the heavens showed him the *"river of the water of life, clear as crystal, coming from the throne of God and of the Lamb, in the middle of its street. On either side of the river was the tree of life, bearing twelve kinds of fruit, yielding its fruit every month; and the leaves of the tree were for the healing of the nations. There will no longer be any curse; and the throne of God and of the Lamb will be in it, and His bond-servants will serve Him; they will see His face, and His name will be on their foreheads. And there will no longer be any night; and they will not have need of the light of a lamp nor the light of the sun, because the Lord God will illumine them; and they will reign forever and ever.*

"And he said to me, 'These words are faithful and true;' and the Lord, the God of the spirits of the prophets, sent His angel to show to His bond-servants the things which must soon take place" (Revelation 22:1-6).

Final Fulfillment of the Eighth Day

The first day of Tabernacles told of Yeshua's Incarnation, of Him dwelling, or tabernacling, among men. This same Greek word, *skenoo*,[209] is used to tell of the Father coming to dwell among men *at the end of the millennium*—thus

---

209 *Strong's* #'s G4637; 4636; 4633.

fulfilling the Eighth Day of Tabernacles. For the Father will once again dwell among us. After Yeshua returns and forevermore establishes His earthly reign, then we will see fulfillment of the Eighth Day of Sukkot. For the Holy One of Israel has promised to spread His *tabernacle* over us. It is written that,"He who sits on the throne will spread His tabernacle [*skenoo*] over them" (Revelation 7:15).

According to friend and Messianic Rabbi Mordechai Silver, "While Sukkot is representative of the Messianic Age and a taste of the Shabbat rest, *Shemini Atzeret* is that time when Yahweh commands Israel to remain with Him for one more day as He desires our company. For this feast is representative of eternity which the number eight represents in Jewish thought." [210]

Soon we will see the final fulfillment of the Eighth Day— we will see the time when the Father will forever set His Sanctuary in our midst. It will be as John the apostle said, *"And I saw the holy city, new Jerusalem, coming down out of heaven from God, made ready as a bride adorned for her husband. And I heard a loud voice from the throne, saying, 'Behold, the **tabernacle** of God is among men, and He will dwell among them, and they shall be His people, and God Himself will be among them'" (Revelation 21:2-3).*

The Great Day

"Near is the great day of YHVH, near and coming very quickly; Listen, the day of YHVH! In it the warrior cries out bitterly" (Zephaniah 1:14).

A day of judgment is coming. It is both a terrible and a great day. It is a Yom HaKippurim day of accounting. For the sinners, it will be a day of wrath, a day in which they will not be able to stand; it will be a day of war against the demons that have so longed opposed the Almighty and His

---

210   Mordechai Silver, Author, *Journey Through Torah Volume I: Commentary on the Torah, Haftarah and Brit Chadoshah Portions for Messianic Israel*, Saint Cloud, FL: Key of David, 2002.

sovereign plan.[211] But for those who love the LORD, for those who long for His appearing, they know they will soon celebrate the Eighth day of Tabernacles, and that will be a day of utter joy.

As stated, a great river of life is coming. However, be warned, for as usual, to pervert and distort and lead astray, the "counterfeiter" will come first.

When Satan knows that his time is short because Israel is being reunited, and thus able to stand, he will come down with a fury. In that time Satan will pour "water like a river out of his mouth after the woman [Israel], so that he might cause her to be swept away with the flood." Satan sends forth, from his mouth, a flood of words in the last days. They are deceptive words, sent forth to deceive, if possible, even the very elect (Revelation 12:12-15; Mark 13:22).

Specifically, Satan, the Accuser of the Brethren, the father of lies, is dedicated to blaspheming the Father's Tabernacle: "He opened his mouth in blasphemies against God, to blaspheme His name and His **tabernacle** that is, those who dwell in heaven. And it was also given to him to make war with the saints...." (Revelation 13:6-7).

We are at war. The question is, will we serve the One who wants to cover us in love, and who promises to conceal us in His *tabernacle* in the day of trouble (Psalm 27:5), or will we serve the one who wants to blaspheme that tabernacle of love?

Protecting the Bride—
Fulfillment of the Eighth Day

We have long been taught that we are the Messiah's bride, and it is good to meditate on the principles that can be learned from this allegory. But we also need to realize that Scripture tells us that the New Jerusalem is our bride.

John the apostle said, "I saw the holy city, new Jerusalem, coming down out of heaven from God, made

---

211 Jude 1:6; Rev 6:17; 16:14.

ready **as a bride** adorned for her husband" (Revelation 21:2).

Moreover, Isaiah prophesied about this coming Bride:

"For Zion's sake I will not keep silent, and for Jerusalem's sake I will not keep quiet, until her righteousness goes forth like brightness, and her salvation like a torch that is burning. The nations will see your righteousness, and all kings your glory; and you will be called by a new name which the mouth of YHVH will designate. You will also be a crown of beauty in the hand of YHVH, and a royal diadem in the hand of your God. It will no longer be said to you, 'Forsaken,' nor to your land will it any longer be said, 'Desolate,' but you will be called, 'My delight is in her,' and your land, 'Married,' for YHVH delights in you, and to Him your land will be married. For as a young man marries a virgin, so your sons will marry you; and as the bridegroom rejoices over the bride, so your God will rejoice over you" (Isaiah 62:1-5).

As sons of Zion, one day we will marry our Heavenly City. We will go into her and forevermore be one with her.

Thus we also need to learn the many principles that can be taught from this type. We especially need to see ourselves as a "protective bridegroom" and so to care about what is happening to our bride. For Isaiah also says of this chosen city: "On your walls, O Jerusalem, I have appointed watchmen; all day and all night they will never keep silent. You who remind YHVH, take no rest for yourselves; and give Him no rest until He establishes and makes Jerusalem a praise in the earth" (Isaiah 62:6-7).

Ephraim was especially called to be a "watchman," and he especially needs to pray for the peace and prosperity of Jerusalem (Hosea 9:8; Psalm 122:6-7).

We who love her must pray and intercede for her. We must long for her appearing, knowing that, when we see the New Jerusalem come down, in that day we will see fulfillment of the Eighth Day of Tabernacles.

Chosen to Choose

The Father has chosen the people of Israel. He has also

left the doors of Israel's commonwealth open to whomsoever would choose to follow Him (Ephesians 2:11-22).

However, collective Israel must realize that she has been *chosen to choose.* "Choose this day whom you will serve O Israel" (Joshua 24:15).

Chosen Israel is called to a "*test.*" For the word *chosen* can also be translated *tested.* "Behold, I have refined you, but not as silver; I have *tested* you in the furnace of affliction" (Isaiah 48:10).

The *Theological Wordbook of the Old Testament,* by Moody Press, says of the Hebrew word, *bachar,* or *chosen:*

"The root idea is evidently to 'take a keen look at'... thus... the connotation of 'testing or examining' found in Isa 48:10....The word is [primarily] used to express the choosing which has ultimate and eternal significance." [212]

To be *chosen, Israel* is to be *tested.* Blessing or curse? Which will Israel choose during her earthly sojourn? Moreover, this eternal call to choose continues on *all* Israel —both houses—Judah and Ephraim.

Shema Yisrael... Hear, understand, and obey, O Israel.

Choose this day whom you will serve, then set your face this day to "pass the test."

---

212 Chicago: Moody, 1985, # 231, Volume 1, p 100.

Restoring David's Fallen Tabernacle

For all the joy of our inspiring celebrations, there is something missing. Our Sukkah is not complete. David's tabernacle is fallen.

David's tabernacle represents the united house of Israel —a house that will only be restored when Israel responds to the Yom Teruah call of the two silver trumpets, which is a call to repentance. And that repentance will surely come, for it is written: "In those days and at that time," declares YHVH, "the sons of Israel will come, both they and the sons of Judah as well; they will go along weeping as they go, and it will be YHVH their God they will seek" (Jeremiah 50:4).

The house of Israel will begin to be fully restored when, like the two cherubim over the Ark, Ephraim and Judah reach out to embrace each other. Then the Father will come and Tabernacle with His children. Then David's Tabernacle will be restored.

King David ruled over the *whole house* of Israel, for "All Israel and Judah loved David" (1 Samuel 18:16). However, sin entered into the camp, and division came to the house.

Israel even told David, "'Look after your own house, David!' And Israel departed to their tents" (1 Kings 12:16).

Years later, Israel found herself scattered among the nations, lost among the heathen. This happened because she had an unfortunate and long-standing penchant for paganism.

Israel has long behaved like their forefather, Jeroboam, who disdained YHVH's prescribed feasts and created his own replacement celebrations (Exodus 31:16-17; Daniel 7:25; 1 Kings 12:27-33). Jeroboam's actions foreshadowed a grievous portrait of "the Church." For, even when being regathered by the Shepherd God, Ephraim Israel, or the "Church system" as we know it, continued to make their own proclamations, changed the Sabbath commandment, and altered the feast days.

Of these sins she must repent.

Virgin Israel must hear the promised call, because the Father *has* promised to rebuild her. She must repent and direct her mind to His highway of holiness. As the Father has said: "Again I will build you and you will be rebuilt, O virgin of Israel! ....Direct your mind to the highway, The way by which you went. Return, O virgin of Israel, Return to these your cities" (Jeremiah 31:4,21).

To do this, Israel must separate herself from error: "Come out from among them, and be ye separate, saith the Lord, and touch not the un-clean thing; and I will receive you" (2 Corinthians 6:17, KJV).

As we earnestly seek the ancient paths of our forefathers, we must "remember," or *zakar,* the feasts, which is to mark, recognize, mention, be mindful of, think on.[213]

As we remember these appointed times, we must also remember that full redemption will not come until both houses repent. Only then will all Israel be reunited. Only then will the fallen booth of David be restored.

---

213 *Strong's* # H2142.

Stumbling Over the Sanctuary

As previously stated, in different ways, both the houses of Israel have stumbled over the One who would be a Sanctuary to them.

That "Sanctuary" is Messiah Yeshua, the One known as the Greater Son of David.[214] To restore David's fallen tabernacle, we must preach the gospel that He declared about the restored Kingdom of Israel (Matthew 4:23; 9:35; 24:14; Mark 1:15; Luke 16:16).

That gospel will not be preached exactly as it has been in the past. It must be a gospel that includes the truth about the Jewish Messiah and the feasts of Israel. It must be a gospel that honors the Shabbat and the Torah, without being legalistic or self-righteous. It must be a gospel that is grounded in the love the God of Israel has for both houses.

That gospel will yet be fully preached because the Holy One yet loves both Judah and Ephraim, and He has sworn to restore them:

"'Is Ephraim My dear son? Is he a delightful child? Indeed, as often as I have spoken against him, I certainly still remember him; therefore My heart yearns for him; I will surely have mercy on him,' declares YHVH'" (Jeremiah 31:20). And, "Thus says YHVH Tsavaot [YHVH of hosts], 'My cities will again overflow with prosperity, and YHVH will again comfort Zion and again choose Jerusalem....YHVH will possess Judah as His portion in the holy land, and will again choose Jerusalem'" (Zechariah 1:17; 2:12).

Believed by the Apostles

The Holy One also has promised, "In that day I will raise up the fallen booth of David, and wall up its breaches; I will also raise up its ruins and rebuild it as in the days of old" (Amos 9:11).

The apostles believed they had entered into that prophesied day of restoration. They were proclaiming the

---

214 Isa 8:13-14; John 2:19-22; Mat 1:1; 22:42.

new covenant promised to both "Israel and Judah" (Jeremiah 31:31-33; Hebrews 8:8-12).

When the Holy Spirit began to be poured out on those of the nations who heard them preaching the gospel of the kingdom, they said , "With this the words of the Prophets agree, as it is written, 'After these things I will return, And I will rebuild the tabernacle of David which has fallen, and I will rebuild its ruins, and I will restore it" (Acts 15:15-16).

The Father promised to build a "house" for His beloved David. He said that after David laid down with his fathers, He would raise up a descendant from him, and would "establish His kingdom forever" (2 Samuel 7:8-16).[215]

That promised heir is Messiah Yeshua, the greater Son of David. To keep His word to David, Yeshua has been gathering from among the nations those called by His name.[216] He has been gathering the lost sheep of Israel.[217] For Yeshua is the prophesied "Branch" sent to *netzer/ preserve*" the cut down and scattered olive tree of Israel (Isaiah 11:1,11-14).[218]

If the apostles were correct, if we are in Israel's time of restoration, and if a day is as a thousand years (2 Peter 3:8), then it is perhaps time for us to heed the prophet Hosea:

"Come, let us return to YHVH, for He has torn us, but He will heal us; He has wounded us, but He will bandage us. He will revive us after two days; He will raise us up on the third day, that we may live before Him. So let us know, let us press on to know YHVH. His going forth is as certain as the dawn; and He will come to us like the rain, like the spring rain watering the earth.

"What shall I do with you, O Ephraim? What shall I do with you, O Judah? For your loyalty is like a morning cloud and like the dew which goes away early.

"Therefore I have hewn them in pieces by the prophets;

---

215 Psa 89:35-37; Isa 9:6-7; 16:5; Eze 21:27; Mat 1:20-23; Luke 1:31-33,69.
216 Amos 9:12; Acts 13:47; 15:17; Rom 15:8-12.
217 Hos 8:8; Amos 9:9; Eze 34.
218 Olive Tree: Jer 11:10,16; 2:18,21; Gen 48:19; Rom 11.

I have slain them by the words of My mouth; and the judgments on you are like the light that goes forth.

"For I delight in loyalty [mercy] rather than sacrifice, and in the knowledge of God rather than burnt offerings. But like Adam they have transgressed the covenant; there they have dealt treacherously against Me" (Hosea 6:1-8).

Weighed in the Balance

The Almighty has weighed us in the balance, and in our divided state we have been found wanting.

Let both the houses of Israel therefore seek to return to the Holy One with clean hands and pure hearts. Let us not try to return to Him in false pride about our many "sacrifices." Instead, let us truly be a humble people of *checed*, or mercy, kindness, goodness.[219] That is how our Messiah came to us, and that is how He wants us to go to others.

David's Tabernacle

"When the Lord has washed away the filth of the daughters of Zion and purged the bloodshed of Jerusalem from her midst, by the spirit of judgment and the spirit of burning, then YHVH will create over the whole area of Mount Zion and over her assemblies a cloud by day, even smoke, and the brightness of a flaming fire by night; for over all the glory will be a canopy. There will be a **sukkah** to give shade from the heat by day, and refuge and protection from the storm and the rain" (Isaiah 4:4-6).

One day the Shekinah glory of God will again tabernacle on Mount Zion, for David built his tabernacle on Mount Zion. In it was found the Ark of the Covenant, and continual praise was lifted up to the Most High.[220] *That* is what the Father wants to restore to His people.

---

219 *Strong's* # H2617.
220 2 Sam 6:17; 1 Chr 15:1; 16:1,4,7,37; 2 Chr 1:4; Psa 76:2; 132:5; Acts 7:45-47; 15:16,17; Amos 9:11-12.

When Israel is purged of her idolatries, the Father will restore David's Tabernacle—we will enter into a time of unending worship and praise.[221]

The Feasts Were and Are Prophetic

To help us enter into that glorious time we must realize that the feasts of Israel are agriculturally based and that they were given to the children of Israel while they were living in the desert and eating manna (Exodus 16:35).

This means that from the very beginning the feasts were prophetic in nature. They are still prophetic in nature. In keeping them, we become living books of godly prophecy to those around us.

Three Divisions

These prophetic convocations were divided into three groups:

- Passover, Unleavened Bread, First Fruits
- Shavuot
- Yom Teruah, Yom HaKippurim, and Sukkot

These three groups generally correspond to the division of the Temple area:

- Outer Court
- The Holy Place
- The Holy of Holies

These Three divisions also help us to see three roles played by our Messiah.

- Priest
- Prophet
- King

The first group of feasts depict our Messiah as our High

---

221 Rev 4:8; 7:15.

Priest.[222] Through His sacrifice, we find forgiveness of our sins and access to the Father. All must come to the Father through Yeshua's priestly sacrifice (John 14:6); and ancient Israel began their approach to the Almighty by first going through the outer court of the Temple where the sacrifices were offered.

The next festal division depicts Messiah Yeshua as our Prophet.[223] Through His ministry, which abounded with signs and wonders, He gave testimony to the world about the things of Yah (God). He foretold the giving of the Ruach HaKodesh on Shavuot, the one who empowers us in our walk.

The altar of sacrifice was located in the Holy Place. It was by the blood that was shed there that the high priest was empowered to continue his walk into the Holy of Holies.

Likewise, we Believers give testimony to the world about the laws, coming judgment, and restoration of the Kingdom of our God. We are empowered to do this by the Ruach HaKodesh; He empowers us to enter into the throne room of grace, and there, we behold the face of our Heavenly Father (Hebrews 4:16).

Having entered into the Temple area, having offered the prescribed sacrifice, we move into the Holy of Holies. In this last segment of appointed times, we see our Messiah as the King of Kings.[224] We see the full restoration of His divided house in these feasts, because the reunion of Judah and Ephraim is crowned by recognition of Messiah Yeshua as the King of Kings and the Lord of Lords. It is also followed by a time when the New Jerusalem will come down and the Father Himself will dwell among His people in all His glory. Then we will truly be dwelling in the Most Holy Place,[225]

---

222 Priest: Heb 2:17; 3:1; 4:14; 6:20; 7:1-3,11,17; 8:1.

223 Prophet: Mat 13:57; 21:11; 21:46; Luke 7:16; 13:33; John 6:14; 7:40; Deu 18:18-19; Acts 3:22.

224 King: Mark 15:12; Mark 15:2; John 19:19; 1 Tim 6:15; Rev 17:14; 19:16.

225 The basic idea of Yeshua as Prophet, Priest and King, is from the book, *The Feasts of the Lord*, Robert Thompson, Medford, OR: Omega Publications, 1975,

(continued...)

and David's Tabernacle of praise will be restored.

We are now being called to lay aside all error and to seek to walk in the truth of the restoration of all Israel to her God-given feasts.

However, let us realize that our first steps down that path will probably lead us into the wilderness.

The Wilderness Experience

Our Father speaks of a day wherein He will "bring" the children of Israel "into the wilderness of the peoples," and there, He says, "I shall enter into judgment with them face to face." At that time, says the Lord, "I shall make you pass under the rod, and I shall bring you into the bond of the covenant; and I shall purge from you the rebels and those who transgress against Me..." (Ezekiel 20:35-38).

The "wilderness of the peoples" speaks of a group that is without wine or water. Many religious organizations qualify for this title, and many Believers find themselves lost in such parched wastelands.

YHVH brings us to this place because "There," He says, "I will confront *you*. There will I state My case against *you*" (New English Bible). "I will deal with *you* there face to face" (Moffatt). *We* are the ones whom the Lord seeks to isolate at this time. As always, it is matter of "If *My* people..."

YHVH also declares that He "will gather those who grieve about the appointed feasts—They came from you, O Zion, and the reproach of exile is a burden on them" (Zephaniah 3:18).

While lost in a dry desert of idolatry, the children of Zion will grieve for the pure, unadulterated feasts of Israel. Being separated from the Land promised to the fathers will be regarded as a reproach. They will long for the comfort of Shabbat. Seeking true reunion with the God of Israel, they will turn from *all* Gentilized, heathen, and false religious practices—be they Jewish, non-Jewish, Babylonian, or

---

225 (...continued)
pp 152-153.

Roman. If the practices are unscriptural, they will turn from them.

While we are in this state of lostness, yet seeking a place where we can finally find the truth, our Father will fulfill a promise: *"Hear the word of the Lord, O house of Jacob, and all the families of the house of Israel... At that time, declares the Lord, I will be the God of all the families of Israel, and they shall be My people... Behold, I will do something new, now it will spring forth; will you not be aware of it? I will even make a roadway in the wilderness..."* (Jeremiah 2:4; 31:1; Isaiah 43:19).

That roadway will not pass through Babylon or Rome. Rather, it is a highway of holiness. It is the way of redemption, and all who trod it must pass through a place of repentance. There, they will remember our Father's plan for full restoration of Judah and Ephraim. That holy highway will lead us to Zion.

All who wish to trod this golden pathway must face the truth about their traditions.

Abba Father, we ask You to forevermore set our feet on Your Holy Highway.
Amen.

Finish

Addendum A

Traditional and Messianic Jewish Celebrations

For the sake of those not familiar with the Traditional Jewish Passover Haggadah, or the Messianic Jewish Passover celebration, we offer the following information.

Often called the "Festival of Freedom," Passover is a celebration of deliverance from slavery. This feast is the oldest of the appointed feasts of Israel. Like *Sukkot* and *Shavuot*, it required a pilgrimage to Jerusalem.

When our forefather, Joseph, was the second most powerful man in Egypt, his family ultimately joined him there. Then, generations later, there arose another Pharaoh —one who knew not Joseph. With his rise to power, the political climate changed. The Hebrew family that once was related to the "Prime-Minister" was reduced to slavery.

Moses was born to a Hebrew slave, but was adopted by Pharaoh's daughter. When he became a man, he was overcome when he saw a fellow Hebrew being mistreated, so he intervened, striking and killing the offender. Then, fearing for his life, he fled into the desert.

Much later, at the Father's insistence, a more subdued, yet stronger, Moses returned and demanded the release of the Hebrews from bondage.

So began the Passover battle between Pharaoh and the Holy One—between worldliness and godliness—between bondage and freedom.

After each of Moses' requests for freedom to worship were refused, the God of Israel struck the Egyptians with a different plague. Finally, Moses threatened a tenth plague, one that would kill all the firstborn Egyptian sons and cattle, because they did not have the blood on their doorposts. Pharaoh foolishly refused to obey, so death came to his son. After the Egyptian firstborn were killed by the angel of death, Pharaoh told the Israelites to leave.

Since they were in a rush to depart, there was not even enough time for their bread to rise. So began the Israelite custom of eating unleavened bread, beginning at Passover.[226]

The Telling of the Story

In most Jewish homes, the first night of Passover features a family dinner that includes retelling the Passover story and singing certain songs. It is called a *Seder*, which means *order, because a particular order* is followed. A book called the *Haggadah*, which means *the telling of the story,* outlines the script for this special night. This instruction book can be small or large, plain or ornate, and often is a family heirloom.

The telling of the story, or *Haggadah*, begins when the youngest child asks the traditional question:

"*Why is this night different from all other nights*"?

With this question, the recounting of the story of great redemption begins.

During the course of the evening four cups of wine are offered. These are said to correspond to the Father's four Exodus promises:"I shall bring you forth, I shall save you, I shall redeem you, I shall take you" (Exodus 6:6-7).

---

226 Exo 7:1; 13:22; Luke 22:1.

The names of the four cups recount these promises. They are called the cups of Sanctification, Deliverance, Redemption, and Praise.

Matzoth (unleavened bread) and *maror* (bitter herbs, usually horseradish) are eaten as reminders of the hasty exodus, and of the bitterness of slavery.

Over the years, rabbis have added other elements to the Passover ritual plate: a green vegetable (*karpas*), a roasted egg, *charoset* (finely chopped apples and nuts mixed with honey and wine to resemble the mortar used for the infamous bricks made in Egypt), and a fifth cup of wine: the cup of Elijah. A place is set at the table and the door left open for him. Elijah's cup traditionally sits on the Passover table, waiting for him to come and drink, and to announce that Messiah has come.

During the service, some *charoset* and *maror* are eaten with a piece of *matzah*. Called a "Hillel Sandwich," it is named after the great rabbi, and it is eaten to remind us that even the most bitter of circumstances can be made sweet—if we hold fast to our hope in the God of Israel.

The Traditional Jewish Seder Table

The traditional Jewish Seder table usually includes a large Seder plate (which may be a family treasure). On this plate there is a roasted lamb shank bone, a hard cooked egg, *maror*, the *charoset* mix, and *karpas* (lettuce, parsley, or watercress). Three *matzoth* are kept on the table under a cover, along with salt water to dip the parsley in, as a reminder of the salty tears of slavery. An ornate cup for the wine is also on the table, with two candles that are lit at the beginning of the Seder as a special blessing is recited.

Passover is a time for the people of Israel to teach their children about the wonderful works of God. It is a time to celebrate the history of the people of Israel. For Messiah's followers this is a time to celebrate, because He fulfills Passover. His sacrificial death brings us into a new Exodus that is a departure from our bondage to sin.

The Messianic Jewish Passover Seder

Messianic Jewish Believers claim that Yeshua was following some form of this tradition when He celebrated His New Covenant Passover.

They also teach that some new truths can be seen in their version of the traditional Jewish Seder:

The three *matzoth* commemorate the unleavened bread of affliction that our forebearers ate in their hasty departure. Some believe the First Century Jewish Believers in Messiah used three *matzoth*,, with the middle one representing the Son who was broken for us. They believe this custom spread throughout Judaism and remains today.[227]

The roasted shank bone is said to speak of the spotless lamb sacrificed on the first Passover. When the Holy One saw the blood of this sacrifice, He passed over our people and did not kill the firstborn. Today, Yeshua is our sinless *Paschal* Lamb, sacrificed once for all (Hebrews 7:27; 9:12; 10:10; 1 Peter 3:18). He paid the ultimate price for our redemption, and if we abide in Him, we too will one day be "passed over" by the angel of the second death.

The roasted egg, or *khagigah*, is said to symbolize eternal life, having no beginning nor end, even as our God is without beginning or end.

Maror, the bitter herb, brings to mind the bitterness of slavery in Egypt, as well as the bitterness of slavery to sin.

Charoset, with its Egyptian brick mortar color, reminds us of the backbreaking labor that comes with bondage.

Karpas, a spring-time vegetable, tells of God's rich bounty, of our spring-time deliverance and our hope in Him.

After searching, a child locates the hidden *afikomen* (the broken half of the middle *matzah*), which is then blessed as the Body of Yeshua, who is the Bread of Life.

---

227 *The Book of Jewish Knowledge* by Nathanel Ausubel (NY: Crown Publishers, 1977), says: "This ceremonial custom [the Seder], in imitation of the patrician manner of banqueting customary in Greco-Roman times, began in the first century, when the Seder was introduced..." See "Passover," p 328.

The third cup of wine drunk during this tradition is called the cup of Redemption. After it is blessed, the participants drink what is said to be the wine of the New Covenant, as lifted up by Yeshua during His "Last Supper."

This cup is followed by a fourth cup of wine and the ceremony is concluded. (See *Messianic Jewish Passover Guide* on the following pages.)

What was Yeshua Doing?

Again we ask, was Yeshua following the *Order* of the Passover that was practiced in His day, or was He initiating a new Passover tradition? (See chapter 8, *The Father's Passover Plan.*)

Yeshua spoke against the traditions of men. Paul likewise warned us about being taken captive by errant traditions. Instead, we are to do all things according to the way of the Messiah (Mark 7:6-8; Colossians 2:8). So we again ask: "How did Yeshua celebrate His New Covenant Passover?"

Beyond Tradition

Other than saying we are fairly certain Yeshua did not have a "Passover plate," as we now know them, and that many of the present Jewish traditions have been added over the centuries, and thus are not Biblical commands, we choose not to argue the finer points of Jewish traditions. Instead, we suggest researching the topic with books like, *The Jewish Book of Why, Volumes One and Two* by Alfred J. Kolatch (Jonathan David Publishers, Inc., 68-22 Eliot Avenue, Middle Village, NY, 11379). Kolatch answers many questions about various traditions.

We prefer incorporating the concept of the *Four Passovers*, as earlier described. Nonetheless, we also offer a *Messianic Jewish Passover Guide* for those who wish to celebrate in a more traditional way. We do this because we realize there is much we can learn by experiencing a

Passover in this manner.

All of our *Passover Guides* are offered for sale in the back of this book. You can order a printed copy, or you may photocopy the four copyrighted pages for your personal use.

However you choose to celebrate, may your celebration be blessed with the Messiah's presence.

Messianic Jewish Passover Haggadah

© 1998, 2002

Angus and Batya Wootten

PO Box 700217, Saint Cloud, FL 34770
Ph. 800 829-8777   Fax 407 348-3770
email: info@mim.net   Web: www.mim.net
Ministering to "both the houses of Israel" (Isaiah 8:14)

Pesach: The Festival of Freedom: *Pesach* is a feminine word meaning, to skip over, to pause or hover over, even as a hen hovers over her chicks.

The Search For Leaven: Leaven swells, puffs up, and permeates, it serves as a symbol for sin. On the 13th of Abib, Jewish fathers begin with a ceremonial search for leaven called *bedikat chametz* (Exo 12:15). They lead the children in a candlelight search using a feather, wooden spoon, and rag or bag. The crumbs (some have been knowingly hidden), feather, spoon and rag then are ceremonially burned.

The Haggadah: *Haggadah* means "the telling, or showing forth." These books often are family heirlooms and are based on answering the "What does this rite mean to you?" question that is to be asked by the youngest child (Exo 12:26-27).

The Seder Table: The table is often adorned with a Menorah and a traditional Passover plate on which we find: a lamb shank-bone, roasted egg, bitter herbs, horseradish, parsley, and *charoset* (mix of chopped apples, nuts, raisins, cinnamon, and wine).

On the table we also find: A dish filled with salt water (for dipping), a wine cup, a cup for Elijah, covers for the *matzoth* (the three pieces of unleavened bread), *afikomen* (half of the one broken and hidden matzoth), and a bowl for washing, with a towel for drying, plus a pillow for leaning. Each of these Passover element pieces may be plain or elaborate.

The Four Cups: According to rabbinic tradition four cups of wine are drunk at the Seder to represent the four expressions of redemption: "I will *free* you," "I will *deliver* you," "I will *redeem* you," "I will *take* you" (Exo 6:6-7). These cups are called: Sanctification, Plagues, Redemption, and Praise.

The Seder (Order):

✡ The head of the house says the *Kiddish* (blessing over the wine) and all drink the first cup of wine, called the cup of *Sanctification*.

✡ The lady of the house takes the bowl around for the washing of the hands.

✡ All dip *karpas* (parsley: a reminder of the *springtime* deliverance) in the salt water (reminder of the tears shed in slavery and of the sea of deliverance), then eat it.

✡ Leader raises the matzah, all recite over the *Bread of Affliction:*

"This is the bread of affliction, the poor bread which our fathers ate in the land of Egypt. Let all who are hungry come and eat. Let all who are in need come and share in the hope of Passover."

✡ Leader breaks the *middle matzah* into two pieces, wraps one half in the *afikomen* bag and then hides it. Later, the children try to find it. Leader *redeems* it from the child who finds it, and they get a reward at *Shavuot* (Pentecost).

✡ The Four Questions are asked by the youngest child:

"On all other nights we eat bread or matzah. On this night *why* do we eat only matzah?

"On all other nights we eat all kinds of vegetables. On this night *why* do we eat only bitter herbs?

"On all other nights we do not dip our vegetables even once. On this night *why* do we dip them twice?

©BRW

"On all other nights we eat our meals sitting or reclining. On this night *why* do we eat only reclining?"

✡ Leader then begins to answer the questions, first explaining and distributing the other half of the broken, "striped and pierced," matzah (Isa 53:5).

✡ All take a piece of matzah with *maror* (horseradish: a reminder of the *bitterness* of slavery in Egypt (Exo 1:12-14)—called a "Hillel Sandwich" after the great rabbi.

✡ Second Dipping: All take a piece of matzoth with *maror*, and dip it into the sweet *charoset* (apple and wine) mix, as a reminder that even the most bitter of circumstances are *sweetened* by hope in our God.

✡ Second cup of wine, *Plagues*, is poured and Leader tells the Passover story. When the ten plagues are recited—blood, frogs, vermin, mixture, pestilence, boils, hail, locusts, darkness, slaying the firstborn—for each plague, a drop of wine (taken from the cup) is sprinkled on the plates. At the end of the story the second cup of wine is drunk.

✡ Leader reclines on pillow, saying, "The first Passover was celebrated by a people enslaved."

✡ All say, "Once we were slaves, but now we are free!"

✡ Leader holds up the *khagigah*, or egg, stating that it reminds us of new birth and eternal life for it has no beginning nor end (may be eaten later with the meal).

✡ The *Dayenu: Dayenu* means, "It would have been sufficient."

Leader: If the Lord had merely rescued us, but had not judged the Egyptians,

All: *Dayenu!*

Leader: If He had only destroyed their gods, but had not parted the Red Sea,

All: *Dayenu!*

Leader: If He had only drowned our enemies, but had not fed us with *manna*,

All: *Dayenu!*

Leader: If He had only led us through the desert, but had not given us the Sabbath,

All: *Dayenu!*

Leader: If He had only given us the Torah, but not the Land of Israel,

All: *Dayenu!*

Leader: But, the Holy One, blessed be He, provided all these things, and many more, for our forefathers—and so He will provide for us—for we are their children!

All: Blesses are You, O Holy One, for You supply all our needs!

✡ It is now time to partake of the Passover Meal

After the meal, the Seder continues...

©BRW

✿ Leader shares the Afikomen and says: "This is My body which is given for you; do this in remembrance of Me" (Luke 22:19)

✿ The third cup of wine is poured, the cup of *Redemption.* Leader says: "This cup which is poured out for you is the new covenant in My blood" (Lk 22:20).

✿ Lift up Elijah's cup and open the door for him (Mal 4:5; Luke 1:17; Matt 11:14).

✿ Leader pours and lifts up the fourth cup of wine, *Praise,* and says:

Give thanks to the Lord, for He is good.
All: His love endures forever.
Leader: Give thanks to the God of gods.
All: His love endures forever.
Leader: Give thanks to the Lord of Lords.
All: His love endures forever.
Leader: To Him who alone does great wonders,
All: His love endures forever.
Leader: Who by His understanding made the heavens,
All: His love endures forever.
Leader: Who spread out the earth above the waters,
All: His love endures forever.
Leader: Who made the great lights,
All: His love endures forever.
Leader: The sun to govern the day,
All: His love endures forever.
Leader: The moon and stars to govern the night,
All: His love endures forever.
Leader: To Him who struck down the firstborn of Egypt
All: His love endures forever.
Leader: And brought Israel out from their midst,
All: His love endures forever.
Leader: With a strong hand and an outstretched arm,
All: His love endures forever.
Leader: To Him who divided the Red Sea asunder,
All: His love endures forever.
Leader: And brought Israel through the midst of it,
Leader: But He overthrew Pharaoh and his army in the Red Sea,
All: His love endures forever.
Leader: To Him who led His people through the wilderness,
All: His love endures forever.
Leader: Give thanks to the God of Heaven!
All: His love endures forever.
    (Psalm 136:1-16,26)

✿ Lift the cup of *Praise* and bless the name of the Lord!
All say: *Next Year In Jerusalem! It Is Finished!*

©BRW

Addendum B

Paul and the Feasts

Did Paul instruct the non-Jewish Believers not to keep the Law, or did he uphold the Torah?

When Paul wanted Timothy to go with him to the Jewish people, Rabbi Paul circumcised him (Acts 16:1-3). Paul also kept a Nazarite vow and paid for others to keep their vows (Acts 18:18; 21:21-28; see Numbers 6:2,5,9,18). Paul instructed us to keep Passover, and he said, "In my inner being I delight in God's law," and, "I have committed no offense either against the Law of the Jews or against the temple or against Caesar." Paul also said, "The Law is **good**, if [IF] one uses it **lawfully**" (Acts 20:16; 1 Corinthians 5:8; Romans 7:22; Acts 24:14; 25:8; 1 Timothy 1:8).

Good, or *kalos*, means beautiful, valuable, virtuous, honest, well, worthy. *Lawfully*, or *nomimos*, means legitimately, lawfully, agreeable to the rules.

Paul did not speak against the law or the feasts but against the errant legalisms of men. He said, "The Law is holy...righteous...good...spiritual," and, "It is not the hearers of the Law who are just before God, it is those who obey the law who will be declared righteous" (Romans 7:12,14; 2:13). Paul's detractors had to put forth "*false*" witnesses to try to prove their lie that he spoke "against Moses" (Acts 6:13).

Paul said he served God the way his "forefathers did," and that he "believed everything that is in accordance with the Law." He also spoke of having the Law written on our hearts, and he said that, "All Scripture is inspired by God and profitable for teaching, for reproof, for correction, for training in righteousness; that the man of God may be adequate, equipped for every good work" (Acts 24:14; Romans 2:13-16; 2 Timothy 1:3; 3:16-17).

When Paul said this, he spoke of Old (First) Covenant Scriptures, because the New Covenant was not yet Canon.[228]

Three Primary Verses

There are three primary Scripture verses in the New Covenant that are often said to prove that the feasts should not be celebrated by New Covenant Believers.

These verses are: *Galatians 4:8-11; Colossians 2:16-17; and Romans 14:1-6.*

For more information on these Scriptures than is provided here, we recommend the article "Does the New Testament Annul the Biblical Appointments?" by author John K. McKee (this article can be found at his web site: www.tnnonline.net). On this topic, and with the understanding that the following books were written from a *Messianic Jewish perspective*, we recommend the relevant comments in the *Jewish New Testament Commentary* by David H. Stern, and also those in the book, *Take Hold* by Ariel and D'vorah Berkowitz.

Galatians 4:8-11

"When you did not know God, you were slaves to those which by nature are no gods. But now that you have come to know God, or rather to be known by God, how is it that you turn back again to the weak and worthless elemental things, to which you desire to be enslaved all over again?

---

228 Note: Torah foretells One Who will speak the words of the Father, and Israel is commanded to listen to Him. Yeshua fulfilled this prophecy and He prayed for those who would believe in Him through the "Words" of His Disciples (Deu 18:18-19; John 5: 46-47; 8:28; 12:49-50; 17:8,17). Thus Torah validates the New Covenant. See, "Has Torah Failed Us? Do We Have The Promised Words of The Prophet?" @ www.mim.net.

*You observe days and months and seasons and years. I fear
for you, that perhaps I have labored over you in vain."*

John McKee states in his paper that some people believe
the problem with the Galatians was that "they thought that
strict obedience to the Law and circumcision would bring
them salvation," and according to them, Paul "feared for
their souls because they had begun to celebrate the Biblical
feast days." McKee continues, "[T]he epistle to the Galatians
was written concerning a situation in Galatia where the
Judaizers had imposed strict legalisms on the non-Jewish
Believers. They asserted that you could only be saved if you
were circumcised and honored the Torah to the letter....
[but] a legalistic attitude will *not* bring eternal salvation....
[that] only comes through being spiritually regenerated
through the atoning work of Messiah Yeshua."

We define "Judaizers" as those who try to bring people
into conformity with Judaism, particularly to adopt rabbinic
interpretations of Torah, much of which is based on oral law
rather than on written Scripture.

David Stern, a commentator with a decidedly Messianic
Jewish slant, says of these verses, "When Gentiles observe
these Jewish holidays neither out of joy in sharing what
God has given the Jewish people nor out of spiritual identifi-
cation with them, but out of fear induced by Judaizers who
have convinced them that unless they do these things, God
will not accept them, then they are not obeying the Torah
but subjecting themselves to legalism; and legalism is just
another species of those weak and miserable elemental
demonic spirits no better than the idols left behind." [229]

Stern suggests the "days, months, seasons and years"
may refer to pagan traditions. This may be so because Paul
spoke of those who were once *foreign* to the God of Israel.
He said: "You were slaves to those which by nature are no
gods," and he asked them, "How is it that you turn back
again to the weak and worthless elemental things?"

---

[229] *Jewish New Testament Commentary* by David H. Stern, Clarksville, MD:
Messianic Jewish Publications, 1995, p 557.

In the same letter, Paul warns of the "elemental things of the world" (Galatians 4:3). Moreover, he warned the Believers of Colosse, "See to it that no one takes you captive ...according to the **elementary principles of the world**, rather than according to Messiah" (Colossians 2:8).

"Things of the world" does not describe the principals of Messiah, nor the Biblical feasts. The feasts are "The LORD's appointed times" (Leviticus 23:2). As McKee notes, they are "*not* weak and miserable principles."

Paul's admonition can be seen both as a warning against returning to heathen practices *and* against being intimidated by Judaizers.

Paul also said of those who were causing the problem: "They eagerly seek you, not commendably, but they wish to shut you out so that you will seek them" (Galatians 4:17).

Judaizers try to put you in bondage to themselves and to their man-made rules. Their actions are not commendable, because they try to get you to seek approval from them, so they can feel important by "shutting you out." In other words, they make you feel unworthy and excluded so they can feel good about themselves.

Such attitudes are not godly or edifying.

Colossians 2:16-17

"Let no one act as your judge in regard to food or drink or in respect to a festival or a new moon or a Sabbath day— things which are a mere shadow of what is to come; but the substance belongs to Messiah."

To understand these verses, we need to look back to verse 8, where Paul warned, "See to it that no one takes you captive through philosophy and empty deception, according to the tradition of men, according to the elementary principles of the world, rather than according to Messiah."

Paul was talking about the traditions of men, and he warned us not to be taken in by them.

However, though Paul repeatedly spoke against such

deceptions, he was nonetheless a rabbi who honored Torah and continually taught from the *Tanach*, the Old Testament. Our interpretations of his writings must be based on this understanding about the apostle from Tarsus.

The New American Standard Bible adds the word "mere" in italics in verse 17. *Italics* means it is not in the Greek text. McKee, who has studied Greek and Hebrew, explains: "The placement of *mere* in the English text is not even implied by the context of the sentence, unlike an under-stood verb or article that was not written by the original author and could legitimately be written in italics. A more accurate translation...comes from the NKJV, which tells us that the feasts 'are a shadow of things to come, but the substance is of Christ.'"

These verses emphasize the truth that the feasts shadow, outline, depict, and portray, our Messiah. Stern puts an even greater emphasis on their connection to Yeshua, saying the verse should be rendered: "These are *definitely* a shadow of things to come." Or: "The festivals do *indeed* have value."

We agree with Stern, because as stated earlier, "shadows cannot be separated from their substance." [230] Moreover, Stern quotes R. C. Lenski, who says, "We should not think lightly of the shadow. It was no less than the divine promise of all the heavenly realities about to arrive."[231]

In these verses, when Paul says to let no one "act as your judge" in these matters, it may be that he was telling the Colossians not to let the *heathen* judge them for "*honoring*" the scriptural feasts, dietary laws, new moon festivals, and the Sabbath (vs 2:16).

We say this because the Jerusalem Council ruled in Acts 15 that the new converts coming to faith were expected to obey certain minimal requirements, as well as go to the synagogue to hear the words of Torah.

---

230 Chapter 2, "Where Do We Go For Answers?" Also see *Who Is Israel?* chapter 22, "Return, O Virgin Israel!"

231 *Jewish New Testament Commentary*, p 611.

Acceptance of these converts might be said to be attached to a "hinge statement." That hinge statement is found in Acts 15:21: "For Moses from ancient generations has in every city those who preach him, since he is read in the synagogues every Sabbath."

Hearing the Torah and having its eternal laws written on our hearts is the very essence of the promised New Covenant (Jeremiah 31:31-33). [232]

In other words, these new Believers were being accepted into the fellowships with minimal behavior requirements, *because* it was assumed that they would soon begin to hear and obey the eternal truths taught by Moses.

Looking through this lens, we see that concerning the Colossian verses in question, Paul was declaring that true meaning and fulfillment of the feast shadows are found in the Messiah. From this perspective, we also see that these verses were meant to *encourage* us to celebrate the feasts, because they depict our Messiah to the world!

To this end, McKee says, "The Biblical feasts explain the pattern of Messiah's life and the plan of redemption and His Second Coming. 'Now these things happened to them as an example, and they were written for our instruction, upon whom the ends of the ages have come' (1 Corinthians 10:11)." And, "If we are the Last Generation 'upon whom the ends of the ages have come,' how are we expected to understand YHVH's redemptive plan for humanity if we do not *honor Messiah* in the holidays that He has specified for us? How are we supposed to properly understand what is to befall Planet Earth? If we do not honor the *orderly* appointed times as God has told us, we are libel to misunderstand His prophetic plan for the ages...." [233]

Just as it could be that the *heathen* were judging the Believers of Colosse for "honoring" the scriptural feasts, so it could be that the *Judaizers* were judging or condemning them for not following their rabbinic teachings.

---

232 *Who Is Israel?* by Batya Wootten, chapter 19, "One Law—One People."
233 McKee.

Romans 14:1-6

"Now accept the one who is weak in faith, but not for the purpose of passing judgment on his opinions. One person has faith that he may eat all things, but he who is weak eats vegetables only. The one who eats is not to regard with contempt the one who does not eat, and the one who does not eat is not to judge the one who eats, for God has accepted him. Who are you to judge the servant of another? To his own master he stands or falls; and he will stand, for the Lord is able to make him stand. One person regards one day above another, another regards every day alike. Each person must be fully convinced in his own mind. He who observes the day, observes it for the Lord, and he who eats, does so for the Lord, for he gives thanks to God; and he who eats not, for the Lord he does not eat, and gives thanks to God" (Romans 14:5-6).

Some believe these verses teach that those who live by the dietary laws of Torah are "weak" in their faith, and that the "strong" ones are those who pay no attention to such laws, believing they were annulled by the New Testament. They then apply this same errant rule to the feast days.

The above verses have to do with how we are to relate to those who are in a different place in their walk of faith. For instance, Paul says, "One person regards one day above another, another regards every day alike. Each person must be fully convinced in his own mind." The point being that we cannot *legislate* observance of the feasts. We must *not* try to force others into believing *what* we believe, *when* we believe it, for the Father instead wants each of His children to become convinced in their own minds.

In their book, *Take Hold*, Ariel and D'vorah Berkowitz explain: "Romans 14 and 15 describes the right behavior in handling an individual who has strong convictions over a disputable matter."

The Berkowitz's define "weak" as "delicate," and say use of the word refers to treating a person "delicately" when they "have strong convictions on a matter on which the Scriptures are not clear and therefore where there is likely to be difference of opinion among other believers."

They suggest being "gracious to such a one. If his strong conviction is not causing a serious problem in the body, give that person space and allow God to move in his life as needed over time (verses 3-4)." And, "According to verses 5-6 believers have room for their own personal convictions that are important to [them]..." [234]

McKee argues that the dispute may be over fasting versus not fasting. This may be so, however, we conclude that, even though eating and how one regards a day are mentioned in the verses, the point being made is about *not passing judgments on people in disputable matters.*

On the other hand, these verses cannot be taken to mean that all days are equal in the sight of the Almighty, or that it is not important whether or not we honor His seventh-day Sabbath or His feast days. We are to observe these days, because—because it is to our benefit to do so.

Romans 14 is not suggesting that people celebrate the Sabbath any time they want, nor is it encouraging replacement holidays for the Father's appointed times. [235]

Again, the issue is our *attitude* toward those who are in a different place in their faith walk.

In Romans 14:1 we are told to "accept the one who is weak in faith, but not for the purpose of passing judgment on his opinions." Stern says some have "strong trust" and some have "weak trust." We find both types among Jewish and non-Jewish Believers. Paul is *not* speaking of "weak Jewish faith" as some suggest. He is simply talking about weak Believers in general, and he is instructing those who are strong to help the weak grow in their faith.

---

234 Ariel & D'vorah Berkowitz, *Take Hold.* Chicago: First Fruits of Zion, 1999, p 218.

235 McKee. *The New Covenant Validates Torah.* www.tnnonline.net

Abbreviations & Bibliography

Abbreviations:
ArtScroll: ArtScroll Tanach Series
BDB: New Brown-Driver-Briggs-Gesenius Hebrew-Aramaic Lexicon
NIV: New International Version Bible
NIV Study Bible: New International Version Study Bible
Strong's: Strong's Exhaustive Concordance
TAB: The Amplified Bible
TWOT: Theological Wordbook of the Old Testament
TNKH: Tanakh The Holy Scriptures

The following is a listing of writings used in making this book.

Adler, Mortimer J. *Ten Philosophical Mistakes*. NY: Macmillian, 1997.

Aharoni, Yohanan; Michael Avi-Yonah. *The Macmillan Bible Atlas*. NY: Macmillan, 1977.

Bacchiocchi, Samuele. *From Sabbath To Sunday*. Maplewood NJ: Hammond, 1979, 2000.

Barraclough, Geoffrey. *The Times Atlas of World History*. The Pontifical Gregorian University Press: Rome, 1977.

Beitzel. Barry J. *Moody Atlas of Bible Lands*. Chicago: Moody, 1985.

Berkowitz. Ariel & D'vorah. *Take Hold*. Chicago: First Fruits of Zion, 1999.

Broadhurst. D. & M. *Passover Before Messiah and After*. Chicago: 1992.

Brown, Frances. *The New Brown-Driver-Briggs-Gesenius Hebrew-Aramaic Lexicon*. Peabody, MA: Hendrickson, 1979.

Buksbazen, Victor. *The Feasts of Israel*. W. Collingswood, NJ: Friends of Israel, 1976.

Bullinger, E.W. *The Witness of the Stars*, Grand Rapids: Kregal, 1981.

Carta's Historical Atlas of Israel. Jerusalem: Carta, 1983.

Cavallaro, Gloria. *My Beloved's Israel*. Saint Cloud: Key of David, 2001.

Chumney, Edward. *The Seven Festivals of the Messiah*. Shippensburg, PA: Destiny Image, 1994.

Cohen, A. *Isaiah*. London: Soncino, 1987.

_____. *The Twelve Prophets*. London: Soncino, 1980.

Conner, Kevin. *The Feasts of Israel*. Portland: City Bible Publishing, 1980.

DeHaan, M. R.. *The Chemistry of the Blood*. Grand Rapids: Zondervan, 1971, 1989.

Dowley, Tim. *The Kregal Pictorial Guide To The Bible*. Grand Rapids: Kregal Publications, 2000.

Eckstein, Yechiel, Rabbi. *What Christiand Should Know About Jews and Judaism*. Waco, TX: Word Books, 1984.

Edersheim, Alfred. *The Life and Times of Jesus the Messiah*. Grand Rapids: Eerdman's, 1979.

_____. *The Temple*. Grand Rapids: Kregal, 1997.

Edidin, Ben M. *Jewish Customs And Ceremonies*. NY: Hebrew Publishing, 1978.

_____. *Encyclopaedia Judaica, 16 Vols*. Jerusalem: Keter, 1972.

Elwell, Walter A., ed. *The Evangelical Dictionary of Theology*. Grand Rapids. Baker, 1984.

Even-Shushan, Avraham. *New Concordance of the Tanach*. Jerusalem: Sivan, 1983.

Fadely, Tony, Rev. Dr. *The Shofar: From Genesis to Revelation*. Whole Loaf Worship Center. Cocoa, FL. 2001.

Fay, Frederdrick L. *A Map Book For Bible Students*. Old Tappan, NJ: Revell, 1966.

Fay, Frederdrick L. *A Map Book For Bible Students*. Old Tappan, NJ: Revell, 1966.

Fellner, Judith. *In the Jewish Tradition, A Year of Food and Festivities*. Middle Village, NY: Jonathan David Publishers. 1995.

Frankel, Ellen, and Betsy Platkin Teutsch. *The Encyclopedia of Jewish Symbols*. Northvale, NJ: Jason Aronson Inc., 1992.

Garborg, Rolf. *The Family Blessing*. Dallas: Word Publishing, 1990.

Gesenius' Hebrew-Chaldee Lexicon To The Old Testament. Grand Rapids. Baker, 1979.

Gilbert, Martin. *Atlas of Jewish History*. NY: William Morrow, 1993.

_____. *Israel: A History*. NY: William Morrow, 1998.

Glaser, Mitch and Zhava. *The Fall Feasts of Israel*. Chicago: Moody Bible Institute, 1987.

Green, Jay P. *The Interlinear Bible*, Hebrew, Greek, English. Grand Rapids: Baker, 1979.

Hagee, *His Glory Revealed*. Nashville: Thomas Nelson Publishers, 1999.

Harris, R. Laird, Gleason L. Archer Jr., and Bruce K. Waltke, eds. *Theological Wordbook of the Old Testament, 2 Vols*. Chicago: Moody, 1981.

Hatch, Edwin, and Henry A. Redpath. *Hatch and Redpath Concordance to the Septuagint, 2 Vols*. Grand Rapids: Baker, 1983.

Hershberger, Ervin N. *Christ In The Tabernacle*. Fairfax, VA: 1999.

Holladay, William L. Editor. *A Concise Hebrew and Aramaic Lexicon of The Old Testament*. Grand Rapids: Eerdman's, 1971.

Houtz, Frank. *A Sign Between You and Me*. Winchester, KY: Dry Bones Restoration Company, 2001.

House of David Herald. Saint Cloud, FL: 1982-2000.

Interpreter's Dictionary of the Bible, 5 Vols. Nashville: Abingdon, 1983.

Jahn, Herb. *The Aramic New Covenant.* Orange, CA: Exegeses, 1996.

Jenkins, Simon. *Bible Mapbook.* Herts, England: Lion, 1985.

Kasden, Barney. *God's Appointed Times.* Baltimore: Lederer. 1993.

Knapp, Christopher. *The Kings of Judah & Israel.* Neptune NJ: Loizeaux, 1983.

Kolatch, Alfred J. *The Jewish book of Why.* Middle Village NY: Jonathan David Publishers, 1981, 1995.

_____. *The Second Jewish Book of Why.* Middle Village NY: Jonathan David Publishers, 1996.

Isaacson, Ben, Dr. David Gross, ed. *Dictionary of the Jewish Religion* Englewood, NJ: Bantam Books, 1979.

Lamsa, George M. *The Holy Bible From Ancient Eastern Manuscripts.* Nashville: Holman, 1968, 1984.

Lascelle, Spector Ruth. *The Passover Feast.* Van Nuys: Bedrock, 1975.

Leil, C.F.; F. Delitzsch. *Commentary on the Old Testament In Ten Volumes.* Grand Rapids: Eerdman's, 1981.

Lindsey, Robert. *Jesus, Rabbi, and Lord.* Oak Creek: Cornerstone, 1990.

_____. *Messianic Israel Herald.* Saint Cloud, 1999-2002.

McKee, John K. When Will the Messiah Return, St. Cloud, FL: Key of David, 2002.

Mordecai, Victor. *Is Fanatic Islam A Global Threat?* Jerusalem: 1996.

The New Encyclopaedia Britannica, 29 Vols. Chicago: Encyclopedia Britannica, 1985.

The New English Bible With the Apocrypha. Oxford, England: Oxford University Press, 1970.

New International Version Study Bible. Grand Rapids: Zondervan, 1985, 1995.

Newsome, James D. Jr., ed. *A Synoptic Harmony of Samuel, Kings and Chronicles.* Grand Rapids: Baker, 1986.

Pearl, Chaim, ed. *The Encyclopedia of Jewish Life and Thought.* Jerusalem: Carta, 1966.

Peterson, Galen, *The Everlasting Tradition,* Grand Rapids: Kregal Publications, 1995.

Pfeiffer, Charles F., Howard F. Vos, and John Rea, eds. *Wycliffe Bible Encyclopaedia.* Chicago: Moody, 1983.

Richards, Lawerence O. *Expository Dictionary of Bible Words.* Grand Rapids: Zondervan, 1985.

Ritchie, John. *Feasts of Jehovah.* Kilmarnock, Scotland: Kregal, 1982.

Scherman, Nosson, and Meir Zlotowitz, eds. *Genesis. ArtScroll Tanach Series.* Brooklyn: Mesorah, 1987.

_____, Rabbis. *The Wisdom In The Hebrew Alphabet.* Brooklyn: Mesorah Publications, 1993.

Smith, William, L.L.D. *Smith's Bible Dictionary.* Peabody, MA: Hendrickson, 1997.

Strong, James. *The New Strong's Exhaustive Concordance*. Nashville: Thomas Nelson, 1984.

Stern, David H. *Jewish New Testament Commentary*. Clarksville, MD: Jewish New Testament Publications, 1995.

TenBoom, Corrie. The Hiding Place. Chosen Books

Tenny, Merrill, ed. *Zondervan Pictorial Encyclopedia of the Bible, 5 Vols.* Grand Rapids: Zondervan, 1976.

Tessler, Gordon S. *The Genesis Diet.* Raleigh, NC: Be Well, 1996.

Thayer, Joseph Henry. *Thayer's Greek-English Lexicon of the New Testament.* Grand Rapids: Baker, 1983.

Thomas, Winton, ed. *Documents from Old Testament Times*. New York: Harper & Row, 1961.

Thompson, Robert. *The Feasts of the Lord.* Medford, OR: Omega Publications, 1975.

Turner, Nigel *Christian Words*. Nashville: Thomas Nelson, 1981.

Unger, Merrill F. *Unger's Bible Dictionary*. Chicago: Moody, 1974, 1996.

Vaughn, Curtis, ed. *26 Translations of the Holy Bible*. Atlanta: Mathis, 1985.

Vincent, Marvin R. *Vincent's Word Studies of the New Testament.* McLean, VA: MacDonald.

Vine, W.E. *The Expanded Vine's Expository Dictionary of New Testament Words*. Minneapolis: Bethany, 1984.

Walton, John H. *Chronological Charts of the Old Testament.* Grand Rapids: Zondervan, 1978.

Webster's Third New International Dictionary, 3 Vols. Chicago: Encyclopedia Britannica, 1981.

Whiston, William, trs. *The Works of Flavius Josephus, 4 Vols.* Grand Rapids: Baker, 1974.

Wilson, William. *Wilson's Old Testament Word Studies, Unabridged Edition*. McLean, VA: MacDonald.

Wootten, Angus. *Restoring Israel's Kingdom*. Saint Cloud, FL: Key of David, 2000.

_____. *Take Two Tablets*. Saint Cloud: Key of David, 2002.

Wootten, Batya Ruth. *In Search of Israel*. Lakewood, NY: Destiny Image/House of David, 1988.

_____. *Ephraim and Judah: Israel Revealed* Saint Cloud: Key of David, 2002.

_____. *Who Is Israel?* Saint Cloud: Key of David, 2000.

Wuest, Kenneth S. *Weust's Word Studies From the Greek New Testament.* Grand Rapids: Eerdman's, 1981.

Yaniv, David. *Birth of the Messiah*. Lynnwood, WA: New West Press, Ltd. 1997.

Zimmerman, Martha. *Celebrate the Feasts*. Grand Rapids: Bethany. 1981.

Batya Ruth Wootten

Batya and her husband, Angus, were early pioneers in the Messianic movement. Decades ago they began publishing the first Messianic Materials Catalogue, created to serve a fledgling new interest in Israel, the Jewish people, and relationships between Christians and Jews.

Batya read countless books about these subjects so she could write informed descriptions of them for the catalogue, and so discovered the great diversity of opinions about Israel's role in the world and about Israel's identity.

Hungering to truly understand "Israel," she began to cry out in desperation to her Heavenly Father, asking Him to show her *His* truth. As promised, He answered: "Call to Me and I will answer you, and I will tell you great and mighty things, which you do not know" (Jeremiah 33:3).

He began to open up the Scriptures to her, which led to her first book, *In Search of Israel,* and then to *The Olive Tree of Israel.* Next she wrote the comprehensive book, *Who Is Israel?* and its companion *Study Guide.* Then came *Ephraim and Judah: Israel Revealed.*

Batya's books represent decades of study, discussion, and prayer on this crucial issue. Readers have been transformed as they read about Israel in all its fullness. Lives continue to be changed as they see the truth about both the houses of Israel—Judah and Ephraim. It is a truth that is helping to restore a brotherhood broken apart long ago.

Batya's emphasis on the need for mercy and grace to both houses is helping to heal the wounds that began when Israel's Kingdom was divided after into the Northern Kingdom of Israel and the Southern Kingdom of Judah.

Her newest book, *Israel's Feasts and Their Fullness,* represents many years of meticulous research, study, and prayerful writing. Several people have said of it: "This is the best book about the feasts that I have ever read."

We hope you will agree.

Batya is married to her best friend, Col. Angus Wootten (Ret.), author of the visionary book, *Restoring Israel's Kingdom,* plus a guide to the Torah commandments, *Take Two Tablets Daily.* Together they have ten children who have blessed them with many grandchildren and great-grandchildren.

Working as a team, Angus and Batya moved forward from the early days of the *House of David Catalogue* and began publishing the enlightening monthly Newsletter, the *House of David Herald,* which ultimately became a magazine, *The Messianic Israel Herald.*

They also developed the informative Messianic Israel web site: *www.mim.net* and *messianicisrael.com*, which in turn led to the founding of the *Messianic Israel Alliance*— a rapidly growing alliance of congregations, synagogues, and home fellowships that agree with *The Hope of Messianic Israel,* the statement of faith of the Messianic Israel Alliance. This cutting-edge Alliance is served by a dedicated Shepherds Council.

Together Angus and Batya continue to publish books that will serve the growing army of Messianic Israel, as well as raising up new leaders and drawing out their giftings. For this assignment they have been uniquely prepared by the God of Abraham, Isaac, and Jacob.

We know you will be blessed as you read their writings.

"Let the one who is taught share all good things with him who teaches" (Galatians 6:6).
If through this book a good thing has been accomplished in your life, please write and share your good news with me.

Batya Wootten
PO Box 700217, Saint Cloud, FL 34770
e-mail: batya@mim.net

The Hope of Messianic Israel

Messianic Israel believes Yeshua Ha'Natsree (Jesus of Nazareth) was and is the true Messiah, the Lion of Judah, the Branch Who will fully reunite all Israel; that He died and rose from the dead and lives at the right hand of the Almighty; and according to the ancient Holy Scriptures, Yeshua is YHVH Elohim appearing in the flesh, as Yeshua demonstrated in Himself (Deu 18:18-19; John 8:58; 10:33; Mat 12:6-8; 9:35; 15:31; Isa 11; 53; Micah 5:2-4; Luke 24:46; Isa 8:14; John 2:22; Acts 3:15-17; Heb 13:20; 1 John 4:2; 2 John 1:7; Rev 5:5; John 1:1).

Messianic Israel believes we are made righteous in Messiah Yeshua. (He is the heart of Abraham's un-conditional covenant.) The sign of the New Covenant is circumcision of the heart, which leads to confession, salvation, faith, grace, and to good works in Messiah. The conditional Mosaic covenant presents the eternal truths of Torah (YHVH's teaching and instructions) to His people, the hearing of which brings about blessing or curse (respond and be blessed, disobey and lack). In the New Covenant, Yeshua's Law is to be written on our hearts by the Spirit (Rom 4:13-16; 5:2; 10:10; 1 Pet 1:19; 2 Cor 5:21; Gal 3:16,29; Titus 3:5; Heb 10:38; 1 John 1:9; Eph 2:8; James 2:14; Deu 28; Ezek 36:26; Jer 31:31-33; Heb 10:16; Gal 2:16; John 5:46; 10;30; 14:2; 15:10).

Messianic Israel is a people whose heart's desire is to fully reunite the olive tree of Israel—both branches —Ephraim and Judah—into one, redeemed, nation of Israel—through Messiah Yeshua. They seek to arouse Ephraim from obscurity, and by example, to awaken Judah to the Messiah—and thus to hasten both Yeshua's return to Earth and the restoration of the promised Kingdom to Israel (Mat 6:10; 12:25; 21:43; 24:43; Luke 22:29-30; Mark 13:34; Luke 22:29-30; 2 Chr 11:4; Eze 37:15-28; Jer 11:10,16; 2:18,21; Rom 11:17,24; Eph 2:11-22; Acts 1:6).

Messianic Israel deems the Jewish people to be the identifiable representatives and offspring of Judah and "the children of Israel, his companions," and that non-Jewish followers of the Messiah from all nations have been, up to now, the unidentifiable represen-tatives and offspring of Ephraim and "all the house of Israel, his companions" (Gen 48:19; Hosea 1-2; 5:3; Eze 37:16; Jer 31:6-9; Gen 15:2-5; 26:3; 28:4; Heb 11:9; Isa 56:3,6-8; Eph 2:11-22).

Messianic Israel affirms that the Jewish people have been kept identifiable as seed of the patriarch Jacob, YHVH's covenant people, to preserve His Holy Torah (Law), Feasts, and Shabbat (Sabbath); that the salvation of the Jewish people through their acceptance of Messiah Yeshua, will be the crowning act of mankind's redemption, and is necessary for the restoration of the Kingdom to Israel. Further, the Father plans that Ephraim, they being the "wild olive branch," stimulate Judah to want what they have; they are called to walk in a way that will make Judah jealous of their relationship with the God of Israel (Gen 48:19; Isa 11:13; 37:31,32; Zec 2:12; Eze 37:15-28; Hosea 1:7; Rom 10:19; 11:11,14; Mat 23:39).

Messianic Israel believes the non-Jewish followers of Yeshua are predominantly returning Ephraim, those who were once among the Gentiles/Goyim/Nations as "LoAmi,"or "Not a people," but have now been restored to the commonwealth of Israel through their covenant with Israel's Messiah; that, they are no more Gentiles/ Goyim/of the Nations, but fulfill the promised restoration of uprooted Ephraim, and Jacob's prophecy that Ephraim would become "melo hagoyim," the "full-ness of the Gentiles/Goyim/ Nations." As Ephraim, they have been kept in mystery until recently, being used to preserve the testimony of Yeshua, the Messiah of all Israel. Their awakening, recognition, and performance as Ephraim, and their union with Judah, is a necessity for salvation of "all" Israel, and the restoration of the Kingdom to Israel (Gen 48:19; Hosea 1:9-10; 5:3; 8:8; Amos 9:9; Jer 31:18-19; Zec 10:7; Rom 9:24-26; 11:26; Eph 2:11-22).

Messianic Israel declares that Believers in Yeshua were not meant to replace Judah as Israel, but as "Ephraim," they are part of the called out ones (ekklesia), and in these latter-days, the Father is leading them to, whenever scripturally possible, join with Judah; that Judah (faithful Jewish ones who will receive Messiah) and Ephraim (faithful non-Jewish Messiah followers) ultimately will fulfill the destiny of the two houses of Israel: that together they might fulfill the prophesies about the one, unified, victorious people of Israel (Jer 31:9; Rom 8:29; Col 1:15,18; 2:12; Heb 12:22-24; Lev 23:2-36; Exo 19:5; 1 Pet 1:1; 2:9; Jer 3:18; 23:6; Zec 8:13; 12:1-5; Mat 25:31-46; Exo 12:48-49; Num 15:15-16; Isa 56:3,6-8).

Messianic Israel maintains that up to this general time "blindness in part" has happened to all (both houses) of Israel, and as the blinders are lifted, non-Jewish followers in Yeshua will gain insight into their role as Ephraim and become defenders of scriptural Torah and of Judah, and due to this character change, many Jewish people will accept Yeshua as Messiah. This process has begun as indicated through the Messianic Jewish movement (Judah), the Christian Zionism movement (Ephraim), and the Messianic Israel movement (union of Judah and Ephraim) (Isa 8:14; 11:13; Rom 11:25,26; Jer 33:14-16; 31:18-19; Ezek 37:15-28).

The reunion and full restoration of the two houses:

This is the hope that burns in the hearts of those of Messianic Israel...

© 1996-2002 Messianic Israel Ministries
PO Box 700217, Saint Cloud, FL 34770
www.mim.net

Who Is Israel?
Enlarged Edition
by Batya Wootten

This phenomenal book is causing an awakening in the Body of Messiah because it clearly explains the truth about "both the houses of Israel," (Isaiah 8:14). It explains who is indeed an Israelite. This awareness has caused a reformation in the Body of Messiah. Read this solution-driven book and see the truth that is inspiring Believers everywhere!

Who is Israel? Why do *you* need to know? Knowing who you are and where you are going is vital to your relationship with the God of Israel.

Reading this book will inspire and encourage you, even change your life. It will help you discover your own Hebraic Heritage and put your feet on the road to Zion. It will enable you to: Understand Israel, the Church, the Bible — The mystery of the "fullness of the Gentiles" — The "blindness of Israel" — The Father's master plan for Israel. It will answer: Why you feel something is missing in your life — Why you have a love for Israel and Jewish people — And why you feel an urge to celebrate the feasts of Israel.

This handbook will move you from religion to relationship. The Biblical truths unveiled in this volume will help: Put an end to "Christian" anti-Semitism and heal divisions in the Body of Messiah, as well as lead us back to our first love: Messiah Yeshua.

This enlightening book includes the following chapters: Believing What Abraham Believed — Israel: A Blessing — Jacob's Firstborn Heir — Ephraim: A Profile — Yankees and Rebels — LoAmmi: Not A People — Many Israels, One Israel — A Priceless Gift — Chosen To Choose — The Blood, The Redeemer, And Physical Israel — Literal or Spiritual? — Israel: A Mystery Until — "Holey" Doctrines — More Tattered Theories — Is Judah All Israel? — Leaving Elementary Things Behind — From Orphans To Heirs — The Olive Tree of Israel — One Law, One People — The Two

Witnesses And Their Fullness — Called to Be Watchmen — Return, O Virgin Israel! — Yeshua: Epitome of All That Is Israel — An Israel Yet To Come. This Enlarged Edition includes Maps and Charts and an Addendum about current Jewish genetic research.
ISBN 1-886987-03-3   Paper, 304 pages $14.95.

Also Available in Spanish!

¿Quién es Israel?

Por Batya Wootten

Traducido al Español por Natalie Pavlik
ISBN 1-886987-08-4 $14.95

Who Is Israel?
A Study Guide

This *Study Guide* is an excellent companion volume to *Who Is Israel?* It can be used as a 12 or 24 week Study Course. The study plan is simple and does not require a great deal of preparation by the leaders. The goal is to help people come to an understanding of Israel and their part in Israel.

The *Study Guide* contains the printed Scripture verses that correspond to each lesson in *Who Is Israel?* These can be read and discussed by the group. Sample questions are listed in the *Study Guide*, with answers in the back. Reading and discussing the selected texts among brethren builds up your faith and makes Scripture come alive with new meaning.

If you want fellowship with Believers of like mind, order a case of these *Study Guides* and get started today!

ISBN 1-886987-08-4   Paper, 288 pages, $12.95
Case of Ten: $85.00 (plus shipping)

Ephraim and Judah
Israel Revealed

by Batya Wootten

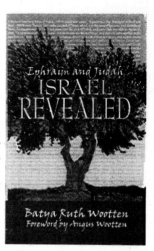

This brief book offers a succinct and updated overview of the material presented in the best-selling seminal classic, *Who Is Israel?*, by Batya Wootten. It includes maps, charts, and lists that clarify misconceptions about Israel's Twelve Tribes. Like Batya's other writings, this book is sure to cause a phenomenal stir among Believers. The truth about both houses of Israel is encouraging a reformation in the Body of Messiah. Read this Scripture-based book and find out what is inspiring Believers in these end times!

This excellent tool will help those of non-Jewish Israel come to know themselves and to see that they too are part of Israel (Jeremiah 31:18-19). It will help both the houses of Israel (Isaiah 8:14) readily see how and where they fit into the Father's divine plan. It will even help bring about the restoration of the Kingdom to the whole House of Israel.

Ephraim and Judah: Israel Revealed—Inexpensive, succinct and easy-to-read, it readily outlines the essence of Messianic Israel teachings.

ISBN 1-886987-11-4   Paper, 80 pages, $ 3.95 plus shipping

All Advertised Books are Distributed by—

Key of David Publishing

Write or Call for a FREE Catalog
PO Box 700217, Saint Cloud, FL 34770
1 800 829-8777
Quantity Discounts Available
Please add appropriate Shipping to all Orders
All Book Prices Are Plus Shipping—Tripled for Overseas

Israel's Feasts and their Fullness

by Batya Wootten

Growing interest in the feasts of Israel has resulted in some confusion and misunderstanding about how Believers in Messiah Yeshua are to celebrate the feasts.

Fortunately, the Father has raised up a voice of clarity in the midst of muddied waters. In her indomitable and delightful style, Batya Wootten has written a clear, concise, informative, well researched, yet entertaining and highly enjoyable book about the feasts of Israel. At last we are told how we can celebrate with the joy and freedom of Messiah Yeshua, yet with reverence for the accuracy of the Holy Scriptures and due respect for the honorable truths of Judaism.

Here you will find trustworthy information on how to celebrate each of the feasts. Included are "Celebration Instruction Guides" for the Sabbath, Havdalah, and Passover. Additionally, there are numerous charts, graphs, tables, and exciting graphics.

Batya continues in the style that has endeared her to so many of her readers. She has written of the need for grace and mercy to both the houses of Israel—Judah and Ephraim. She encourages us to begin to dance and sing and celebrate the presence of the Almighty in our midst!

Get ready for a delightful ride into the Kingdom of God's feasts. This is a book you can't put down and one that you will to refer to for years to come.

ISBN 1-886987-02-5   Paper 384 pages $17.95

Color Printed Celebration Instruction Guides

$2.00 each (includes shipping).
Please specify:
- Shabbat Guide
- Havdalah Guide
- Passover Guide
- Messianic Jewish Passover Guide

Restoring Israel's Kingdom

by Angus Wootten

What was the last question Messiah Yeshua's disciples asked their teacher as they stood on the Mount of Olives, knowing that He was about to depart? What mattered most to them?

As followers of Israel's Messiah, we must ask the question that mattered so much to His chosen twelve: "Lord, is it at this time You are restoring the kingdom to Israel?" (Acts 1:6).

Yeshua's disciples, who had been trained by Him for more than three years, asked this question because He taught them to pray to our Father in Heaven, "'Your kingdom come. Your will be done, On earth as it is in heaven" (Matthew 6:10).

Since we are a people dedicated to bringing Yeshua's Kingdom to this earth, we must not lose sight of the vision that burned in the hearts of His first disciples.

We have lost sight of our heritage as part Israel and have often forgotten this important goal, but just as Judah is beginning to see the Messiah, the veil is likewise being lifted from our "partially blinded" Israelite eyes (Genesis 48:19; Romans 11).

Restoring Israel's Kingdom offers the following challenging chapters: Are You Prepared? — Can We Make A Difference? — Learning the Lessons of History — A Brief History of Israel — Lessons Learned — The Voice of The People — Who Told You? — Who Is A Jew? A Look At Israel's Bloodline — Our Hope of Glory And The Mystery of The Gentiles — The Way of The Gentiles — Ephraim, Once Again A Mighty Man — Ephraim Should Know More About Judah — From Roman Roads To The World Wide Web — The Jubilee Generation — A Mandate For Ephraim — Restoring The Kingdom To Israel — The Messianic Vision — When Will Yeshua Return? — And Preparing For The Final Battle.

This exciting book will help you keep your eye on the goal: The restoration of the Kingdom to the restored house of Israel.

ISBN 1-886987-04-1   Paper, 304 pages, $14.95 plus shipping

The 10 Commandments
and the 613 Laws

Angus Wootten

Take Two Tablets Daily
The 10 Commandments and 613 Laws
by Angus Wootten

"You're trying to put me under the Law!" This cry is often heard from Christians when they are presented with the laws and commandments of the God of Abraham, Isaac and Jacob.

Is their cry justified? This valuable book will help you thoughtfully examine the laws the Holy One gave to His people through Moses. Read it and see that the Father's instructions were given for the physical and spiritual guidance of His people. His judgments and precepts were not given to punish Israel, but to guide them as individuals and as a nation. They were given to enable the people of Israel to become strong, courageous, healthy and blessed.

This handy guide conveniently lists the 613 laws, divided into Mandatory Commandments and Prohibitions (according to Jewish custom), plus the Scripture verse(s) from which each law is derived. Chapter titles include: Under the Law? — Yeshua's Attitude Toward the Law — Our Need For Law And Order — YHVH's Law or Man's Law? — Paul and the Law — Principles of the Protestant Reformation — What Should Be Our Attitude Toward the Law? — The Decalogue: The Ten Commandments.

YHVH's Word is like medicinal ointment, and nothing is more symbolic of His Word than the two tablets on which He wrote His desires for us. Taken daily, these "Two Tablets" will give us life more abundantly. This reference book should be in every Believers library. It is a must read!

ISBN1-886987-06-8   96 Informative pages, $4.95

Journey Through Torah Volume I:
Commentary on the Torah, Haftarah and Brit Chadoshah Portions for Messianic Israel
by Rav Mordechai Silver

Rav Silver offers 52 encouraging Torah teachings especially for Messianic Israel—all based on the Jewish tradition of reading certain "portions" of the Torah and the Prophets each week. Comments are founded on the truth that Yahweh is presently reuniting the two sticks of Judah and Ephraim. Silver, a Jewish Believer in the Messiah, repeatedly reaffirms that reunion. Corroborating teachings from the Brit Chadoshah (New Covenant) are included, plus a calendar that lists each of the portions.

Inspiring regular readings in a spiral-bound book for those seeking to return to their Hebraic roots. Those who long for Israel's full restoration won't want to miss these enlightening teachings.

ISBN 1-886987-10-6   Paper, 288 pages $15.00

Want More Torah Teachings?

Register to receive weekly email Torah teachings from Rav Silver and other Messianic Israel leaders and teachers.
Go to Torah Teachings at <messianicisrael.com>.

When Will The Messiah Return?
by John K. McKee

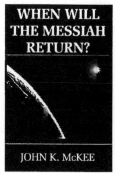

WHEN WILL THE MESSIAH RETURN?

JOHN K. McKEE

If we are to understand what is coming in the future, we must look to the Scriptures for answers. *When Will the Messiah Return?* is an exhaustive study about how Messianic Israel fits into the Father's end time scenario. This well-researched volume addresses the subject of the Second Coming and discusses the theology of Messianic Israel in relation to the idea of post-tribulationism. This will prove to be an exciting book for exciting times. ISBN 1-886987-14-9   Paper, 224 pages $15.00

My Beloved's Israel
by Gloria Cavallaro

Deepen your personal relationship with your Bridegroom. Embark on an intimate journey into the heart of our Heavenly Father. Experience relationship with the Holy One of Israel like David described in his Psalms. Know intimacy with the Bridegroom like Solomon spoke of in the Song of Songs. A Spirit-filled Believer, Gloria chronicles her visions and dreams, then interprets and journals them in light of scriptural reflection. This journal exhorts and encourages intimacy with the Holy One. It helps prepare the hearts of Israelites for reunion and restoration so they will be ready for coming challenges.

ISBN 1-886987-05-X   Paper, 384 pages, $16.95.

All Israel Dances
Toward the Tabernacle
by Chester Anderson

This inspiring book will help you understand the dynamics of worship. It takes you beyond the pale of other worship books and answers your many dance related questions. For example, What is dance? — How did it originate? — What if I don't know how to dance? — Does something special happen in the heavenlies when we dance? — What attitude should be in our hearts when we are dancing and why? — Why do I feel so drawn to Hebraic dance? — Why has Davidic dance become so popular? — How does dance come into play in the restoration of both the houses of Israel?

This book will fill your heart with hope for the Glory that is soon to be upon us! It will put a yearning in your heart to dance before the Holy One of Israel.

ISBN 1-886987-09-2 Paper, 192 pages. $12.95 plus shipping.

Key of David Publications

The
Messianic
Israel
Herald
Magazine

Informative! Challenging! Inspiring!
Stay Informed! Subscribe Today! $24.00 per Year
(Back Issues Available)
Visit Us At Our Cutting Edge Website

Messianic Israel Ministries
www.mim.net

For a Free Catalogue of our Books, and Messianic
Materials, plus a Sample Messianic Israel Magazine,
Write To—
Messianic Israel Ministries
PO Box 700217, Saint Cloud, FL 34770
Ph: 800 829 8777 (Orders) Fax: 407 870 8986

Unlocking *your* future...

All Advertised Books are Distributed by—

Key of David Publishing

Write or Call for a Free Catalog
PO Box 700217, Saint Cloud, FL 34770
1 800 829-8777
All Book Prices Are Plus Shipping—Tripled for Overseas
Please add appropriate Shipping to all Orders

Index

7/7/04

Notes

<u>Feasts</u>

Identity is blinding Israel

Judah begins to see Ephraiose spiritual joy
+ future life

Watchmen — must have knowledge of feasts

Seventh day Sabbath says G-d

Gregorian cal. — ours 365½

Lunar mo, 348 days

G add 1 more mo. every 7 yrs

Notes